Perfect Score . . . 43 | Name Tiffanie Tabor

Deduct . . . . . . ___ | Date 9-3-96 Class ______

Your Score . . . ___ | Checked by ______

STUDY GUIDE

UNIT A—Identifying Accounting Terms

DIRECTIONS: Select the one term in Column I that best fits each definition in Column II. Print the letter identifying your choice in the Answers column.

Column I

- **A.** account
- **B.** account balance
- **C.** account title
- **D.** accounting
- **E.** accounting equation
- **F.** accounting records
- **G.** accounting system
- **H.** asset
- **I.** balance sheet
- **J.** capital
- **K.** equities
- **L.** liability
- **M.** owner's equity
- **N.** proprietorship
- **O.** service business
- **P.** transaction

Column II	Answers	For Scoring
0. Anything of value that is owned	H	**0.** ✓
1. An amount owed by a business	L	**1.**
2. The name given to an account	C	**2.**
3. Financial rights to the assets of a business	K	**3.**
4. A financial statement that reports assets, liabilities, and owner's equity on a specific date	I	**4.**
5. A business owned by one person	N	**5.**
6. The amount remaining after the value of all liabilities is subtracted from the value of all assets	M	**6.**
7. Planning, recording, analyzing, and interpreting financial information	D	**7.**
8. A record summarizing all the information pertaining to a single item in the accounting equation	A	**8.**
9. A planned process for providing financial information that will be useful to management	G	**9.**
10. The account used to summarize the owner's equity in the business	J	**10.**
11. An equation showing the relationship among assets, liabilities, and owner's equity	E	**11.**
12. A business activity that changes assets, liabilities, or owner's equity	P	**12.**
13. Organized summaries of a business' financial activities	F	**13.**
14. A business that performs an activity for a fee	O	**14.**
15. The amount in an account	B	**15.**

UNIT B—Analyzing a Balance Sheet

DIRECTIONS: The parts of the balance sheet on the right are identified with capital letters. For each of the following items, decide which part is being described. Print the letter identifying your choice in the Answers column.

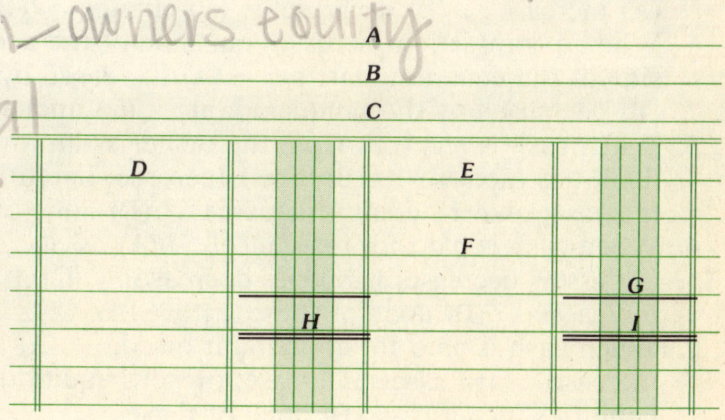

	Answers	For Scoring
0. The name of the business	A	**0.** ✓
1. The total amount of equity in the business	I	**1.**
2. The label Assets	D	**2.**
3. The total amount owned by the business	H	**3.**
4. The label Owner's Equity	F	**4.**

	Answers	For Scoring
5. The date of the balance sheet	C	**5.**
6. The label Liabilities	E	**6.**
7. The name of the report	B	**7.**
8. The amount of owner's equity	G	**8.**

UNIT C—Analyzing How Transactions Change an Accounting Equation

DIRECTIONS: For each of the following transactions, select the two accounts in the accounting equation that are changed. Decide if each account is increased or decreased. Place a "+" in the column if the account is increased. Place a "−" in the column if the account is decreased.

Trans. No.	Assets			= Liabilities		+ Owners' Equity	For Scoring	
	Cash	+ Supplies	+ Prepaid Insurance	= Eastside Supply Company	+ Fairmont Company	+ Mary Gazda, Capital		
0–0.	−	+					0. ✓	0. ✓
1–2.	+					+	1.	2.
3–4.	−				−		3.	4.
5–6.	−		+				5.	6.
7–8.	−			−			7.	8.
9–10.		+		+			9.	10.

Transactions

0–0. Paid cash for supplies.
1–2. Received cash from owner as an investment.
3–4. Paid cash on account to Fairmont Company.
5–6. Paid cash for insurance.
7–8. Paid cash on account to Eastside Supply Company.
9–10. Bought supplies on account from Eastside Supply Company.

UNIT D—Identifying Accounting Concepts and Practices

DIRECTIONS: For each of the following items, select the choice that best completes the statement. Print the letter identifying your choice in the Answers column.

0. When financial records for a business and for its owner's personal belongings are not mixed, this is an application of the accounting concept **(A)** business entity **(B)** going concern **(C)** unit of measurement **(D)** none of these ...

1. In the United States, recording and reporting financial information in dollars and cents is an application of the accounting concept **(A)** business entity **(B)** going concern **(C)** unit of measurement **(D)** none of these...............

2. Assets = Liabilities + Owner's Equity is known as the **(A)** accounting system **(B)** transaction **(C)** accounting equation **(D)** none of these ....

3. For each transaction, at least two accounts on the accounting equation **(A)** increase **(B)** decrease **(C)** change **(D)** none of these....................

4. When a transaction increases one side of the accounting equation, the other side of the equation must be **(A)** increased by the same amount **(B)** decreased by the same amount **(C)** unchanged **(D)** none of these.......

5. When cash is received from the owner as an investment, **(A)** assets increase; liabilities increase **(B)** assets increase; liabilities decrease **(C)** assets increase; owner's equity increases **(D)** none of these...............................

6. When cash is paid for insurance, **(A)** assets increase; assets decrease **(B)** assets decrease; liabilities decrease **(C)** assets increase; owner's equity increases **(D)** none of these ....

7. When cash is paid for an amount owed, **(A)** assets decrease; liabilities increase **(B)** assets decrease; owner's equity decreases **(C)** assets increase; liabilities increase **(D)** none of these ....

8. When supplies are bought on account, **(A)** assets increase; liabilities increase **(B)** assets increase; liabilities decrease **(C)** liabilities increase; owner's equity increases **(D)** none of these ....

9. When cash is paid for supplies, **(A)** assets increase; liabilities decrease **(B)** assets increase; liabilities increase **(C)** assets increase; assets decrease **(D)** none of these ....

10. Preparing financial statements with the expectation that a business will remain in operation indefinitely is an application of the concept **(A)** business entity **(B)** going concern **(C)** unit of measurement **(D)** none of these...............

Answers	For Scoring
A	0. ✓
C	1.
C	2.
C	3.
A	4.
C	5.
A	6.
D	7.
A	8.
C	9.
B	10.

Name ______________________________ Date ________ Class ______ *DRILL 1-D1, p. 14*

Classifying assets, liabilities, and owner's equity

Items	Asset	Liability	Owner's Equity
1. Cash	✓		
2. Alice Jones, Capital			✓
3. Prepaid Insurance	✓		
4. Steward Supply Company		✓	
5. Supplies	✓		
6. Any amount owed		✓	
7. Owner's capital account			✓
8. Anything owned	✓		

Determining how transactions change an accounting equation *DRILL 1-D2, p. 15*

Trans. No.	Assets =	Liabilities +	Owner's Equity
1.	+	+	
2.	− +		
3.	+		+
4.	− +		
5.	−	−	

Determining where items are listed on a balance sheet *DRILL 1-D3, p. 15*

1	2	3
	Balance Sheet	
Items	Left side	Right side
1. Cash	Asset	
2. Gretchen Murphy, Capital		
3. Supplies		
4. Prepaid Insurance		
5. Action Laundry		
6. Anything owned		
7. Any amount owed		
8. Owner's capital account		

Determining how transactions change an accounting equation *PROBLEM 1-1, p. 15*

	Assets			=	Liabilities		+	Owner's Equity
Trans. No.	Cash +	Supplies +	Prepaid Insurance	=	Swan's Supply Company +	York Company +		Frank March, Capital
Beg. Bal. 1.	0 +2,000	0	0		0	0		0 +2,000 (investment)
New Bal. 2.	2,000 −600	0	0 +600		0	0		2,000
New Bal. 3.	1400	0 +100	600		0 +100	0		2,000
New Bal. 4.	1400	100 +500	600		100	0 +500		2000
New Bal. 5.	1400 −100	600	600		100 −100	500		2000
New Bal. 6.	1300 −300	600	600		0	500 −300		2000
New Bal. 7.	1000 −500	600 +500	600		0	200		2000
New Bal. 8.	500 +500	1100	600		0	200		2000 +500
New Bal.	1000	1100	600		0	200		2500

Name ______________________ Date ________ Class ______ *PROBLEM 1-2, p. 16*

Preparing a balance sheet from information in an accounting equation

Steffens Company
Balance Sheet
September 30, 1996

Assets		Liabilities	
Cash	1200 –	Morton Company	250 –
Supplies	150 –	Owners Equity	
Prepaid insurance	300 –	Steve Steffens, Capital	1400 –
total assets	1650 –	total Liabilities & owners	1650 –

Extra form

Determining how transactions change an accounting equation and preparing a balance sheet

PROBLEM 1-3, p. 16

[1]

Trans. No.	Assets			=	Liabilities	+	Owner's Equity
	Cash +	Supplies +	Prepaid Insurance	=	Helfrey Company	+	Nancy Dirks, Capital
Beg. Bal.	0	0	0		0		0
1.	+350						+350 (investment)
New Bal.	350	0	0		0		350
2.		+100			+100		
New Bal.	350	100	0		100		350
3.	-150		+150				
New Bal.	200	100	150		100		350
4.	-50	+50					
New Bal.	150	150	150		100		350
5.	+300						+300
New Bal.	450	150	150		100		650
6.	- 75				- 75		
New Bal.	375	150	150		25		650

[2]

Dirks Company
Balance Sheet
July 31, 1996

Assets		Liabilities	
Cash	375 —	Helfrey Company	25 —
Supplies	150 —	Owners Equity	
Prepaid Insurance	150 —	Nancy Dirks, Capital	650 —
Total assets	675 —	Tot. Liab. & Owners Eq.	675 —

Name ______________________ Date ________ Class ______

MASTERY PROBLEM 1-M, p. 17

[1]

Determining how transactions change an accounting equation and preparing a balance sheet

Trans. No.	Assets			= Liabilities	+ Owner's Equity
	Cash +	Supplies +	Prepaid Insurance	= Limo Supply Company	+ Gregory Morgan, Capital
Beg. Bal. 1.	0 +2,000	0	0	0	0 +2,000 (investment)
New Bal. 2.	2,000 -250	0 +250	0	0	2,000
New Bal. 3.	1750	250 +300	0	0 +300	2000
New Bal. 4.	1750 -600	550	0 +600	300	2000
New Bal. 5.	1150 -150	550	600	300 -150	2000
New Bal.	1000	550	600	150	2000

[2]

Luxury Limo
Balance Sheet
February 5, 1996

Assets		Liabilities	
Cash	1000 —	Limo Supply Comp.	150 —
Supplies	550 —	Owners Equity	
Prepaid Insurance	600 —	Gregory Morgan, Cap	2000 —
Total assets	2150 —	Total Liab. & Owners	2150 —

Applying accounting concepts to determine how transactions change the accounting equation

CHALLENGE PROBLEM 1-C, p. 18

Trans. No.	Assets			=	Liabilities		+	Owner's Equity
	Cash	+ Supplies	+ Prepaid Insurance	=	Mutual Savings Bank	+ Nelson Supply Company	+	Jerome Olson, Capital
Beg. Bal.	0	0	0		0	0		0
1.	+1,500							+1,500 (investment)
New Bal.	1,500	0	0		0	0		1,500
2.								
New Bal.								
3.								
New Bal.								
4.								
New Bal.								
5.								
New Bal.								
6.								
New Bal.								

Extra form

Perfect Score..... 40   Name ____________________

Deduct......... ___   Date ____________ Class ____________

Your Score..... ___   Checked by ____________________

STUDY GUIDE 2

UNIT A—Analyzing How Transactions Change an Accounting Equation

DIRECTIONS: For each of the following transactions, select the two accounts in the accounting equation that are changed. Decide if each account is increased or decreased. Print the letters identifying your choices in the proper Answers column to show whether the accounts are increased (+) or decreased (−).

Accounting Equation

Assets					=	Liabilities	+	Owner's Equity
Cash	+	Supplies	+	Prepaid Insurance	=	Best Supply Company	+	Mary Gaston, Capital
A		*B*		*C*		*D*		*E*

Transactions	Answers Increase (+)	Answers Decrease (−)	For Scoring	
0–0. Paid cash for supplies	B	A	**0.** ✓	**0.** ✓
1–2. Received cash from sales	A E		**1.**	**2.**
3–4. Paid cash for equipment repairs		A E	**3.**	**4.**
5–6. Paid cash on account to Best Supply Company		A D	**5.**	**6.**
7–8. Received cash from owner as an investment	A E		**7.**	**8.**
9–10. Paid cash for telephone bill		A E	**9.**	**10.**
11–12. Paid cash to owner for personal use		A E	**11.**	**12.**
13–14. Paid cash for rent		A E	**13.**	**14.**
15–16. Paid cash for insurance	C	A	**15.**	**16.**
17–18. Paid cash for advertising		A E	**17.**	**18.**

UNIT B—Analyzing a Balance Sheet

DIRECTIONS: Place a check mark in the proper Answers column to show whether each of the following statements is true or false.

	Answers True	Answers False	For Scoring
0. The balance sheet reports the balances of the asset, liability, and owner's equity accounts	✓		**0.** ✓
1. A balance sheet may be prepared on any date	X		**1.**
2. The accounts shown on the left side of an accounting equation are shown on the left side of the balance sheet	X		**2.**
3. The heading of a balance sheet contains the name of the business, name of the report, and date of the report	X		**3.**
4. Asset accounts are shown on the right side of a balance sheet		X	**4.**
5. Owner's equity accounts are presented above liability accounts on the balance sheet		X	**5.**
6. The total of the amounts on the left side of a balance sheet must equal the total of the amounts on the right side of the balance sheet	X		**6.**
7. Most businesses prepare a balance sheet every week		X	**7.**

UNIT C—Identifying Accounting Terms

DIRECTIONS: Select the one term in Column I that best fits each definition in Column II. Print the letter identifying your choice in the Answers column.

Column I	*Column II*	Answers	For Scoring
A. expense	**0.** A normal business activity that changes assets, liabilities, and owner's equity	C	**0.** ✓
B. revenue	**1.** An increase in owner's equity resulting from the operation of a business	B	**1.**
C. transaction	**2.** A decrease in owner's equity resulting from the operation of a business	a	**2.**
D. withdrawals	**3.** Assets taken out of a business for the owner's personal use	D	**3.**

UNIT D—Identifying Accounting Concepts and Procedures Related to Changes that Affect Owner's Equity

DIRECTIONS: For each of the following items, select the choice that best completes the statement. Print the letter identifying your choice in the Answers column.

Item	Answers	For Scoring
0. The statement Assets = Liabilities + Owner's Equity is known as **(A)** equity **(B)** an accounting equation **(C)** a financial statement **(D)** none of these	B	**0.** ✓
1. When cash is received from sales, **(A)** assets increase; owner's equity decreases **(B)** assets increase; owner's equity increases **(C)** assets decrease; owner's equity decreases **(D)** none of these	B	**1.**
2. When cash is paid for an expense, **(A)** assets decrease; owner's equity decreases **(B)** assets decrease; owner's equity increases **(C)** assets increase; owner's equity increases **(D)** none of these	A	**2.**
3. When cash is paid to the owner for personal use, **(A)** assets increase; owner's equity increases **(B)** assets increase; owner's equity decreases **(C)** assets decrease; owner's equity decreases **(D)** none of these	C	**3.**
4. When cash is received from the owner as an investment, **(A)** assets increase; owner's equity increases **(B)** assets increase; owner's equity decreases **(C)** assets decrease; owner's equity decreases **(D)** none of these	A	**4.**
5. Expenses of a business could include **(A)** supplies **(B)** liabilities **(C)** withdrawal **(D)** none of these	D	**5.**
6. Owner's equity is increased by **(A)** withdrawals **(B)** revenue **(C)** expenses **(D)** none of these	B	**6.**
7. When a transaction causes a decrease in cash and an increase in supplies, there is **(A)** an increase in total assets **(B)** a decrease in owner's equity **(C)** no change in total assets **(D)** none of these	C	**7.**
8. When cash is paid for insurance, **(A)** two assets decrease **(B)** owner's equity increases **(C)** liabilities decrease **(D)** none of these	D	**8.**
9. Recording an expense transaction in an accounting equation causes liabilities to **(A)** increase **(B)** decrease **(C)** remain unchanged **(D)** none of these	C	**9.**
10. Cash is increased by **(A)** revenue **(B)** expenses **(C)** withdrawals **(D)** none of these	A	**10.**
11. Owner's equity is decreased by **(A)** investments **(B)** expenses **(C)** revenue **(D)** none of these	B	**11.**
12. A transaction that increases cash and decreases owner's equity is **(A)** revenue **(B)** expense **(C)** withdrawal **(D)** none of these	D	**12.**

Name ______________ Date ________ Class ________ *DRILL 2-D1, p. 28*

Determining how revenue, expense, and withdrawal transactions change an accounting equation

Trans. No.	Assets			=	Liabilities	+	Owner's Equity
	Cash	+ Supplies	+ Prepaid Insurance	=	Maxwell Company	+	Susan Sanders, Capital
1.	+						+
2.	+						+
3.	−						−
4.	−						−
5.	−						−
6.	−						−
7.	+						+
8.	−						−

Determining how transactions change an accounting equation *DRILL 2-D2, p. 28*

Trans. No.	Assets			=	Liabilities	+	Owner's Equity
	Cash	+ Supplies	+ Prepaid Insurance	=	Barrett Company	+	Sue Marist, Capital
1.		+			+		
2.	−						−
3.	+						+
4.	−		+				
5.	+						+
6.	−						−
7.	−	+					
8.	−						−
9.	−				+		
10.	−						−

Determining how revenue, expense, and withdrawal transactions change an accounting equation

PROBLEM 2-1, p. 29

Trans. No.	Assets			=	Liabilities	+	Owner's Equity
	Cash	+ Supplies	+ Prepaid Insurance	=	Kline Company	+	Peter Smith, Capital
Beg. Bal. 1.	625 −300	375	300		200		1,100 −300 (expense)
New Bal. 2.	325 −150	375	300		200		800 −150 wd
New Bal. 3.	175 +800	375	300		200		650 +800 R
New Bal. 4.	975 −100	375	300		200		1450 −100 EX
New Bal. 5.	875 −60	375	300		200		1350 −60 EX
New Bal. 6.	815 +650	375	300		200		1290 +650 R
New Bal. 7.	1465 −35	375	300		200		1940 −35 EX
New Bal. 8.	1430 −25	375	300		200		1905 −25 EX
New Bal.	1405	375	300		200		1880

Extra form

Name ______________________ Date ________ Class ________

PROBLEM 2-2, p. 30
[1]

Determining how transactions change an accounting equation and preparing a balance sheet

Trans. No.	Assets			= Liabilities	+ Owner's Equity
	Cash +	Supplies +	Prepaid Insurance =	Teale Company +	Doris Becker, Capital
Beg. Bal.	500	260	300	100	960
1.	−50				−50 (expense)
New Bal.	450	260	300	100	910
2.	+325				+325 R
New Bal.	775	260	300	100	1235
3.	−200	+200			
New Bal.	575	460	300	100	1235
4.		+1200		+1200	
New Bal.	575	1660	300	1300	1235
5.	−200				−200 EX
New Bal.	375	1660	300	1300	1035
6.	+280				+280 R
New Bal.	655	1660	300	1300	1315
7.	−60				−60 EX
New Bal.	595	1660	300	1300	1255
8.	−400		+400		
New Bal.	195	1660	700	1300	1255
9.	−125				−125 WD
New Bal.	70	1660	700	1300	1130
10.	+260				+260 R
New Bal.	330	1660	700	1300	1390
11.	−45				−45 EX
New Bal.	285	1660	700	1300	1345
12.	−25				−25 EX
New Bal.	260	1660	700	1300	1320
13.	+300				+300 R
New Bal.	560	1660	700	1300	1620
14.	−100			−100	
New Bal.	460	1660	700	1200	1620
15.	+1000				+1000 INV
New Bal.	1460	1660	700	1200	2620
16.	−600				−600 EX
New Bal.	860	1660	700	1200	2020
17.	+430				+430 R
New Bal.	1290	1660	700	1200	2450
18.	−750			−750	
New Bal.	540	1660	700	450	2450

Quick Type
Balance Sheet
July 17, 1996

Assets		Liabilities	
Cash	540 —	Teale Company	450 —
Supplies	1660 —	Owner's Equity	
Prepaid Insurance	700 —	Doris Becker, Capital	2450 —
Total assets	2900	Tot. Liab. & Owners equity	2900 —

Extra form

Name ______________________ Date ________ Class ________

MASTERY PROBLEM 2-M, p. 31
[1]

Determining how transactions change an accounting equation and preparing a balance sheet

3905 2905 2905

Trans. No.	Assets: Cash	+	Supplies	+	Prepaid Insurance	=	Liabilities: Sickle Company	+	Owner's Equity: Fred Nance, Capital
Beg. Bal.	1,400		300		400		1,500		600
1.	−100								−100 (expense)
New Bal.	1,300		300		400		1,500		500
2.	+200								+200 INV
New Bal.	1500		300		400		1500		700
3.	-500								-500 EX
New Bal.	1000		300		400		1500		200
4.	-100								-100 EX
New Bal.	900		300		400		1500		100
5.	+895								+895 R
New Bal.	1795		300		400		1500		995
6.			+600				+600		
New Bal.	1795		900		400		2100		995
7.	-15								-15 EX
New Bal.	1780		900		400		2100		980
8.	-30								-30 EX
New Bal.	1740		900		400		2100		940
9.	+920								+920 R
New Bal.	2660		900		400		2100		1860
10.	-50								-50 EX
New Bal.	2610		900		400		2100		1810
11.	-10								-10 EX
New Bal.	2600		900		400		2100		1800
12.	-400		+400						
New Bal.	2200		1300		400		2100		1800
13.	-250								-250 EX
New Bal.	1950		1300		400		2100		1550
14.	+795								+795 R
New Bal.	2745		1300		400		2100		2345
15.	-1500						-1500		
New Bal.	1245		1300		400		600		2345
16.	-250				+250				
New Bal.	995		1300		650		600		2345
17.	+960								+960 R
New Bal.	1955		1300		650		600		3305
18.	-1000								-1000 WD
New Bal.	965		1300		650		600		2305

Determining how transactions change an accounting equation and preparing a balance sheet

MASTERY PROBLEM 2-M, concluded
[2]

Nance Company
Balance Sheet
April 30, 1996

Assets		Liability	
Cash	965 —	Sickle Company	600 —
Supplies	1300 —	Owners Equity	
Prepaid Insurance	650 —	Fred Nance, Capital	2315 —
Total assets	2915 —	Tot. Liab. & Owners Equity	2915 —

Calculating the missing amounts in an accounting equation

CHALLENGE PROBLEM 2-C, p. 32
[1-3]

Statement	Assets					=	Liabilities	+	Owner's Equity
	Cash	+	Supplies	+	Prepaid Insurance	=	Dexter Company	+	Pat Bouwman, Capital
1.	400		300		800		500		1,000
		Total:	1,500				Total:	1,500	
2.	200		______		400		250		900
		Total:	______				Total:	______	
3.	300		1,000		750		______		1,200
		Total:	______				Total:	______	
4.	______		2,000		1,200		2,400		3,500
		Total:	______				Total:	______	
5.	100		2,700		______		1,100		2,500
		Total:	______				Total:	______	
6.	250		400		300		______		500
		Total:	______				Total:	______	
7.	600		2,200		900		500		______
		Total:	______				Total:	______	
8.	______		100		400		150		500
		Total:	______				Total:	______	

Perfect Score..... 43 Name ______________________

Deduct......... ___ Date ______________ Class ______________

Your Score..... ___ Checked by ______________________

STUDY GUIDE 3

UNIT A—Identifying Accounting Terms

DIRECTIONS: Select the one term in Column I that best fits each definition in Column II. Print the letter identifying your choice in the Answers column.

Column I

A. account
B. chart of accounts
C. contra account
D. credit
E. debit
F. T account

Column II	Answers	For Scoring
0. A summary of all the information pertaining to a single element in an accounting equation................	A	0. ✓
1. An amount recorded on the left side of a T account..	B	1.
2. An amount recorded on the right side of a T account .	E	2.
3. A list of accounts used by a business	D	3.
4. An accounting device used to analyze transactions	F	4.
5. An account that reduces a related account on a financial statement	C	5.

UNIT B—Analyzing Transactions into Debit and Credit Parts

DIRECTIONS: Analyze each of the following transactions into debit and credit parts. Print the letter identifying your choice in the proper Answers columns.

Account Titles

A. Cash
B. Supplies
C. Prepaid Insurance
D. Burns Supplies
E. David Glancy, Capital
F. David Glancy, Drawing
G. Sales
H. Miscellaneous Expense
I. Rent Expense
J. Repair Expense
K. Utilities Expense

Transactions	Answers Debit	Answers Credit	For Scoring Debit	For Scoring Credit
0–0. Paid cash for rent..	I	A	0. ✓	0. ✓
1–2. Received cash from owner as an investment..................	A	E	1.	2.
3–4. Paid cash for supplies..	E	A	3.	4.
5–6. Paid cash for insurance......................................	C	A	5.	6.
7–8. Bought supplies on account from Burns Supplies	B	D	7.	8.
9–10. Paid cash on account to Burns Supplies	D	A	9.	10.
11–12. Received cash from sales	A	G	11.	12.
13–14. Paid cash for repairs	J	A	13.	14.
15–16. Paid cash for telephone bill	K	A	15.	16.
17–18. Paid cash to owner for personal use	F	A	17.	18.

UNIT C—Identifying Changes in Accounts

DIRECTIONS: For each of the following items, select the choice that best completes the statement. Print the letter identifying your choice in the Answers column.

	Answers	For Scoring
0. Decreases in any asset account are shown on a T account's **(A)** debit side **(B)** credit side **(C)** balance side **(D)** none of these	B	**0.** ✓
1. Decreases in any liability account are shown on a T account's **(A)** debit side **(B)** credit side **(C)** balance side **(D)** none of these	A	**1.**
2. Decreases in any owner's capital account are shown on a T account's **(A)** debit side **(B)** credit side **(C)** right side **(D)** none of these	A	**2.**
3. Decreases in a revenue account are shown on a T account's **(A)** debit side **(B)** credit side **(C)** balance side **(D)** none of these	A	**3.**
4. Decreases in any expense account are shown on a T account's **(A)** debit side **(B)** credit side **(C)** left side **(D)** none of these	B	**4.**
5. Increases in a contra capital account are shown on a T account's **(A)** debit side **(B)** credit side **(C)** right side **(D)** none of these	A	**5.**
6. The normal balance side of any asset account is the **(A)** debit side **(B)** credit side **(C)** right side **(D)** none of these	A	**6.**
7. The normal balance side of any liability account is the **(A)** debit side **(B)** credit side **(C)** left side **(D)** none of these	B	**7.**
8. The normal balance side of any revenue account is the **(A)** debit side **(B)** credit side **(C)** left side **(D)** none of these	B	**8.**
9. The normal balance side of any expense account is the **(A)** debit side **(B)** credit side **(C)** right side **(D)** none of these	A	**9.**
10. The normal balance side of an owner's capital account is the **(A)** debit side **(B)** credit side **(C)** left side **(D)** none of these	B	**10.**
11. The normal balance side of an owner's drawing account is the **(A)** debit side **(B)** credit side **(C)** right side **(D)** none of these	A	**11.**
12. Debits must equal credits **(A)** in a T account **(B)** in all transactions **(C)** on the equation's left side **(D)** none of these	B	**12.**
13. The total amounts on an equation's left side and the total amounts on an equation's right side must be **(A)** debits **(B)** credits **(C)** equal **(D)** none of these	C	**13.**
14. Increases in any asset account are shown on a T account's **(A)** debit side **(B)** credit side **(C)** right side **(D)** none of these	A	**14.**
15. Increases in any liability account are shown on a T account's **(A)** debit side **(B)** credit side **(C)** left side **(D)** none of these	B	**15.**
16. Increases in any owner's capital account are shown on a T account's **(A)** debit side **(B)** credit side **(C)** left side **(D)** none of these	B	**16.**
17. Increases in any revenue account are shown on a T account's **(A)** debit side **(B)** credit side **(C)** left side **(D)** none of these	B	**17.**
18. Increases in any expense account are shown on a T account's **(A)** debit side **(B)** credit side **(C)** right side **(D)** none of these	A	**18.**
19. The left side of any T account is also referred to as the **(A)** debit side **(B)** credit side **(C)** balance side **(D)** none of these	A	**19.**
20. The right side of any T account is also referred to as the **(A)** debit side **(B)** credit side **(C)** balance side **(D)** none of these	B	**20.**

Name ____________ Date ________ Class ________

Determining the normal balance, increase, and decrease sides for accounts **[1-2]**

Cash	
Debit side Normal Balance Increase	Credit side Decrease

Supplies	
dr NB +	cr −

Prepaid Insurance	
dr NB +	cr −

Miller Supplies	
dr −	cr NB +

Wayne Office Supplies	
dr −	cr NB +

Jeff Dixon Capital	
dr −	cr NB +

Jeff Dixon, Drawing	
dr NB +	cr −

Sales	
dr −	cr NB +

Advertising Expen	
dr NB +	cr −

Miscellaneous Ex	
dr NB +	cr −

Rent Expence	
dr NB +	cr −

Repair Expence	
dr NB +	cr −

Utility Expence	
dr NB +	cr −

1	2	3	4	5	6	7	8	9
Trans. No.	**Accounts Affected**	**Account Classification**	**Account's Normal Balance**		**How Is Account Affected?**		**Entered in Account as a**	
			Debit	**Credit**	**+**	**−**	**Debit**	**Credit**
1.	Cash	Asset	✓		✓		✓	
	Jeff Dixon, Capital	Owner's Equity		✓	✓			✓
2.	cash	asset	X			X		X
	Supplies	asset	X		X		X	
3.	Cash	asset	X			X		X
	Insurance	asset	X		X		X	
4.	Miller Supp.	Liability		X	X			X
	Supplies	asset	X		X		X	
5.	Cash	asset	X		X		X	
	Sales	revenue		X	X			X
6.	Cash	asset	X			X		X
	Miller Supplies	Liability		X		X	X	
7.	Cash	asset	X			X		X
	Rent	expence	X		X		X	
8.	Cash	asset	X			X		X
	repairs	expence	X		X		X	
9.								
10.								
11.	Cash	asset	X			X		X
	Jeff Dixon Drawing	Contra Capital	X		X		X	

Name ______________________ Date ________ Class ______

PROBLEM 3-1, p. 47
[1,2]

Analyzing transactions into debit and credit parts

April

1.

Cash	
5,000.00	

Dixie Conastar, Capital	
	5,000.00

2.

Supplies	
50	

Cash	
	50

3.

Prepaid Insurance	
75	

Cash	
	75

6.

Supplies	
100	

Bales Office Supplies	
	100

7.

Cash	
400	

Sales	
	400

8.

Utilities Expence	
25	

Cash	
	25

9.

13.

Bales Office Supplies	
50	

Cash	
	50

14.

Cash	
400	

Sales	
	400

15.

16.

Dixie Conastar Drawing	
50	

Cash	
	50

18.

Rent Expence	
250	

Cash	
	250

[1,2]

Cash

(1) 2000	(25) 90
(7) 400	(6) 500
(14) 500	(11) 250
(21) 750	(13) 80
(28) 520	(15) 600
(31) 400	(19) 240
	(21) 500
	(26) 130
	(28) 15
	(29) 600
+ 4570	− 3005

(1565)

Supplies

(15) 600	
(4) 500	
(20) 50	
(21) 500	
1650	

Prepaid Insurance

(19) 240	
240	

Fortune Supplies

	(20) 50
	50

Herdle Office Supplies

(11) 250	(4) 500
250	500

(250)

Butlah VanBorne, Cap

	(1) 2000
	2000

Butlah VanBorne, Draw

(29) 600	
600	

Sales

	(7) 400
	(14) 500
	(21) 750
	(28) 520
	(31) 400
	2570

(8125)

Advertising Ex.

(26) 130	
130	

Miscellaneous Expence

(28) 15	
15	

Rent expence

(6) 500	
500	

Repair expence

(13) 80	
80	

Utilities Expence

(25) 90	
90	

8125

Name ______________________ Date ________ Class ________

MASTERY PROBLEM 3-M, p. 48
[1,2]

Analyzing transactions into debit and credit parts

Cash

Debit	Credit
(1) 3000	(2) 60
(4) 350	(4) 200
(1) 900	(5) 10
(11) 300	(10) 100
(18) 400	(15) 5
(25) 220	(16) 50
(30) 100	(22) 35
	(23) 30
	(26) 600
5270	1090

(4180)

(6910)

James Lants, Cap.

Debit	Credit
	(1) 3000
	(1) 900
	3900

James Lants, Draw.

Debit	Credit
(26) 600	
600	

Sales

Debit	Credit
	(4) 350
	(11) 300
	(18) 400
	(25) 220
	(30) 100
	1370

Supplies

Debit	Credit
(2) 60	
(9) 500	
(12) 50	
610	

Advertising

Debit	Credit
(23) 30	
30	

Prepaid Insurance

Debit	Credit
(10) 100	
100	

Misc. Ex.

Debit	Credit
(15) 5	
5	

Rent Expence

Debit	Credit
(4) 200	
200	

Vanitor Supplies

Debit	Credit
(16) 50	(9) 500
50	500

(450)

Repair Expence

Debit	Credit
(5) 10	
10	

Derner Office Supplies

Debit	Credit
	(12) 50
	50

6910

Utilities Expence

Debit	Credit
(22) 35	
35	

[1-4]

1	2	3	4	5	6
Trans. No.	**Accounts Affected**	**Account Classification**	**Entered in Account as a**		**Description of Transaction**
			Debit	**Credit**	
1.	Cash	Asset	✓		Received cash from owner as an investment
	Edward Burns, Capital	Owner's Equity		✓	
2.					
3.					
4.					
5.					
6.					
7.					
8.					
9.					
10.					
11.					
12.					

Perfect Score..... 37 Name ____________________

Deduct......... ___ Date ______________ Class ______________

Your Score..... ___ Checked by ____________________

STUDY GUIDE 4

UNIT A — Identifying Accounting Terms

DIRECTIONS: Select the one term in Column I that best fits each definition in Column II. Print the letter identifying your choice in the Answers column.

Column I	*Column II*	Answers	For Scoring
A. check	**0.** A form for recording transactions in chronological order..	E	**0.** ✓
B. double-entry accounting	**1.** A form on which a brief message is written describing a transaction..	G	**1.**
C. entry	**2.** A journal with two amount columns in which all kinds of entries can be recorded..............	D	**2.**
D. general journal	**3.** Information for each transaction recorded in a journal..	C	**3.**
E. journal	**4.** The recording of debit and credit parts of a transaction..	B	**4.**
F. journalizing			
G. memorandum			
H. receipt			
I. source document			

	Answers	For Scoring
5. A business paper from which information is obtained for a journal entry........	I	**5.**
6. A business form ordering a bank to pay cash from a bank account...............	A	**6.**
7. A business form giving written acknowledgement for cash received..............	H	**7.**
8. Recording transactions in a journal..	F	**8.**

UNIT B — Identifying Accounting Concepts and Practices

DIRECTIONS: For each item below, select the choice that best completes the sentence. Print the letter identifying your choice in the Answers column.

	Answers	For Scoring
0. Before information is recorded in a general journal, transactions are **(A)** analyzed into debit and credit parts **(B)** journalized **(C)** placed on an accounting equation **(D)** none of these...	A	**0.** ✓
1. Preparing a check for all cash payments is an application of the accounting concept **(A)** objective evidence **(B)** unit of measurement **(C)** business entity **(D)** none of these	A	**1.**
2. The kind of journal a business uses is determined by the **(A)** total amount of sales for a month **(B)** nature and number of transactions **(C)** total expenses for a week **(D)** none of these..	B	**2.**
3. On a single journal page, the month is written **(A)** in full for each entry **(B)** for each entry **(C)** once on a page **(D)** none of these	D	**3.**
4. At the same time a business prepares a check the business also prepares a **(A)** receipt **(B)** check stub **(C)** memorandum **(D)** none of these..........	B	**4.**
5. A memorandum includes a **(A)** stub **(B)** brief statement describing the transaction **(C)** new balance **(D)** none of these................................	B	**5.**
6. When a page of a journal is full except for a single blank line at the bottom of the page, **(A)** the next entry is split between this page and the next page **(B)** entries are verified to assure that debits equal credits **(C)** a new journal page is started **(D)** none of these..	C	**6.**
7. On a single journal page, the day of the month is written **(A)** in full for each entry **(B)** for each entry **(C)** once on a page **(D)** none of these....	B	**7.**
8. On a single journal page, the year is written **(A)** in full for each entry **(B)** for each entry **(C)** once on a page **(D)** all of these	C	**8.**
9. The source document number in the general journal Doc. No. column is a **(A)** cross reference from the journal to the source document **(B)** page number **(C)** number assigned at the time an entry is recorded **(D)** none of these..	A	**9.**
10. In accounting, words are **(A)** abbreviated whenever possible **(B)** written above the line **(C)** written in full when space permits **(D)** none of these ...	C	**10.**

UNIT C—Analyzing a General Journal

DIRECTIONS: Some items of the general journal are identified with capital letters. For each item below, decide which item is being described. Print the letter identifying your choice in the Answers column.

GENERAL JOURNAL PAGE

	DATE		ACCOUNT TITLE	Doc. No.	POST. REF.	DEBIT	CREDIT	
1	A B	C	D	E	F	G		1
2			H				I	2
3								3

	Answers	For Scoring
0. Write the year for the first entry on a journal page	A	**0.** ✓
1. Write the name of the month for the first entry	B	**1.**
2. Write the title of an account to be debited	D	**2.**
3. Write the title of an account to be credited	H	**3.**
4. Write the amount debited to Rent Expense	G	**4.**
5. Write the amount credited to Sales	I	**5.**
6. Write the debit amount when cash is received from sales	G	**6.**
7. Write the credit amount when cash is received from the owner as an investment	I	**7.**
8. Write the source document number for an entry	E	**8.**
9. Write the day of the month for an entry	C	**9.**
10. Write the title of the account debited when the electric bill is paid	D	**10.**

SECTION D—Recording Transactions in a General Journal

DIRECTIONS: Decide in which general journal amount column to record the amount described for each item below. Place a check mark in the appropriate Answers column to identify your decision.

Transactions	Answers Journal Amount Debit	Answers Journal Amount Credit	For Scoring
0. Entry to Cash when cash is paid for rent		✓	**0.** ✓
1. Entry to owner's drawing account when cash is paid for personal use	X		**1.**
2. Entry to Prepaid Insurance when cash is paid for insurance	X		**2.**
3. Entry to Supplies when supplies are bought on account	X		**3.**
4. Entry to Supplies when cash is paid for supplies	X		**4.**
5. Entry to Cash when cash is paid for Miscellaneous Expense		X	**5.**
6. Entry to a liability account when cash is paid on account	X		**6.**
7. Entry to owner's capital account when cash is received cash from owner as an investment		X	**7.**
8. Entry to Sales when cash is received from revenue		X	**8.**
9. Entry to Utilities Expense when cash is paid for electric bill	X		**9.**

Name ______________ Date ______ Class ______

DRILL 4-D1, p. 67
[1, 2]

Analyzing transactions

1.

Supplies	
100.00	

Cash	
	100.00

2.

3.

4.

5.

6.

7.

8.

9.

10.

11.

12.

DRILL 4-D2, p. 68
[1–4]

1	2	3	4	5	6	7
Trans No.	**Accounts Affected**	**Account Classification**	**How Is Account Affected?**		**Entered in Account as a**	
			+	**–**	**Debit**	**Credit**
1.	Advertising Expense	Expense	✓		✓	
	Cash	Asset		✓		✓
2.						
3.						
4.						
5.						
6.						
7.						
8.						
9.						
10.						
11.						
12.						

Name ______________________ Date ________ Class ________

PROBLEM 4-1, p. 69
[1]

Journalizing transactions in a general journal

GENERAL JOURNAL

PAGE 1

DATE		ACCOUNT TITLE	DOC. NO.	POST. REF.	DEBIT	CREDIT
1996 Feb	1	Cash	R1		12000 —	
		Dorothy Gilbert, Capital				12000 —
	3	rent expence	C1		600 —	
		Cash				600 —
	4	Prepaid Insurance	C2		1200 —	
		Cash				1200 —
	5	Supplies	M1		1500 —	
		Mertz Supplies				1500 —
	6	Supplies	C3		1000 —	
		Cash				1000 —
	7	Mertz Supplies	C4		750 —	
		Cash				750 —
	7	Cash	T7		500 —	
		Sales				500 —
	10	miscellaneous expence	C5		5 —	
		Cash				5 —
	14	Cash	T14		450 —	
		Sales				450 —
	17	repair expence	C6		75 —	
		Cash				75 —
	21	Cash	T21		2090 —	
		Sales				2090 —
	25	Utility expence	C7		50 —	
		Cash				50 —
	26	advertising expence	C8		90 —	
		Cash				90 —
	28	Dorothy Gilbert, Drawing	C9		250 —	
		Cash				250 —
	28	Cash	T28		1650 —	
		Sales				1650 —

[1]

GENERAL JOURNAL

PAGE

DATE		ACCOUNT TITLE	DOC. NO.	POST. REF.	DEBIT	CREDIT

Name ______________ Date ________ Class ________

PROBLEM 4-2, concluded

[2]

GENERAL JOURNAL

PAGE

DATE		ACCOUNT TITLE	DOC. NO.	POST. REF.	DEBIT	CREDIT

[1]

GENERAL JOURNAL

PAGE 1

DATE		ACCOUNT TITLE	DOC. NO.	POST. REF.	DEBIT	CREDIT
1996 June	1	Cash	R1		18000 —	
		Rachel Frank, Capital				18000 —
	2	rent expense	C1		900 —	
		Cash				900 —
	3	Supplies	C2		1500 —	
		Cash				1500 —
	4	Supplies	M1		3000 —	
		Delancy Supplies				3000 —
	5	Prepaid Insurance	C3		4500 —	
		Cash				4500 —
	5	Cash	T5		750 —	
		Sales				750 —
	8	Delancy Supplies	C4		1500 —	
		cash				1500 —
	9	Utilities expense	C5		75 —	
		cash				75 —
	9	Misc. expense	C6		7 —	
		cash				7 —
	10	Utilities expense	C7		1000 —	
		cash				1000 —
	10	advertising expense	C8		35 —	
		cash				35 —
	11	repair expense	C9		100 —	
		cash				100 —
	12	Cash	T12		850 —	
		Sales				850 —
	15	Rachel Frank, Drawing	C10		350 —	
		Cash				350 —
	16	Supplies	C11		1500 —	
		Cash				1500 —
	17	Supplies	M2		750 —	
		Long Supplies				750 —
	19	Cash	T19		3550 —	
		Sales				3550 —

Name ______________________ Date ________ Class ________

MASTERY PROBLEM 4-M, concluded

[2]

GENERAL JOURNAL

PAGE 2

DATE		ACCOUNT TITLE	DOC. NO.	POST. REF.	DEBIT	CREDIT
1996 June	22	Supplies	M3		80 —	
		Long Supplies				80 —
	23	advertising expense	C12		130 —	
		Cash				130 —
	24	utilities expense	C13		60 —	
		Cash				60 —
	26	Cash	T26		3000 —	
		Supplies				3000 —
	29	Supplies	C14		70 —	
		Cash				70 —
	30	Rachel Frank, Drawing	C15		375 —	
		Cash				375 —
	30	Cash	T30		1550 —	
		Sales				1550 —

27700
12102 =15598

CHALLENGE PROBLEM 4-C, p. 72

[1]

GENERAL JOURNAL

PAGE 2

DEBIT	DATE	ACCOUNT TITLE	DOC. NO.	POST. REF.	CREDIT

GENERAL JOURNAL [2]

PAGE

DEBIT	DATE	ACCOUNT TITLE	DOC. NO.	POST. REF.	CREDIT

Extra form

GENERAL JOURNAL

PAGE

DATE		ACCOUNT TITLE	DOC. NO.	POST. REF.	DEBIT	CREDIT

Perfect Score..... 49	Name ______________	
Deduct......... ___	Date ______________	Class ______________
Your Score..... ___	Checked by ______________	

STUDY GUIDE 5

UNIT A — Identifying Accounting Terms

DIRECTIONS: Select the one term in Column I that best fits each definition in Column II. Print the letter identifying your choice in the Answers column.

Column I	*Column II*	Answers	For Scoring
A. account number	**0.** The number assigned to an account	A	**0.** ✓
B. file maintenance	**1.** A group of accounts		**1.**
C. general ledger	**2.** A ledger that contains all accounts needed to prepare financial statements		**2.**
D. ledger	**3.** Transferring information from a journal entry to a ledger account		**3.**
E. opening an account	**4.** Writing an account title and number on the heading of an account		**4.**
F. posting			
G. proving cash			
	5. The procedure for arranging accounts in a general ledger, assigning account numbers and keeping records current		**5.**
	6. Determining that the amount of cash agrees with the accounting records		**6.**

UNIT B—Analyzing Accounting Practices

DIRECTIONS: Place a check mark in the proper Answers column to show whether each of the following statements is true or false.

	Answers True	Answers False	For Scoring
0. The procedure for transferring information from a journal to ledger accounts is called journalizing		✓	**0.** ✓
1. A journal is a permanent record of the debit and credit parts of each transaction recorded in chronological order			**1.**
2. A separate form is used to summarize in one place all the changes to a single account			**2.**
3. The T account is a useful device for journalizing all transactions			**3.**
4. The second division of Rugcare's chart of accounts is the owner's equity division			**4.**
5. The name given to an account is the account title			**5.**
6. The first digit of account numbers for accounts in Rugcare's owner's equity ledger division is 3			**6.**
7. When adding a new liability account between accounts numbered 220 and 230, the new account is assigned the account number 225			**7.**
8. When adding a new expense account between accounts numbered 510 and 520, the new account is assigned the account number 515			**8.**
9. When adding a new asset account between accounts numbered 130 and 140, the new account is assigned the account number 150			**9.**
10. When adding an account at the end of a ledger division, the next number in a sequence of 100's is used			**10.**
11. Account numbers on a chart of account always consist of three digits regardless of the type of business			**11.**
12. The last step in posting is to put the journal page number in the account's Post. Ref. column			**12.**
13. An account is opened in a general ledger by writing the account title and number in the account heading			**13.**

UNIT C—Identifying Accounting Concepts

DIRECTIONS: Place a check mark in the proper Answers column to show whether each of the following statements is best described as a debit or a credit.

	Statement	Answers: Debit	Answers: Credit	For Scoring
0.	Normal balance of Cash	✓		**0.** ✓
1.	Normal balance of Sales			**1.**
2.	Normal balance of owner's capital account			**2.**
3.	Normal balance of a liability account			**3.**
4.	Normal balance of Rent Expense			**4.**
5.	Column in an asset account in which an increase is shown			**5.**
6.	Column in a liability account in which an increase is shown			**6.**
7.	Column in a revenue account in which an increase is shown			**7.**
8.	Column in an expense account in which an increase is shown			**8.**
9.	Column in an asset account in which a decrease is shown			**9.**
10.	Column in a liability account in which a decrease is shown			**10.**
11.	Column in a revenue account in which a decrease is shown			**11.**
12.	Column in an expense account in which a decrease is shown			**12.**
13.	Account balance column in which the account balance is recorded when total debit entries exceed the total credit entries			**13.**
14.	Account balance column in which the account balance is recorded when total credit entries exceed the total debit entries			**14.**
15.	Account balance column in which the new account balance is recorded when previous balance is a debit of $500.00 and the current entry is a credit of $200.00			**15.**

UNIT D—Analyzing Posting from a Journal to a General Ledger

DIRECTIONS: In the journal below, some items are identified with capital letters. In the general ledger accounts, locations to which items are posted are identified with numbers. For each number in a general ledger account, select the letter in the journal that will be posted to the account. Print the letter identifying your choice in the Answers column.

GENERAL JOURNAL — PAGE A

	Date		Account Title	Doc. No.	Post. Ref.	Debit	Credit	
1	19-- May	2	Cash	R1		1 000 00		1
2			Adam Oliver, Capital				1 000 00	2
3		4	Supplies	M1		200 00		3
4			Hathaways				200 00	4
5		6	Prepaid Insurance	C1		500 00		5
6			Cash				500 00	6
7	B	C	D	E		F	G	7

ACCOUNT Cash — ACCOUNT NO. 110

Date		Item	Post. Ref.	Debit	Credit	Balance Debit	Balance Credit
0	1		2	3			

ACCOUNT Supplies — ACCOUNT NO. 120

Date		Item	Post. Ref.	Debit	Credit	Balance Debit	Balance Credit
4	5		6	7			

ACCOUNT Prepaid Insurance — ACCOUNT NO. 130

Date		Item	Post. Ref.	Debit	Credit	Balance Debit	Balance Credit
8	9		10	11			

ACCOUNT Hathaways — ACCOUNT NO. 210

Date		Item	Post. Ref.	Debit	Credit	Balance Debit	Balance Credit
12	13		14		15		

Bold Numbers in Ledger Accounts	Answers	For Scoring
0.	B	**0.** ✓
1.		**1.**
2.		**2.**
3.		**3.**
4.		**4.**
5.		**5.**
6.		**6.**
7.		**7.**
8.		**8.**
9.		**9.**
10.		**10.**
11.		**11.**
12.		**12.**
13.		**13.**
14.		**14.**
15.		**15.**

Name ______________________ Date ________ Class ________

DRILL 5-D1, p. 92
[1–4]

Preparing a chart of accounts

1	2
Account Description	**Account Number**
1. The first asset account	110
2. The first liability account	210
3. The first owner's equity account	310
4. The first revenue account	410
5. The first expense account	510
6. The third asset account	130
7. The fourth expense account	540
8. The owner's drawing account	320
9. The cash account	110
10. The sales account	421
11. The owner's capital account	310

Analyzing posting from a general journal

DRILL 5-D2, p. 92
[1, 2]

	1	2	3
Trans. No.	**Accounts Affected**	**How Accounts Are Affected**	
		Debit	**Credit**
1.	Cash	✓	
	Ben Furman, Capital		✓
2.	Ben Furman, Drawing	X	
	Cash		X
3.	Supplies	X	
	Cash		X
4.	Supplies	X	
	Butler Cleaning Supplies		X
5.	Butler Cleaning Supplies		X
	Cash		X
6.	Rent Expense	X	
	Cash		X
7.	Prepaid Insurance	X	
	Cash		X
8.	Utilities Expense	X	
	Cash		X
9.	Miscellaneous Expense	X	
	Cash		X
10.	Cash	X	
	Sales		X
11.	Advertising Expense	X	
	Cash		X

Preparing a chart of accounts

PROBLEM 5-1, p. 93
[1, 2]

Extra form

Name ______________________ Date ________ Class ______ *PROBLEM 5-2, p. 93*
[2]

Posting to a general ledger

GENERAL JOURNAL

PAGE 1

DATE		ACCOUNT TITLE	DOC. NO.	POST. REF.	DEBIT	CREDIT
19-- Nov.	1	Cash	R1	110	5000 00	
		Don Ley, Capital		310		5000 00
	3	Supplies	C1	120	780 00	
		Cash		110		780 00
	6	Prepaid Insurance	C2	130	900 00	
		Cash		110		900 00
	9	Supplies	M1	120	620 00	
		Donard Supplies		210		620 00
	12	Rent Expense	C3	530	200 00	
		Cash		110		200 00
	13	Utilities Expense	C4	540	25 00	
		Cash		110		25 00
	13	Cash	T13	110	300 00	
		Sales		410		300 00
	16	Donard Supplies	C5	210	310 00	
		Cash		110		310 00
	17	Miscellaneous Expense	C6	520	25 00	
		Cash		110		25 00
	20	Advertising Expense	C7	510	30 00	
		Cash		110		30 00
	20	Cash	T20	110	510 00	
		Sales		410		510 00
	25	Miscellaneous Expense	C8	520	40 00	
		Cash		110		40 00
	27	Cash	T27	110	1110 00	
		Sales		410		1110 00
	30	Supplies	M2	120	100 00	
		Fell Office Supplies		220		100 00
	30	Don Ley, Drawing	C9	320	50 00	
		Cash		110		50 00
	30	Cash	T30	110	230 00	
		Sales		410		230 00

GENERAL LEDGER

ACCOUNT   ACCOUNT NO.

DATE		ITEM	POST. REF.	DEBIT	CREDIT	BALANCE DEBIT	BALANCE CREDIT
1996 Nov	1		1	5000 –		5000 –	
	3		1		780 –	4220 –	
	6		1		900 –	3320 –	
	12		1		200 –	3120 –	
	13		1		25 –	3095 –	
	13		1	300 –		3395 –	
	16		1		310 –	3085 –	
	17		1		25 –	3060 –	
	20		1		30 –	3030 –	
	20		1	510 –		3540 –	
	25		1		40 –	3500 –	
	27		1	1110 –		4610 –	
	30		1		50 –	4560 –	
	30		1	230 –		4790 –	

ACCOUNT Supplies   ACCOUNT NO. 120

DATE		ITEM	POST. REF.	DEBIT	CREDIT	BALANCE DEBIT	BALANCE CREDIT
1996 Nov	3		1	780 –		780 –	
	9		1	620 –		1400 –	
	30		1	100 –		1500 –	

ACCOUNT Prepaid Insurance   ACCOUNT NO. 130

DATE		ITEM	POST. REF.	DEBIT	CREDIT	BALANCE DEBIT	BALANCE CREDIT
1996 Nov	6		1	900 –		900 –	

ACCOUNT Dohard Supplies   ACCOUNT NO. 210

DATE		ITEM	POST. REF.	DEBIT	CREDIT	BALANCE DEBIT	BALANCE CREDIT
1996 Nov	9		1		620 –		620 –
	16		1	310 –			310 –

ACCOUNT   ACCOUNT NO. 220

DATE		ITEM	POST. REF.	DEBIT	CREDIT	BALANCE DEBIT	BALANCE CREDIT
1996 Nov	30		1		100 –		100 –

GENERAL LEDGER

ACCOUNT Don Ley Capital ACCOUNT NO. 310

DATE		ITEM	POST. REF.	DEBIT	CREDIT	BALANCE DEBIT	BALANCE CREDIT
1996 Nov	1		1		5000 –		5000 –

ACCOUNT Don Ley Drawing ACCOUNT NO. 320

DATE		ITEM	POST. REF.	DEBIT	CREDIT	BALANCE DEBIT	BALANCE CREDIT
1996 Nov	30		1	50 –		50 –	

ACCOUNT Sales ACCOUNT NO. 410

DATE		ITEM	POST. REF.	DEBIT	CREDIT	BALANCE DEBIT	BALANCE CREDIT
1996 Nov	13		1		300 –		300 –
	20		1		510 –		810 –
	27		1		1110 –		1920 –
	30		1		230 –		2150 –

ACCOUNT Advertising expense ACCOUNT NO. 510

DATE		ITEM	POST. REF.	DEBIT	CREDIT	BALANCE DEBIT	BALANCE CREDIT
1996 Nov	20		1	30 –		30 –	

ACCOUNT ACCOUNT NO. 520

DATE		ITEM	POST. REF.	DEBIT	CREDIT	BALANCE DEBIT	BALANCE CREDIT
1996 Nov	17		1	25 –		25 –	
	25		1	40 –		65 –	

ACCOUNT ACCOUNT NO. 530

DATE		ITEM	POST. REF.	DEBIT	CREDIT	BALANCE DEBIT	BALANCE CREDIT
1996 Nov	12		1	200 –		200 –	

ACCOUNT ACCOUNT NO. 540

DATE		ITEM	POST. REF.	DEBIT	CREDIT	BALANCE DEBIT	BALANCE CREDIT
1996 Nov	13		1	25 –		25 –	

[1, 2]

GENERAL JOURNAL

PAGE

DATE		ACCOUNT TITLE	DOC. NO.	POST. REF.	DEBIT	CREDIT
1996 Nov	1	Cash	R1	110	7000 —	
		Al Hiatt, Capital		310		7000 —
	3	Rent expense	C1	530	300 —	
		Cash		110		300 —
	5	Prepaid Insurance	C2	130	200 —	
		Cash		110		200 —
	6	Cash	T6	110	400 —	
		Sales		410		400 —
	9	Misc. expense	C3	510	5 —	
		Cash		110		5 —
	11	Supplies	C4	120	500 —	
		Cash		110		500 —
	13	Supplies	M1	120	600 —	
		Major supplies		210		600 —
	13	Cash	T13	110	350 —	
		Sales		410		350 —
	16	Utilities expense	C5	540	40 —	
		Cash		110		40 —
	18	Major Supplies	C6	210	300 —	
		Cash		110		300 —
	20	Advertising expense	C7	510	30 —	
		Cash		110		30 —
	20	Cash	T20	110	700 —	
		Sales		410		700 —
	25	Supplies	C8	120	150 —	
		Cash		110		150 —
	27	Supplies	C9	120	100 —	
		Cash		110		100 —
	27	Cash	T27	110	1920 —	
		Sales		410		1920 —
	30	Al Hiatt Drawing	C10	320	300 —	
		Cash		110		300 —
	30	Cash	T30	110	410 —	
		Sales		410		410 —

[2, 3]

GENERAL LEDGER

ACCOUNT Cash — ACCOUNT NO. 110

DATE		ITEM	POST. REF.	DEBIT	CREDIT	BALANCE DEBIT	BALANCE CREDIT
1996 Nov	1		1	7000 —		7000 —	
	3		1		300 —	6700 —	
	5		1		200 —	6500 —	
	6		1	400 —		6900 —	
	9		1		5 —	6895 —	
	11		1		500 —	6395 —	
	13		1	350 —		6745 —	
	16		1		40 —	6705 —	
	18		1		300 —	6405 —	
	20		1		30 —	6375 —	
	20		1	700 —		7075 —	
	25		1		150 —	6925 —	
	27		1		100 —	6825 —	
	27		1	1920 —		8745 —	
	30		1		300 —	8445 —	
	30		1	410 —		8855 —	

ACCOUNT Supplies — ACCOUNT NO. 120

DATE		ITEM	POST. REF.	DEBIT	CREDIT	BALANCE DEBIT	BALANCE CREDIT
1996 Nov	11		1	500 —		500 —	
	13		1	600 —		1100 —	
	25		1	150 —		1250 —	
	27		1	100 —		1350 —	

ACCOUNT Prepaid Insurance — ACCOUNT NO. 130

DATE		ITEM	POST. REF.	DEBIT	CREDIT	BALANCE DEBIT	BALANCE CREDIT
1996 Nov	5		1	200 —		200 —	

ACCOUNT Major Supplies — ACCOUNT NO. 210

DATE		ITEM	POST. REF.	DEBIT	CREDIT	BALANCE DEBIT	BALANCE CREDIT
1996 Nov	13		1		600 —		600 —
	18		1	300 —			300 —

MASTERY PROBLEM 5-M, concluded

[2]

GENERAL LEDGER

ACCOUNT Al Hiatt, Capital — ACCOUNT NO. 310

DATE		ITEM	POST. REF.	DEBIT	CREDIT	BALANCE DEBIT	BALANCE CREDIT
1996 Nov.	1		1		7000—		7000—

ACCOUNT Al Hiatt, Drawing — ACCOUNT NO. 320

DATE		ITEM	POST. REF.	DEBIT	CREDIT	BALANCE DEBIT	BALANCE CREDIT
1998 Nov.	30		1	300—		300—	

ACCOUNT Sales — ACCOUNT NO. 410

DATE		ITEM	POST. REF.	DEBIT	CREDIT	BALANCE DEBIT	BALANCE CREDIT
1998 Nov.	6		1		400—		400—
	13		1		350—		750—
	20		1		700—		1450—
	27		1		1920—		3370—
	30		1		410—		3780—

ACCOUNT Advertising Expense — ACCOUNT NO. 510

DATE		ITEM	POST. REF.	DEBIT	CREDIT	BALANCE DEBIT	BALANCE CREDIT
1996 Nov.	26		1	30—		30—	

ACCOUNT Miscellaneous Expense — ACCOUNT NO. 520

DATE		ITEM	POST. REF.	DEBIT	CREDIT	BALANCE DEBIT	BALANCE CREDIT
1996 Nov.	9		1	5—		5—	

ACCOUNT Rent Expense — ACCOUNT NO. 530

DATE		ITEM	POST. REF.	DEBIT	CREDIT	BALANCE DEBIT	BALANCE CREDIT
1998 Nov.	3		1	300—		300—	

ACCOUNT Utilities Expense — ACCOUNT NO. 540

DATE		ITEM	POST. REF.	DEBIT	CREDIT	BALANCE DEBIT	BALANCE CREDIT
1998 Nov.	10		1	40—		40—	

Name ______________________ Date ________ Class ______

CHALLENGE PROBLEM 5-C, p. 94
[1, 2]

Journalizing in a general journal and posting to a general ledger

GENERAL JOURNAL

PAGE

DEBIT	DATE	ACCOUNT TITLE	DOC. NO.	POST. REF.	CREDIT

CHALLENGE PROBLEM 5-C, continued
[2, 3]

GENERAL LEDGER

ACCOUNT Cash — ACCOUNT NO. 110

DATE		ITEM	POST. REF.	DEBIT	CREDIT	BALANCE	
						DEBIT	CREDIT

ACCOUNT Supplies — ACCOUNT NO. 120

DATE		ITEM	POST. REF.	DEBIT	CREDIT	BALANCE	
						DEBIT	CREDIT

ACCOUNT Prepaid Insurance — ACCOUNT NO. 130

DATE		ITEM	POST. REF.	DEBIT	CREDIT	BALANCE	
						DEBIT	CREDIT

ACCOUNT Hartwood Supplies — ACCOUNT NO. 210

DATE		ITEM	POST. REF.	DEBIT	CREDIT	BALANCE	
						DEBIT	CREDIT

ACCOUNT Dee Worthy, Capital — ACCOUNT NO. 310

DATE		ITEM	POST. REF.	DEBIT	CREDIT	BALANCE	
						DEBIT	CREDIT

Name ______________________ Date ________ Class ________

CHALLENGE PROBLEM 5-C, concluded

[2]

GENERAL LEDGER

ACCOUNT Dee Worthy, Drawing — ACCOUNT NO. 320

DATE	ITEM	POST. REF.	DEBIT	CREDIT	BALANCE DEBIT	BALANCE CREDIT

ACCOUNT Sales — ACCOUNT NO. 410

DATE	ITEM	POST. REF.	DEBIT	CREDIT	BALANCE DEBIT	BALANCE CREDIT

ACCOUNT Advertising Expense — ACCOUNT NO. 510

DATE	ITEM	POST. REF.	DEBIT	CREDIT	BALANCE DEBIT	BALANCE CREDIT

ACCOUNT Miscellaneous Expense — ACCOUNT NO. 520

DATE	ITEM	POST. REF.	DEBIT	CREDIT	BALANCE DEBIT	BALANCE CREDIT

ACCOUNT Rent Expense — ACCOUNT NO. 530

DATE	ITEM	POST. REF.	DEBIT	CREDIT	BALANCE DEBIT	BALANCE CREDIT

ACCOUNT Utilities Expense — ACCOUNT NO. 540

DATE	ITEM	POST. REF.	DEBIT	CREDIT	BALANCE DEBIT	BALANCE CREDIT

GENERAL LEDGER

ACCOUNT ACCOUNT NO.

DATE		ITEM	POST. REF.	DEBIT	CREDIT	BALANCE DEBIT	BALANCE CREDIT

ACCOUNT ACCOUNT NO.

DATE		ITEM	POST. REF.	DEBIT	CREDIT	BALANCE DEBIT	BALANCE CREDIT

ACCOUNT ACCOUNT NO.

DATE		ITEM	POST. REF.	DEBIT	CREDIT	BALANCE DEBIT	BALANCE CREDIT

ACCOUNT ACCOUNT NO.

DATE		ITEM	POST. REF.	DEBIT	CREDIT	BALANCE DEBIT	BALANCE CREDIT

ACCOUNT ACCOUNT NO.

DATE		ITEM	POST. REF.	DEBIT	CREDIT	BALANCE DEBIT	BALANCE CREDIT

Perfect Score..... 37	Name Tiffanie Tabor	
Deduct......... ___	Date ______	Class 2nd
Your Score..... ___	Checked by ______	

STUDY GUIDE 6

UNIT A — Identifying Accounting Terms

DIRECTIONS: Select the one term in Column I that best fits each definition in Column II. Print the letter identifying your choice in the Answers column.

Column I

A. bank statement
B. blank endorsement
C. checking account
D. dishonored check
E. endorsement
F. postdated check
G. petty cash
H. petty cash slip
I. restrictive endorsement
J. special endorsement

Column II	Answers	For Scoring
0. A bank account from which payments can be ordered by a depositor	C	**0.** ✓
1. A form showing proof of a petty cash payment	H	**1.**
2. An endorsement consisting only of the endorser's signature	B	**2.**
3. An endorsement indicating a new owner of a check	J	**3.**
4. An endorsement restricting further transfer of a check's ownership	I	**4.**
5. A check with a future date on it	F	**5.**
6. A report of deposits, withdrawals, and bank balance sent to a depositor by a bank	A	**6.**
7. A check that a bank refuses to pay	D	**7.**
8. An amount of cash kept on hand and used for making small payments	G	**8.**
9. A signature or stamp on the back of a check transferring ownership	E	**9.**

UNIT B—Analyzing Transactions in a Cash Control System

DIRECTIONS: Analyze each of the following transactions into debit and credit parts. Print the letters identifying your choices in the proper Answers columns.

Account Titles

A. Cash
B. Miscellaneous Expense
C. Petty Cash
D. Rent Expense
E. Supplies

Transactions	Answers Debit	Answers Credit	For Scoring Debit	For Scoring Credit
0–0. Paid cash for rent	D	A	**0.** ✓	**0.** ✓
1–2. Paid cash to establish a petty cash fund	C	A	**1.**	**2.**
3–4. Received bank statement showing bank service charge	B	A	**3.**	**4.**
5–6. Paid cash to replenish petty cash fund, $15.00: supplies, $10.00; miscellaneous expense, $5.00	BE	A	**5.**	**6.**
7–8. Received notice from the bank of a dishonored check	B	A	**7.**	**8.**

UNIT C—Analyzing Accounting Practices

DIRECTIONS: Place a check mark in the proper Answers column to show whether each of the following statements is true or false.

Statement	Answers: True	Answers: False	For Scoring
0. A bank requires that the signature of the person authorized to sign checks be on the signature card	✓		**0.** ✓
1. When a depositor places money in a bank account, the bank issues a receipt	✓		**1.**
2. Each deposit made to a bank account should be recorded as a debit to cash in the journal	✓		**2.**
3. The amount of a check is written twice on each check	✓		**3.**
4. If an error is made on a check, tear up the check and dispose of the remains		✓	**4.**
5. Preparing a check stub for a cash payments transactions is the application of the accounting concept Objective Evidence	✓		**5.**
6. A check stub should be prepared before its corresponding check is written	✓		**6.**
7. A check with a blank endorsement on it can be cashed by whomever has the check	✓		**7.**
8. A stamped endorsement is not acceptable by most banks		✓	**8.**
9. Each time a payment is made from a petty cash fund, a petty cash slip should be prepared	✓		**9.**
10. Petty cash is replenished only when the amount in the petty cash box is low		✓	**10.**
11. The petty cash slip is the source document for the entry to replenish petty cash		✓	**11.**
12. The petty cash account is classified as an expense		✓	**12.**
13. When the petty cash fund is replenished, the balance of the petty cash account increases		✓	**13.**
14. Petty cash slips in a petty cash box represent cash payments that need to be journalized	✓		**14.**
15. Writing checks for all cash payments is not a cost effective cash control	✓		**15.**
16. Using a petty cash fund usually decreases the number of checks that have to be written	✓		**16.**
17. A memorandum is the source document for the entry to record establishing a petty cash fund		✓	**17.**
18. A special endorsement restricts the further transfer of ownership of a check		✓	**18.**
19. An outstanding check is one that has been issued but not yet reported on a bank statement by the bank	✓		**19.**
20. A restrictive endorsement restricts further transfer of a check's ownership	✓		**20.**

Name ______________________ Date ________ Class ________ *DRILL 6-D1, p. 116*

Reconciling a bank statement

RECONCILIATION OF BANK STATEMENT

____
(Date)

Balance On Check Stub No. ___ .... $

DEDUCT BANK CHARGES:

Description	Amount	
	$	

Total bank charges ▶

Adjusted Check Stub Balance .... $

Balance On Bank Statement....................... $

ADD OUTSTANDING DEPOSITS:

Date	Amount	
	$	

Total outstanding deposits ▶

TOTAL .... $

DEDUCT OUTSTANDING CHECKS:

Ck. No.	Amount		Ck. No.	Amount	

Total outstanding checks ▶

Adjusted Bank Balance .... $

Reconciling a bank statement *DRILL 6-D2, p. 117*

RECONCILIATION OF BANK STATEMENT

____
(Date)

Balance On Check Stub No. ___ .... $

DEDUCT BANK CHARGES:

Description	Amount	
	$	

Total bank charges ▶

Adjusted Check Stub Balance .... $

Balance On Bank Statement....................... $

ADD OUTSTANDING DEPOSITS:

Date	Amount	
	$	

Total outstanding deposits ▶

TOTAL .... $

DEDUCT OUTSTANDING CHECKS:

Ck. No.	Amount		Ck. No.	Amount	

Total outstanding checks ▶

Adjusted Bank Balance .... $

Replenishing a petty cash fund *DRILL 6-D3, p. 117*

Endorsing checks *PROBLEM 6-1, p. 117*

[1–3]

ENDORSE HERE
X Tiffanie Tabor
DO NOT WRITE, STAMP, OR SIGN BELOW THIS LINE RESERVED FOR FINANCIAL INSTITUTION USE

ENDORSE HERE
X pay to the order
of Delbert Richardson
Tiffanie Tabor
DO NOT WRITE, STAMP, OR SIGN BELOW THIS LINE RESERVED FOR FINANCIAL INSTITUTION USE

ENDORSE HERE
X for deposit only
Odd Jobs
Tiffanie Tabor
DO NOT WRITE, STAMP, OR SIGN BELOW THIS LINE RESERVED FOR FINANCIAL INSTITUTION USE

Writing checks

NO. **50** $ 138.00
Date October 30, 19 96
To Corner Garage
For repairs

BAL. BRO'T. FOR'D.	1396	75
AMT. DEPOSITED 10 30 96 (Date)	390	—
SUBTOTAL	1786	35
BANK CHARGES:		
SUBTOTAL:	1786	35
AMT. THIS CHECK	138	—
BAL. CAR'D. FOR'D.	1648	35

ODDJOBS
154 Main Street
Billings, MT 50001

NO. **50** 93-109/929

October 30 19 96

PAY TO THE ORDER OF Corner Garage $ 138.00

One hundred thirty eight & no/100 DOLLARS

For Classroom Use Only

peoples national bank
Billings, MT 59101-2320

FOR repairs Tiffanie Tabor

⑆0929010941⑆ 291⑈36118⑈

NO. **51** $ 50.00
Date October 30 19 96
To Office World
For supplies

BAL. BRO'T. FOR'D.	1648	35
AMT. DEPOSITED (Date)		
SUBTOTAL	1648	35
BANK CHARGES:		
SUBTOTAL:	1648	35
AMT. THIS CHECK	50	—
BAL. CAR'D. FOR'D.	1598	35

ODDJOBS
154 Main Street
Billings, MT 50001

NO. **51** 93-109/929

October 30 19 96

PAY TO THE ORDER OF Office Supplies $ 50.00

fifty & no/100 DOLLARS

For Classroom Use Only

peoples national bank
Billings, MT 59101-2320

FOR Supplies Tiffanie Tabor

⑆0929010941⑆ 291⑈36118⑈

NO. **52** $ 15.00
Date October 30 19 96
To Dixon Papers
For supplies

BAL. BRO'T. FOR'D.	1598	35
AMT. DEPOSITED (Date)		
SUBTOTAL	1598	35
BANK CHARGES:		
SUBTOTAL:	1598	30
AMT. THIS CHECK	15	—
BAL. CAR'D. FOR'D.	1584	35

ODDJOBS
154 Main Street
Billings, MT 50001

NO. **52** 93-109/929

October 30 19 96

PAY TO THE ORDER OF Dixon Papers $ 15.00

fifteen & no/100 DOLLARS

For Classroom Use Only

peoples national bank
Billings, MT 59101-2320

FOR Supplies Tiffanie Tabor

⑆0929010941⑆ 291⑈36118⑈

SECURITY NATIONAL BANK
Pittsburgh, Pa 15209-7634

STATEMENT OF ACCOUNT FOR
GolfPro
119 Matlock Street
Pittsburgh, PA 15237-4403

ACCOUNT NUMBER: 398-24534

STATEMENT DATE: August 28, 19--

BALANCE FROM PREVIOUS STATEMENT	NO. OF CHECKS	AMOUNT OF CHECKS	NO. OF DEPOSITS	AMOUNT OF DEPOSITS	SERVICE CHARGES	STATEMENT BALANCE
0.00	11	4,675.00	4	12,955.00	5.00	8,275.00

DATE	CHECK	AMOUNT	CHECK	AMOUNT	DEPOSITS	BALANCE
08/01/--						0.00
08/01/--					12,000.00	12,000.00
08/04/--	151	1,577.00				10,423.00
08/08/--	152	200.00			125.00	10,348.00
08/13/--	154	250.00	156	135.00		9,963.00
08/15/--	153	1,560.00	158	75.00	260.00	8,588.00
08/17/--	155	205.00	159	98.00		8,285.00
08/18/--	160	140.00				8,145.00
08/20/--	157	250.00				7,895.00
08/22/--					570.00	8,465.00
08/25/--	162	185.00				8,280.00
08/27/--	SC	5.00				8,275.00

PLEASE EXAMINE AT ONCE - IF NO ERRORS ARE REPORTED WITHIN 10 DAYS THE ACCOUNT WILL BE CONSIDERED CORRECT. REFER ANY DISCREPANCY TO OUR ACCOUNTING DEPARTMENT IMMEDIATELY.

GolfPro, 119 Matlock Street, Pittsburgh, PA 15237-4403 — NO. 151 — 8-17/430 — August 4, 19-- — PAY TO THE ORDER OF Montag Company $1577.00

GolfPro, 119 Matlock Street, Pittsburgh, PA 15237-4403 — NO. 152 — 8-17/430 — August 5, 19-- — PAY TO THE ORDER OF Pirin Company $200.00

GolfPro, 119 Matlock Street, Pittsburgh, PA 15237-4403 — NO. 153 — 8-17/430 — August 8, 19-- — PAY TO THE ORDER OF Thomson Company $1560.00

GolfPro, 119 Matlock Street, Pittsburgh, PA 15237-4403 — NO. 154 — 8-17/430 — August 8, 19-- — PAY TO THE ORDER OF Metro Insurance Co. $250.00

GolfPro, 119 Matlock Street, Pittsburgh, PA 15237-4403 — NO. 155 — 8-17/430 — August 10, 19-- — PAY TO THE ORDER OF City Electric Company $205.00

GolfPro, 119 Matlock Street, Pittsburgh, PA 15237-4403 — NO. 156 — 8-17/430 — August 10, 19-- — PAY TO THE ORDER OF Patterson Supplies $135.00
One hundred thirty five dollars — 00/100 DOLLARS
SECURITY NATIONAL BANK, Pittsburgh, Pa 15209-7634
FOR payment on account — John Walker
⑆043000177⑆ 398⑈24534⑈

GolfPro, 119 Matlock Street, Pittsburgh, PA 15237-4403 — NO. 157 — 8-17/430 — August 13, 19-- — PAY TO THE ORDER OF John Walker $250.00

GolfPro, 119 Matlock Street, Pittsburgh, PA 15237-4403 — NO. 158 — 8-17/430 — August 14, 19-- — PAY TO THE ORDER OF Pennsylvania Telephone Co. $75.00

GolfPro, 119 Matlock Street, Pittsburgh, PA 15237-4403 — NO. 159 — 8-17/430 — August 15, 19-- — PAY TO THE ORDER OF Ace Cleaning Company $98.00

GolfPro, 119 Matlock Street, Pittsburgh, PA 15237-4403 — NO. 160 — 8-17/430 — August 15, 19-- — PAY TO THE ORDER OF Tri-State Agency $140.00

GolfPro, 119 Matlock Street, Pittsburgh, PA 15237-4403 — NO. 162 — 8-17/430 — August 22, 19-- — PAY TO THE ORDER OF Dowd Company $185.00
One hundred eighty five dollars — 00/100 DOLLARS
SECURITY NATIONAL BANK, Pittsburgh, Pa 15209-7634
FOR payment on account — John Walker
⑆043000177⑆ 398⑈24534⑈

[3]

RECONCILIATION OF BANK STATEMENT

August 29, 1990
(Date)

Balance On Check Stub No. 165	$8068 —
DEDUCT BANK CHARGES:	

Description	Amount
Service charge	$ 5 —

Total bank charges ▶	5 —
Adjusted Check Stub Balance	$8063 —

Balance On Bank Statement	$8275 —
ADD OUTSTANDING DEPOSITS:	

Date	Amount
8-28-90	$430 —

Total outstanding deposits ▶	430 —
TOTAL	$8705 —
DEDUCT OUTSTANDING CHECKS:	

Ck. No.	Amount	Ck. No.	Amount
161	375 —		
163	17 —		
164	250 —		

Total outstanding checks ▶	1042 —
Adjusted Bank Balance	$8063 —

[4]

GENERAL JOURNAL

PAGE 8

	DATE		ACCOUNT TITLE	DOC. NO.	POST. REF.	DEBIT	CREDIT	
1								1
2								2
3								3
4								4
5								5
6								6
7								7
8								8
9								9
10								10
11								11
12								12
13								13
14								14
15								15

NO. 151 $ 1,577.00
Date August 1, 19--
To Mantag Company
For Supplies

BAL. BRO'T. FOR'D.	0	00
AMT. DEPOSITED 8/1	12,000	00
SUBTOTAL	12,000	00
BANK CHARGES:		
SUBTOTAL	12,000	00
AMT. THIS CHECK	1,577	00
BAL. CAR'D. FOR'D.	10,423	00

NO. 152 $ 200.00
Date August 5, 19--
To Perin Company
For Rent

BAL. BRO'T. FOR'D.	10,423	00
AMT. DEPOSITED		
SUBTOTAL	10,423	00
BANK CHARGES:		
SUBTOTAL	10,423	00
AMT. THIS CHECK	200	00
BAL. CAR'D. FOR'D.	10,223	00

NO. 153 $ 1,560.00
Date August 8, 19--
To Thomson Company
For Supplies

BAL. BRO'T. FOR'D.	10,223	00
AMT. DEPOSITED 8/8	125	00
SUBTOTAL	10,348	00
BANK CHARGES:		
SUBTOTAL	10,348	00
AMT. THIS CHECK	1,560	00
BAL. CAR'D. FOR'D.	8,788	00

NO. 154 $ 250.00
Date August 8, 19--
To Metro Insurance Company
For Insurance

BAL. BRO'T. FOR'D.	8,788	00
AMT. DEPOSITED		
SUBTOTAL	8,788	00
BANK CHARGES:		
SUBTOTAL	8,788	00
AMT. THIS CHECK	250	00
BAL. CAR'D. FOR'D.	8,538	00

NO. 155 $ 205.00
Date August 10, 19--
To City Electric Company
For Utilities

BAL. BRO'T. FOR'D.	8,538	00
AMT. DEPOSITED		
SUBTOTAL	8,538	00
BANK CHARGES:		
SUBTOTAL	8,538	00
AMT. THIS CHECK	205	00
BAL. CAR'D. FOR'D.	8,333	00

NO. 156 $ 135.00
Date August 10, 19--
To Patterson Supplies
For Payment on Account

BAL. BRO'T. FOR'D.	8,333	00
AMT. DEPOSITED		
SUBTOTAL	8,333	00
BANK CHARGES:		
SUBTOTAL	8,333	00
AMT. THIS CHECK	135	00
BAL. CAR'D. FOR'D.	8,198	00

NO. 157 $ 250.00
Date August 13, 19--
To John Walker
For Owner's withdrawal

BAL. BRO'T. FOR'D.	8,198	00
AMT. DEPOSITED		
SUBTOTAL	8,198	00
BANK CHARGES:		
SUBTOTAL	8,198	00
AMT. THIS CHECK	250	00
BAL. CAR'D. FOR'D.	7,948	00

NO. 158 $ 75.00
Date August 14, 19--
To Pennsylvania Telephone Company
For Utilities

BAL. BRO'T. FOR'D.	7,948	00
AMT. DEPOSITED		
SUBTOTAL	7,948	00
BANK CHARGES:		
SUBTOTAL	7,948	00
AMT. THIS CHECK	75	00
BAL. CAR'D. FOR'D.	7,873	00

NO. 159 $ 98.00
Date August 15, 19--
To Ace Cleaning Company
For Cleaning

BAL. BRO'T. FOR'D.	7,873	00
AMT. DEPOSITED		
SUBTOTAL	7,873	00
BANK CHARGES:		
SUBTOTAL	7,873	00
AMT. THIS CHECK	98	00
BAL. CAR'D. FOR'D.	7,775	00

NO. 160 $ 140.00
Date August 15, 19--
To Tri-State Agency
For Miscellaneous

BAL. BRO'T. FOR'D.	7,775	00
AMT. DEPOSITED 8/15	260	00
SUBTOTAL	8,035	00
BANK CHARGES:		
SUBTOTAL	8,035	00
AMT. THIS CHECK	140	00
BAL. CAR'D. FOR'D.	7,895	00

NO. 161 $ 375.00
Date August 19, 19--
To Pittsburgh Enquirer
For Advertising

BAL. BRO'T. FOR'D.	7,895	00
AMT. DEPOSITED		
SUBTOTAL	7,895	00
BANK CHARGES:		
SUBTOTAL	7,895	00
AMT. THIS CHECK	375	00
BAL. CAR'D. FOR'D.	7,520	00

NO. 162 $ 185.00
Date August 22, 19--
To David Company
For Payment on Account

BAL. BRO'T. FOR'D.	7,520	00
AMT. DEPOSITED 8/22	570	00
SUBTOTAL	8,090	00
BANK CHARGES:		
SUBTOTAL	8,090	00
AMT. THIS CHECK	185	00
BAL. CAR'D. FOR'D.	7,905	00

NO. 163 $ 17.00
Date August 23, 19--
To Jason North
For Miscellaneous

BAL. BRO'T. FOR'D.	7,905	00
AMT. DEPOSITED		
SUBTOTAL	7,905	00
BANK CHARGES:		
SUBTOTAL	7,905	00
AMT. THIS CHECK	17	00
BAL. CAR'D. FOR'D.	7,888	00

NO. 164 $ 250.00
Date August 28, 19--
To John Walker
For Owner's withdrawal

BAL. BRO'T. FOR'D.	7,888	00
AMT. DEPOSITED 8/28	430	00
SUBTOTAL	8,318	00
BANK CHARGES:		
SUBTOTAL	8,318	00
AMT. THIS CHECK	250	00
BAL. CAR'D. FOR'D.	8,068	00

NO. 165 $ 6.00
Date August 29 19--
To
For

BAL. BRO'T. FOR'D.	8,068	00
AMT. DEPOSITED		
SUBTOTAL	8,068	00
BANK CHARGES:		
SUBTOTAL		
AMT. THIS CHECK		
BAL. CAR'D. FOR'D.		

Name ______________ Date ________ Class ________

PROBLEM 6-4, p. 117
[1]

Establishing and replenishing a petty cash fund

GENERAL JOURNAL

PAGE 10

DATE	ACCOUNT TITLE	DOC. NO.	POST. REF.	DEBIT	CREDIT

Reconciling a bank statement; journalizing a bank service charge, a dishonored check, and petty cash transactions

MASTERY PROBLEM 6-M, p. 118

[1, 3]

GENERAL JOURNAL

PAGE 20

	DATE		ACCOUNT TITLE	DOC. NO.	POST. REF.	DEBIT	CREDIT	
1	1994 Aug	21	Petty cash fund		601	100 —		1
2			cash				100 —	2
3		24	Repairs		602	135 —		3
4			cash				135 —	4
5		26	Supplies		603	40 —		5
6			cash				40 —	6
7		27						7
8								8
9								9
10								10
11								11
12								12
13								13
14								14
15								15
16								16
17								17

[2]

RECONCILIATION OF BANK STATEMENT

August 31, 1994
(Date)

Balance On Check Stub No. 607	$ 1601 —
DEDUCT BANK CHARGES:	
Description: Service charge — Amount: $ 5 —	
Total bank charges	5 —
Adjusted Check Stub Balance	$ 1606 —

Balance On Bank Statement	$ 1521 —
ADD OUTSTANDING DEPOSITS:	
Date: 8-31-94 — Amount: $ 430 —	
Total outstanding deposits	430
TOTAL	$ 1951 —
DEDUCT OUTSTANDING CHECKS:	
Ck. No. 605 — Amount 300 —	
Ck. No. 606 — Amount 110 —	
Total outstanding checks	410 —
Adjusted Bank Balance	$ 1541 —

Name ______________________ Date ________ Class ________

CHALLENGE PROBLEM 6-C, p. 119
[3]

Reconciling a bank statement

RECONCILIATION OF BANK STATEMENT

November 30, 19--
(Date)

Balance On Check Stub No. *507* .... $ *11,723.00*

DEDUCT BANK CHARGES:

Description	Amount
Service Charge	$ *3.00*

Total bank charges ▶ *3.00*

Adjusted Check Stub Balance .... $ *11,720.00*

Balance On Bank Statement .... $ *11,830.00*

ADD OUTSTANDING DEPOSITS:

Date	Amount
	$

Total outstanding deposits ▶ *0.00*

TOTAL .... $ *11,830.00*

DEDUCT OUTSTANDING CHECKS:

Ck. No.	Amount	Ck. No.	Amount
504	*25.00*		
505	*129.00*		
506	*500.00*		
507	*89.00*		

Total outstanding checks ▶ *743.00*

Adjusted Bank Balance .... $ *11,087.00*

RECONCILIATION OF BANK STATEMENT

____
(Date)

Balance On Check Stub No. ____ .... $

DEDUCT BANK CHARGES:

Description	Amount
	$

Total bank charges ▶

Adjusted Check Stub Balance .... $

Balance On Bank Statement .... $

ADD OUTSTANDING DEPOSITS:

Date	Amount
	$

Total outstanding deposits ▶

TOTAL .... $

DEDUCT OUTSTANDING CHECKS:

Ck. No.	Amount	Ck. No.	Amount

Total outstanding checks ▶

Adjusted Bank Balance .... $

[1–3]

NO. 500 $ 15.00
Date November 24, 19--
To Robin Office Supply
For Supplies

BAL. BRO'T. FOR'D.	12,377	00
AMT. DEPOSITED (Date)		
SUBTOTAL	12,377	00
BANK CHARGES:		
SUBTOTAL:	12,377	00
AMT. THIS CHECK	15	00
BAL. CAR'D. FOR'D.	12,362	00

NO. 501 $ 1,009.00
Date November 24, 19--
To Wallace Company
For Payment on Account

BAL. BRO'T. FOR'D.	12,362	00
AMT. DEPOSITED (Date)		
SUBTOTAL	12,362	00
BANK CHARGES:		
SUBTOTAL:	12,362	00
AMT. THIS CHECK	1,009	00
BAL. CAR'D. FOR'D.	11,353	00

NO. 502 $ 35.00
Date November 25, 19--
To Mason Repair Company
For Repairs

BAL. BRO'T. FOR'D.	11,353	00
AMT. DEPOSITED (Date)		
SUBTOTAL	11,353	00
BANK CHARGES:		
SUBTOTAL:	11,353	00
AMT. THIS CHECK	35	00
BAL. CAR'D. FOR'D.	11,318	00

NO. 503 $ 125.00
Date November 26, 19--
To The Examiner
For Advertising

BAL. BRO'T. FOR'D.	11,318	00
AMT. DEPOSITED 11 26 -- (Date)	640	00
SUBTOTAL	11,958	00
BANK CHARGES:		
SUBTOTAL:	11,958	00
AMT. THIS CHECK	152	00
BAL. CAR'D. FOR'D.	11,833	00

NO. 504 $ 25.00
Date November 28, 19--
To Robin Office Supply
For Supplies

BAL. BRO'T. FOR'D.	11,806	00
AMT. DEPOSITED (Date)		
SUBTOTAL	11,806	00
BANK CHARGES:		
SUBTOTAL:	11,806	00
AMT. THIS CHECK	25	00
BAL. CAR'D. FOR'D.	11,781	00

NO. 505 $ 129.00
Date November 29, 19--
To Secure Insurance Company
For Insurance

BAL. BRO'T. FOR'D.	11,781	00
AMT. DEPOSITED (Date)		
SUBTOTAL	11,808	00
BANK CHARGES:		
SUBTOTAL:	11,808	00
AMT. THIS CHECK	129	00
BAL. CAR'D. FOR'D.	11,652	00

NO. 506 $ 500.00
Date November 29, 19--
To Julie Johnson
For Owner's withdrawal

BAL. BRO'T. FOR'D.	11,652	00
AMT. DEPOSITED (Date)		
SUBTOTAL	11,652	00
BANK CHARGES:		
SUBTOTAL:	11,652	00
AMT. THIS CHECK	500	00
BAL. CAR'D. FOR'D.	11,252	00

NO. 507 $ 89.00
Date November 30, 19--
To Petty Cash
For Replenishment

BAL. BRO'T. FOR'D.	11,252	00
AMT. DEPOSITED 11 30 -- (Date)	560	00
SUBTOTAL	11,812	00
BANK CHARGES:		
SUBTOTAL:	11,812	00
AMT. THIS CHECK	89	00
BAL. CAR'D. FOR'D.	11,723	00

Perfect Score..... 44 Name ______

Deduct......... ___ Date ______ Class ______

Your Score..... ___ Checked by ______

STUDY GUIDE 7

UNIT A—Identifying Accounting Terms

DIRECTIONS: Select the one term in Column I that best fits each definition in Column II. Print the letter identifying your choice in the Answers column.

Column I	Column II	Answers	For Scoring
A. adjustments **B.** fiscal period	**0.** The length of time for which a business summarizes and reports financial information	B	**0.** ✓
C. income statement **D.** net income	**1.** A financial statement showing the revenue and expenses for a fiscal period		**1.**
E. net loss **F.** trial balance	**2.** A proof of the equality of debits and credits in a general ledger		**2.**
G. work sheet	**3.** Changes recorded on a work sheet to update general ledger accounts at the end of a fiscal period		**3.**
	4. A columnar accounting form used to summarize the general ledger information needed to prepare financial statements		**4.**
	5. The difference between total revenue and total expenses when total revenue is greater		**5.**
	6. The difference between total revenue and total expenses when total expenses is greater		**6.**

UNIT B—Analyzing the Preparation of a Trial Balance on a Work Sheet

DIRECTIONS: For each account title listed below, decide whether the account balance is recorded in the Trial Balance Debit or Trial Balance Credit column. Place a check mark in the proper Answers column identifying your choice.

	Trial Balance Debit	Trial Balance Credit	For Scoring
0. Advertising Expense	✓		**0.** ✓
1. Ben Furman, Capital			**1.**
2. Ben Furman, Drawing			**2.**
3. Butler Cleaning Supplies			**3.**
4. Cash			**4.**
5. Miscellaneous Expense			**5.**

	Trial Balance Debit	Trial Balance Credit	For Scoring
6. Petty Cash			**6.**
7. Prepaid Insurance			**7.**
8. Rent Expense			**8.**
9. Repair Expense			**9.**
10. Sales			**10.**
11. Supplies			**11.**
12. Utilities Expense			**12.**

UNIT C—Analyzing Adjustments and Extending Account Balances on a Work Sheet

DIRECTIONS: For each account listed below, determine in which work sheet column(s) an amount typically will be written. Place a check mark in the proper Answers column to show your answer.

	Adjustments		Income Statement		Balance Sheet		For Scoring
	Debit	Credit	Debit	Credit	Debit	Credit	
0. Insurance Expense	✓		✓				**0.** ✓
1. Advertising Expense							**1.**
2. Ben Furman, Capital							**2.**
3. Ben Furman, Drawing							**3.**
4. Butler Cleaning Supplies							**4.**
5. Cash							**5.**
6. Miscellaneous Expense							**6.**
7. Petty Cash							**7.**
8. Prepaid Insurance							**8.**
9. Rent Expense							**9.**
10. Repair Expense							**10.**
11. Sales							**11.**
12. Supplies							**12.**
13. Supplies Expense							**13.**
14. Utilities Expense							**14.**

UNIT D—Analyzing Accounting Practices Related to a Work Sheet

DIRECTIONS: Place a check mark in the proper True or False Answers column to show whether each of the following statements is true or false.

	Answers		For Scoring
	True	False	
0. On December 31 of the current year, a business' advertising expense account has a debit balance because the accounts debits exceed its credits	✓		**0.** ✓
1. The four questions asked when analyzing anadjustment are: 1. Why? 2. Where? 3. When? and 4. How?			**1.**
2. The information written on the second line of the heading for a work sheet is the report's date			**2.**
3. A work sheet summarizes and reports the financial information of a business for a fiscal period			**3.**
4. The account balance for the cash account is recorded in the Trial Balance Debit and Balance Sheet Credit columns of a work sheet			**4.**
5. A net loss results when the total revenue is greater than the total expenses			**5.**
6. A net income results when the total revenue is greater than the total expenses			**6.**
7. The two accounts affected by the adjustment for the supplies account are Supplies and Supplies Expense			**7.**
8. The two accounts affected by the adjustment for insurance are Prepaid Insurance Expense and Insurance			**8.**
9. If the two totals of a work sheet's Trial Balance columns are not equal, and the difference between the two totals is $1.00, the error is likely in posting			**9.**
10. If the two totals of the Adjustment columns are not equal, and the difference between the two totals is $18.00, the error is likely a transposition or a slide			**10.**
11. If the two totals of the Balance Sheet columns are not equal, and the difference between the two totals is $15.00, the error is probably in addition			**11.**
12. If the two totals of the Income Statement columns are not equal, and the error does not appear to be in arithmetic, the next thing to check is whether the account balances have been transferred correctly from the Trial Balance columns			**12.**

Extending account balances on a work sheet [1–3]

		1	2	5	6	7	8
	Account Title	Trial Balance		Income Statement		Balance Sheet	
		Debit	Credit	Debit	Credit	Debit	Credit
1.	Advertising Expense	✓		✓			
2.							
3.							
4.							
5.							
6.							
7.							
8.							
9.							
10.							
11.							
12.							

	Income Statement		Balance Sheet	
	Debit	**Credit**	**Debit**	**Credit**
COMPANY A				
1. Column totals	$9,000	$9,500	$35,500	$35,000
2. Net Income	500			500
3. Proving totals	9,500	9,500	35,500	35,500
COMPANY B				
1. Column totals				
2.				
3. Proving totals				
COMPANY C				
1. Column totals				
2.				
3. Proving totals				
COMPANY D				
1. Column totals				
2.				
3. Proving totals				
COMPANY E				
1. Column totals				
2.				
3. Proving totals				

Completing a work sheet [1–6]

Clean Lawn
Worksheet
For Month ended September 30, 1996

	Account Title	Trial Balance Debit (1)	Trial Balance Credit (2)	Adjustments Debit (3)	Adjustments Credit (4)	Income Statement Debit (5)	Income Statement Credit (6)	Balance Sheet Debit (7)	Balance Sheet Credit (8)
	Cash	3000—						3000—	
	Petty Cash	100—						100—	
	Supplies	2000—			(a) 900—			1100—	
Assets	Prepaid Insurance	900—			(b) 300—			600—	
	Bix Supplies		600—						600—
L	Officeworld		100—						100—
	Dorothy Daily, Cap		4100—						4100—
C	Dorothy Daily, Dra	200—						200—	
	Income Summary	—	—						
	Sales		2505—				2505—		
	Advertising expense	75—				75—			
	Insurance expense	—		(b) 300—		300—			
	Misc. expense	110—				110—			
	Rent expense	600—				600—			
	Repair expense	180—				180—			
	Supplies expense	—		(a) 900—		900—			
	Utilities expense	140—				140—			
		7305—	7305—	1200—	1200—	2305—	2505—	5000—	4800—
	Net Income					200—			200—
						2505—	2505—	5000—	5000—

Village Service Co.
Work Sheet
For month ended October 31, 1996

	ACCOUNT TITLE	1 TRIAL BALANCE DEBIT	2 TRIAL BALANCE CREDIT	3 ADJUSTMENTS DEBIT	4 ADJUSTMENTS CREDIT	5 INCOME STATEMENT DEBIT	6 INCOME STATEMENT CREDIT	7 BALANCE SHEET DEBIT	8 BALANCE SHEET CREDIT	
1	Cash	4900 —						4900 —		1
2	Petty Cash	300 —						300 —		2
3	Supplies	2500 —			(a) 1000 —			1500 —		3
4	PrePaid Insurance	2100 —			(b) 1200 —			900 —		4
5	National Supplies		1400 —						1400 —	5
6	Office Distributors		1200 —						1200 —	6
7	Wensk Movies		800 —						800 —	7
8	Susan Haile, Cap		6000 —						6000 —	8
9	Susan Haile, Dra	1200 —						1200 —		9
10	Income Summary									10
11	Sales		20100 —				20100 —			11
12	Advertising Ex	4200 —				4200 —				12
13	Insurance Expense			(b) 1200 —		1200 —				13
14	Misc Expense	600 —				600 —				14
15	Rent expense	8000 —				8000 —				15
16	Repair expense	2400 —				2400 —				16
17	Supplies expense			(a) 1000 —		1000 —				17
18	Utilities expense	3300 —				3300 —				18
19		29500 —	29500 —	2200 —	2200 —	20700 —	20100 —	8800 —	9400 —	19
20							600	600 —		20
21						20700 —	20700 —	9400 —	9400 —	21
22										22
23										23
24										24
25										25
26										26
27										27
28										28
29										29
30										30
31										31
32										32

Name ______________________ Date ________ Class ________

PROBLEM 7-3, p. 144
[1, 2]

Finding and correcting errors in accounting records

GENERAL LEDGER

ACCOUNT Cash — ACCOUNT NO. 110

DATE		ITEM	POST. REF.	DEBIT	CREDIT	BALANCE DEBIT	BALANCE CREDIT
19-- Sept.	1		1	5,000.00		5,000.00	
	30		2	7,000.00		~~15,000.00~~ 12,000—	
	30		2		6,750.00	~~8,000.00~~ 5250—	

ACCOUNT Supplies — ACCOUNT NO. 120

DATE		ITEM	POST. REF.	DEBIT	CREDIT	BALANCE DEBIT	BALANCE CREDIT
19-- Sept.	2		1	600.00		600.00	
	25		2	425.00		~~725.00~~ 1025—	

ACCOUNT Prepaid Insurance — ACCOUNT NO. 130

DATE		ITEM	POST. REF.	DEBIT	CREDIT	BALANCE DEBIT	BALANCE CREDIT
19-- Sept.	3		1	150.00		150.00	
	20		2	150.00		~~400.00~~ 300—	

ACCOUNT Powers Supply — ACCOUNT NO. 210

DATE		ITEM	POST. REF.	DEBIT	CREDIT	BALANCE DEBIT	BALANCE CREDIT
19-- Sept.	4		1		300.00		300.00
	15		2	150.00			150.00

ACCOUNT Paul Coty, Capital — ACCOUNT NO. 310

DATE		ITEM	POST. REF.	DEBIT	CREDIT	BALANCE DEBIT	BALANCE CREDIT
19-- Sept.	1		1		5,000.00		5,000.00

GENERAL LEDGER

ACCOUNT Paul Coty, Drawing — ACCOUNT NO. 320

DATE		ITEM	POST. REF.	DEBIT	CREDIT	BALANCE DEBIT	BALANCE CREDIT
19-- Sept.	30		2	300 00		300 00	

ACCOUNT Income Summary — ACCOUNT NO. 330

DATE		ITEM	POST. REF.	DEBIT	CREDIT	BALANCE DEBIT	BALANCE CREDIT

ACCOUNT Sales — ACCOUNT NO. 410

DATE		ITEM	POST. REF.	DEBIT	CREDIT	BALANCE DEBIT	BALANCE CREDIT
19-- Sept.	30		2		1900 00		~~1875 00~~
							1900 —

ACCOUNT Insurance Expense — ACCOUNT NO. 510

DATE		ITEM	POST. REF.	DEBIT	CREDIT	BALANCE DEBIT	BALANCE CREDIT

ACCOUNT Miscellaneous Expense — ACCOUNT NO. 520

DATE		ITEM	POST. REF.	DEBIT	CREDIT	BALANCE DEBIT	BALANCE CREDIT
19-- Sept.	9		1	150 00		150 00	
	27		2	25 00		~~125 00~~	
						175 —	

ACCOUNT Supplies Expense — ACCOUNT NO. 530

DATE		ITEM	POST. REF.	DEBIT	CREDIT	BALANCE DEBIT	BALANCE CREDIT

[1]

ERRORS

[1]

LeafyLift
Work Sheet
For Month Ended September 30, 19--

	ACCOUNT TITLE	1 TRIAL BALANCE DEBIT	2 TRIAL BALANCE CREDIT	3 ADJUSTMENTS DEBIT	4 ADJUSTMENTS CREDIT	5 INCOME STATEMENT DEBIT	6 INCOME STATEMENT CREDIT	7 BALANCE SHEET DEBIT	8 BALANCE SHEET CREDIT	
1	Cash	8000 00						8000 00		1
2	Supplies	725 00		(a) 390 00				1115 00		2
3	Prepaid Insurance	400 00		(b) 95 00				495 00		3
4	Powers Supply		150 00						150 00	4
5	Paul Coty, Capital		5000 00						5000 00	5
6	Paul Coty, Drawing	300 00							300 00	6
7	Income Summary									7
8	Sales		1875 00				1875 00			8
9	Insurance Expense				(b) 95 00		95 00			9
10	Miscellaneous Expense	125 00				152 00				10
11	Supplies Expense				(a) 390 00		390 00			11
12		9550 00	7025 00	485 00	485 00	152 00	2360 00	9610 00	5450 00	12
13	Net Income					2208 00			4160 00	13
14						2360 00	2360 00	9610 00	9610 00	14

Fastgrow
Work Sheet
For month ended april 30, 1996

	ACCOUNT TITLE	TRIAL BALANCE DEBIT	TRIAL BALANCE CREDIT	ADJUSTMENTS DEBIT	ADJUSTMENTS CREDIT	INCOME STATEMENT DEBIT	INCOME STATEMENT CREDIT	BALANCE SHEET DEBIT	BALANCE SHEET CREDIT
1	Cash	5800—						5800—	
2	petty cash	200—						200—	
3	Supplies	4000—			(a) 1950—			2050—	
4	prepaid Insurance	1000—			(b) 550—			450—	
5	Wheaton Supplies		200—						200—
6	Norton Company		115—						115—
7	Roger Bently, Cap.		7200—						7200—
8	Roger Bently, Dra.	400—						400—	
9	Income Summery								
10	Sales		5300—				5300—		
11	advertising expense	325—				325—			
12	Insurance expense			(b) 550—		550—			
13	Misc expense	140—				140—			
14	Rent expense	500—				500—			
15	Supplies expense			(b) 1950—		1950—			
16	Utilities expense	450—				450—			
17		12815—	12815—	2500—	2500—	3915—	5300—	8900—	7515—
18	Net income					1385—			1385—
19						5300—	5300—	8900—	8900—

[3]

	ACCOUNT TITLE	1 TRIAL BALANCE DEBIT	2 TRIAL BALANCE CREDIT	3 ADJUSTMENTS DEBIT	4 ADJUSTMENTS CREDIT	5 INCOME STATEMENT DEBIT	6 INCOME STATEMENT CREDIT	7 BALANCE SHEET DEBIT	8 BALANCE SHEET CREDIT	
1										1
2										2
3										3
4										4
5										5
6										6
7										7
8										8
9										9
10										10
11										11
12										12
13										13
14										14
15										15
16										16
17										17
18										18
19										19
20										20
21										21
22										22
23										23
24										24
25										25
26										26
27										27
28										28
29										29
30										30
31										31
32										32

Completing a work sheet [1–2]

	ACCOUNT TITLE	TRIAL BALANCE		ADJUSTMENTS		INCOME STATEMENT		BALANCE SHEET		
		1 DEBIT	2 CREDIT	3 DEBIT	4 CREDIT	5 DEBIT	6 CREDIT	7 DEBIT	8 CREDIT	
1										1
2										2
3										3
4										4
5										5
6										6
7										7
8										8
9										9
10										10
11										11
12										12
13										13
14										14
15										15
16										16
17										17
18										18
19										19
20										20
21										21
22										22
23										23
24										24
25										25
26										26
27										27
28										28
29										29
30										30
31										31
32										32

	ACCOUNT TITLE	1 TRIAL BALANCE DEBIT	2 TRIAL BALANCE CREDIT	3 ADJUSTMENTS DEBIT	4 ADJUSTMENTS CREDIT	5 INCOME STATEMENT DEBIT	6 INCOME STATEMENT CREDIT	7 BALANCE SHEET DEBIT	8 BALANCE SHEET CREDIT	
1										1
2										2
3										3
4										4
5										5
6										6
7										7
8										8
9										9
10										10
11										11
12										12
13										13
14										14
15										15
16										16
17										17
18										18
19										19
20										20
21										21
22										22
23										23
24										24
25										25
26										26
27										27
28										28
29										29
30										30
31										31
32										32

Perfect Score..... 39 Name ____________________

Deduct......... ___ Date ______________ Class ______________

Your Score..... ___ Checked by ____________________

STUDY GUIDE 8

UNIT A—Analyzing an Income Statement

DIRECTIONS: The parts of the income statement on the right are identified with capital letters. Decide the location of each of the following items. Print the letter identifying your choice in the Answers column.

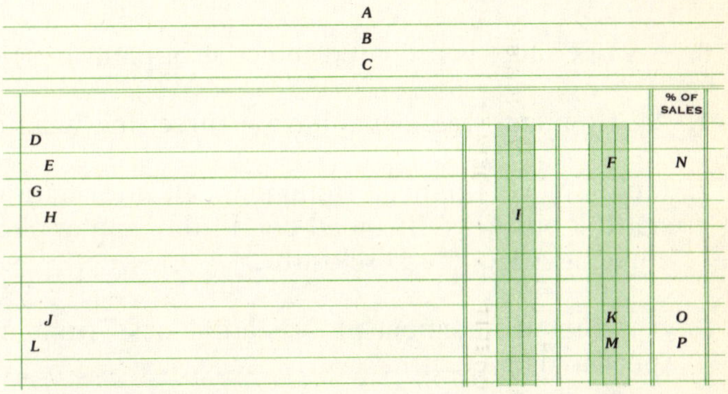

	Answers	For Scoring
0. Date of the income statement....................	C	**0.** ✓
1. The amount of net income or net loss		**1.**
2. Business name.............		**2.**
3. Expense account balances		**3.**
4. Expense account titles ...		**4.**
5. Heading of expense section		**5.**
6. Heading of revenue section		**6.**
7. Net Income or net loss component percentage....		**7.**

	Answers	For Scoring
8. Revenue account title		**8.**
9. Sales component percentage		**9.**
10. Statement name		**10.**
11. Total amount of revenue		**11.**
12. Total expenses component percentage		**12.**
13. Words *Net Income* or *Net Loss*		**13.**
14. Words *Total Expenses*		**14.**

UNIT B—Analyzing a Balance Sheet

DIRECTIONS: The parts of the balance sheet on the right are identified with capital letters. Decide the location of each of the following items. Print the letter identifying your choice in the Answers column.

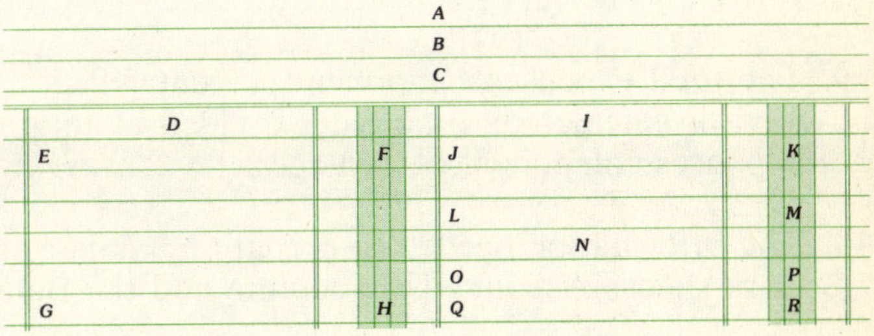

	Answers	For Scoring
0. Name of the Statement...	B	**0.** ✓
1. Amount of total assets ...		**1.**
2. Amount of total liabilities and owner's equity.........		**2.**
3. Asset account balances...		**3.**
4. Liability account balances		**4.**
5. Owner's capital account balance		**5.**
6. Heading for the assets section		**6.**
7. Heading for the liabilities section		**7.**

	Answers	For Scoring
8. Heading for the owner's equity section		**8.**
9. Liability account titles ...		**9.**
10. Asset account titles		**10.**
11. Owner's capital account title		**11.**
12. Words *Total Assets*		**12.**
13. Words *Total Liabilities and Owner's Equity*........		**13.**

DIRECTIONS: Place a check mark in the proper Answers column to show whether each of the following statements is true or false.

	Answers True	False	For Scoring
0. A work sheet is prepared to assist in planning financial statements	✓		**0.** ✓
1. All financial statements have a three-line heading			**1.**
2. Including on financial statements all information necessary to understand a business' financial condition is an application of the accounting concept Adequate Disclosure			**2.**
3. An income statement reports a business' financial condition on a specific date			**3.**
4. A balance sheet reports a business' financial condition on a specific date			**4.**
5. Reporting revenue earned and expenses incurred to earn that revenue in the same fiscal period is an application of the accounting concept Matching Expenses with Revenue			**5.**
6. Information from a work sheet's Account Title column and Trial Balance columns is used in preparing the revenue section of an income statement			**6.**
7. Single lines ruled across an amount column of a income statement indicate that amounts are to be added			**7.**
8. Double lines are ruled across the income statement amount columns below the amount of net income to show that the amount has been verified as correct			**8.**
9. The total expenses component percentage shown on an income statement is calculated: Total Sales divided by total expenses equals total expenses component percentage			**9.**
10. The information needed to prepare a balance sheet is obtained from a work sheet's Account Title column and the Balance Sheet columns			**10.**
11. The right side of a balance sheet consists of the assets and liability information for a specific date			**11.**
12. The place of the total asset line is determined after the equities section is prepared			**12.**

Name ______________________ Date __________ Class ________

DRILL 8-D1, p. 159
[1–3]

Classifying accounts

1	2	3	4	5	6	7	8
	Account Classification					Financial Statement	
Account Title	**Asset**	**Liab.**	**Owner's Equity**	**Revenue**	**Expense**	**Income Statement**	**Balance Sheet**
1. Cash	✓						✓
2. Alice Wayne, Capital			✓				✓
3. Alice Wayne, Drawing			✓				✓
4. Advertising expense					✓	✓	
5. Coen office Supplies		✓					✓
6. Insurance Expense					✓	✓	
7. Misc. expense					✓	✓	
8. Mercer Supplies		✓					✓
9. Prepaid Insurance	✓						✓
10. Rent expense					✓	✓	
11. Sales				✓		✓	
12. Supplies	✓						✓
13. Supplies expense					✓	✓	

p. 147

income statement indicates the progress of a business
balance sheet indicates the financial condition of a business

DRILL 8-D2, p. 160

Figuring net income or net loss and owner's current capital [1–3]

	1	2	3	4	5	6	7	8	9
Company	Total Assets	Total Liabilities	Balance of Capital	Balance of Drawing	Total Revenue	Total Expenses	Net Income	Net Loss	Ending Capital
A	$ 5,600	$2,000	$ 2,320	$120	$ 2,300	$ 900			
B	7,300	2,600	2,945	145	3,100	1,200			
C	7,000	3,200	4,840	200	3,600	4,440			
D	9,560	2,835	4,995	160	3,150	1,260			
E	10,680	3,850	4,035	220	4,725	1,710			
F	14,500	5,770	10,475	325	7,380	8,800			
G	13,620	4,900	4,940	270	6,250	2,200			
H	14,325	7,880	14,465	420	10,000	17,600			

Use the space below for calculations.

B:

C:

D:

E:

F:

G:

H:

Preparing an income statement

LawnMow
Income statement
For month ended June 30, 1996

	Subtotal	Total	% OF SALES
Revenue:			
Sales		3100 —	100
Expenses:			
advertising expense	30 —		
Insurance expense	140 —		
misc expense	65 —		
rent expense	800 —		
Supplies expense	400 —		
Utilities expense	75 —		
total expenses		1510 —	48.7
Net income		1590 —	51.3

Preparing a balance sheet *Problem 8-2, p. 162*

Lawnmow
Balance Sheet
June 30, 1996

Assets		Liabilities	
Cash	7530 —	Barker Supplies	4400 —
Petty Cash	200 —	Richmond Office Supplies	1300 —
Supplies	6860 —	Total Liabilities	5700 —
Prepaid Insurance	2500 —	Owners Equity	
		Clem Sitter, Capital	11390 —
total assets	17090 —	total Liab. & Owners. EQ	17090 —

[1]

Ace Delivery Service
Income Statement
for month ended July 31, 199--

			% OF SALES
Revenue:			
Sales		5670 —	100
Expenses:			
Advertising expense	390 —		
Insurance expense	190 —		
Miscellaneous expense	150 —		
Rent expense	3000 —		
Supplies expense	200 —		
Utilities expense	140 —		
Total expenses		4070 —	71.7
Net income		1600 —	28.3

[2]

Ace Delivery Service
Balance Sheet
June 30, 199--

Assets		Liabilities	
Cash	7500 —	Down Supplies	4700 —
Petty Cash	200 —	Melton office supplies	1200 —
Supplies	7800 —	Total Liabilities	5900 —
Prepaid Insurance	2600 —	Owner's Equity	
		Clark Smith, Cap	12200 —
Total assets	18100 —	Total Liab & Owner's EQ	18100 —

[1]

Preparing financial statements with two sources of revenue and a loss

			% OF SALES

[2]

			% OF SALES

Perfect Score..... 43 Name ______________________

Deduct......... ___ Date ______________ Class ______________

Your Score..... ___ Checked by ______________________

STUDY GUIDE 9

UNIT A—Identifying Accounting Terms

DIRECTIONS: Select the one term in Column I that best fits each definition in Column II. Print the letter identifying your choice in the Answers column.

Column I	*Column II*	Answers	For Scoring
A. accounting cycle **B.** adjusting entries	**0.** Journal entries recorded to update general ledger accounts at the end of a fiscal period..................	B	**0.** ✓
C. closing entries **D.** permanent accounts	**1.** Accounts used to accumulate information until it is transferred to the owner's capital account.............	F	**1.**
E. post-closing trial balance	**2.** Accounts used to accumulate information from one fiscal period to the next..................................	D	**2.**
F. temporary accounts	**3.** Journal entries used to prepare temporary accounts for a new fiscal period..................................	C	**3.**
	4. A trial balance prepared after the closing entries are posted..........................	E	**4.**
	5. The series of accounting activities included in recording financial information for a fiscal period..................................	A	**5.**

UNIT B—Analyzing Accounts Affected by Adjusting and Closing Entries

DIRECTIONS: Use the partial chart of accounts given below. For each adjusting or closing entry described, decide which accounts are debited and credited. Write the account numbers identifying your choice in the proper Answers column.

Partial Chart of Accounts

ACCOUNT TITLE	ACCT. NO.
Supplies..............................	120
Prepaid Insurance..................	130
Jill Glenn, Capital..................	310
Jill Glenn, Drawing................	320
Income Summary....................	330
Sales..................................	410
Advertising Expense..............	510
Insurance Expense.................	520
Supplies Expense..................	530

	Accounts to be Debited	Accounts to be Credited	For Scoring Debit	For Scoring Credit
0–0. Adjusting entry for Supplies........................	530	120	**0.** ✓	**0.** ✓
1–2. Adjusting entry for Prepaid Insurance...............	520	130	**1.**	**2.**
3–4. Closing entry for revenue account........................	318	410	**3.**	**4.**
5–6. Closing entry for all expense accounts			**5.**	**6.**
7–8. Closing entry for Income Summary with a net income.........................			**7.**	**8.**
9–10. Closing entry for Income Summary with a net loss...			**9.**	**10.**
11–12. Closing entry for owner's drawing account			**11.**	**12.**

UNIT C—Analyzing Accounts After Closing Entries are Posted

DIRECTIONS: For each account listed below, decide whether the account will normally appear on a post-closing trial. Place a check mark in the proper Answers column to show your answer.

	Appear on a Post-Closing Trial Balance: Yes	No	For Scoring
0. Advertisement Expense		✓	**0.** ✓
1. Cash......................			**1.**
2. Income Summary......			**2.**
3. Insurance Expense			**3.**
4. Mel Dorset, Capital ...			**4.**
5. Mel Dorset, Drawing..			**5.**
6. Miscellaneous Expense			**6.**
7. Rent Expense...........			**7.**

	Appear on a Post-Closing Trial Balance: Yes	No	For Scoring
8. Richmond Office Supplies..................			**8.**
9. Repair Expense			**9.**
10. Sales.....................			**10.**
11. Stutzman Supplies.....			**11.**
12. Supplies..................			**12.**
13. Utilities Expense			**13.**

UNIT D—Analyzing Adjusting and Closing Entries

DIRECTIONS: For each of the following items, select the choice that best completes the statement. Print the letter identifying your choice in the Answers column.

	Answers	For Scoring
0. A post-closing trial balance shows **(A)** the net income for a fiscal period **(B)** the owner's drawing account balance **(C)** that debits equal credits after closing entries are posted **(D)** that assets equal liabilities	C	**0.** ✓
1. The information needed for journalizing the adjusting entries is obtained from the **(A)** general ledger account Balance columns **(B)** income statement **(C)** work sheet's Adjustments columns **(D)** balance sheet..........................		**1.**
2. After adjusting entries are posted, the supplies account balance will be equal to **(A)** the value of supplies used during the fiscal period **(B)** the value of the supplies on hand at the end of the fiscal period **(C)** zero **(D)** none of these..........................		**2.**
3. After adjusting entries are posted, the insurance expense account balance will be equal to **(A)** the value of insurance premiums used during the fiscal period **(B)** the value of unused prepaid insurance at the end of the fiscal period **(C)** zero **(D)** none of these		**3.**
4. Information needed for recording the closing entries is obtained from **(A)** the general ledger accounts' Debit Balance columns the **(B)** work sheet's Income Statement columns **(C)** balance sheet **(D)** income statement..................		**4.**
5. Income Summary is a(an) **(A)** asset account **(B)** liability account **(C)** temporary capital account **(D)** a permanent account		**5.**
6. After closing entries are posted, the net income appears in the **(A)** income summary account as a credit **(B)** owner's capital account as a credit **(C)** owner's capital account as a debit **(D)** owner's drawing account............		**6.**
7. After closing entries are posted, a net loss appears in the **(A)** income summary account as a debit **(B)** owner's capital account as a credit **(C)** owner's capital account as a debit **(D)** owner's drawing account............		**7.**
8. Information needed to journalize a closing entry for revenue is obtained from the **(A)** work sheet's Income Statement Credit column **(B)** work sheet's Income Statement Debit column **(C)** work sheet's Adjustments Debit column **(D)** work sheet's Adjustments Credit column..........................		**8.**
9. Information needed to journalize a closing entry for expenses is obtained from the **(A)** work sheet's Income Statement Credit column **(B)** work sheet's Income Statement Debit column **(C)** work sheet's Adjustments Debit column **(D)** work sheet's Adjustments Credit column..........................		**9.**
10. Information needed to journalize a closing entry for the income summary account is obtained from **(A)** the general ledger accounts **(B)** a work sheet's net income or net loss line **(C)** an income statement **(D)** a balance sheet..		**10.**
11. Information needed to journalize a closing entry for the owner's drawing account is obtained from the **(A)** work sheet's balance sheet debit column **(B)** work sheet's balance sheet credit column **(C)** income statement **(D)** work sheet's income statement debit column..........................		**11.**
12. After the closing entries are posted, the owner's capital account balance should be the same as **(A)** shown on the balance sheet for the fiscal period **(B)** shown in the work sheet's Balance Sheet Debit column **(C)** shown in the work sheet's Balance Sheet Credit column **(D)** shown in the work sheet's Income Statement Debit column		**12.**
13. The accounts listed on a post-closing trial balance are **(A)** those that have balances after the closing entries are posted **(B)** all general ledger accounts **(C)** those that have no balances after adjusting and closing entries are posted **(D)** those that appear in the work sheet's Trial Balance columns		**13.**

Name ______________________________ Date ________ Class ________

DRILL 9-D1, p. 184
[1–4]

Determining accounts affected by adjusting and closing entries

1	2	3	4	5	6	7
Account Title	**Account is Affected by an Adjusting Entry**		**Account is Affected by a Closing Entry**		**After Closing Entries are Posted, Account has a Balance**	
	Yes	**No**	**Yes**	**No**	**Yes**	**No**
1. Advertising Expense		✓	✓			✓
2. Baer Supplies						
3. Cash						
4. Gates Office Supplies						
5. Irma Downs, Capital						
6. Irma Downs, Drawing						
7. Income Summary						
8. Insurance Expense						
9. Miscellaneous Expense						
10. Prepaid Insurance						
11. Rent expense						
12. Sales						
13. Supplies ~~Expense~~						
14. Supplies Expense						
15. Utilities expense						

Journalizing and posting adjusting and closing entries; preparing a post-closing trial balance

Problem 9-1, p. 184

[1, 2]

GENERAL JOURNAL

PAGE 3

	DATE		ACCOUNT TITLE	DOC. NO.	POST. REF.	DEBIT	CREDIT	
1			Adjusting entries					1
2	19-- Oct	31	Supplies expense		540	145—		2
3			Supplies		120		145—	3
4		31	Insurance expense		510	190—		4
5			Prepaid Insurance		130		190—	5
6			Closing entries					6
7		31	Sales		410	1188—		7
8			Income summery		330		1180—	8
9		31	Income Summery		330	720—		9
10			Inshrance expense		510		190—	10
11			Misc expense		520		65—	11
12			Rent expense		530		320—	12
13			Supplies expense		540		145—	13
14		31	Income summery		330	380—		14
15			Norma Delk, Capital		310		380—	15
16		31	Norma Delk, Capital		310	250—		16
17			Norma Delk, drawing		320		250—	17

GENERAL LEDGER

[1–3]

ACCOUNT Cash ACCOUNT NO. 110

DATE		ITEM	POST. REF.	DEBIT	CREDIT	BALANCE DEBIT	BALANCE CREDIT
19-- Oct.	31	Balance	✓			2 6 0 0 00	

ACCOUNT Supplies ACCOUNT NO. 120

DATE		ITEM	POST. REF.	DEBIT	CREDIT	BALANCE DEBIT	BALANCE CREDIT
19-- Oct.	31	Balance	✓			7 0 5 00	
	31		3		145—	560—	

ACCOUNT Prepaid Insurance ACCOUNT NO. 130

DATE		ITEM	POST. REF.	DEBIT	CREDIT	BALANCE DEBIT	BALANCE CREDIT
19-- Oct.	31	Balance	✓			4 0 0 00	
	31		3		190—	210—	

Name ______________________ Date ________ Class _______

PROBLEM 9-1, continued
[1–3]

GENERAL LEDGER

ACCOUNT Kurtz Supplies — ACCOUNT NO. 210

DATE		ITEM	POST. REF.	DEBIT	CREDIT	BALANCE DEBIT	BALANCE CREDIT
19-- Oct.	31	Balance	✓				300 00

ACCOUNT Wiley Supplies — ACCOUNT NO. 220

DATE		ITEM	POST. REF.	DEBIT	CREDIT	BALANCE DEBIT	BALANCE CREDIT
19-- Oct.	31	Balance	✓				90 00

ACCOUNT Norma Delk, Capital — ACCOUNT NO. 310

DATE		ITEM	POST. REF.	DEBIT	CREDIT	BALANCE DEBIT	BALANCE CREDIT
19-- Oct.	31	Balance	✓				2850 00
	31		3		380—		3230—
	31		3	250—			2980—

ACCOUNT Norma Delk, Drawing — ACCOUNT NO. 320

DATE		ITEM	POST. REF.	DEBIT	CREDIT	BALANCE DEBIT	BALANCE CREDIT
19-- Oct.	31	Balance	✓			250 00	
	31		3		250—	—	—

ACCOUNT Income Summary — ACCOUNT NO. 330

DATE		ITEM	POST. REF.	DEBIT	CREDIT	BALANCE DEBIT	BALANCE CREDIT
19-- Oct	31		3		1100—		1100—
	31		3	720—			380—
	31				380—	—	—

ACCOUNT Sales — ACCOUNT NO. 410

DATE		ITEM	POST. REF.	DEBIT	CREDIT	BALANCE DEBIT	BALANCE CREDIT
19-- Oct.	31	Balance	✓				1100 00
	31		3	1100—		—	—

ACCOUNT Insurance Expense — ACCOUNT NO. 510

DATE		ITEM	POST. REF.	DEBIT	CREDIT	BALANCE DEBIT	BALANCE CREDIT
19-- Oct	31		3	190—		190—	
	31		3		190—	—	—

GENERAL LEDGER

ACCOUNT Miscellaneous Expense **ACCOUNT NO.** 520

DATE		ITEM	POST. REF.	DEBIT	CREDIT	BALANCE DEBIT	BALANCE CREDIT
19-- Oct.	31	Balance	✓			65 00	
	31		3		65—	—	—

ACCOUNT Rent Expense **ACCOUNT NO.** 530

DATE		ITEM	POST. REF.	DEBIT	CREDIT	BALANCE DEBIT	BALANCE CREDIT
19-- Oct.	31	Balance	✓			320 00	
	31		3		320—	—	—

ACCOUNT Supplies Expense **ACCOUNT NO.** 540

DATE		ITEM	POST. REF.	DEBIT	CREDIT	BALANCE DEBIT	BALANCE CREDIT
1996 Oct	31		3	145—		145—	
	31		3		145—	—	—

[3]

Eilers Company
Post Closing trial balance
October 31, 1996

ACCOUNT TITLE	DEBIT	CREDIT
Cash	2600—	
Supplies	560—	
Prepaid Insurance	210—	
Kurtz Supplies		300—
Wiley Supplies		90—
Norma Deir, Capital		2980—
Totals	3370—	3370—

Name ______________________ Date ________ Class ________

MASTERY PROBLEM 9-M, p. 185
[1, 2]

Journalizing and posting adjusting and closing entries; preparing a post-closing trial balance

GENERAL JOURNAL

PAGE 3

DATE		ACCOUNT TITLE	DOC. NO.	POST. REF.	DEBIT	CREDIT
		Adjusting Entries		[illegible]		
Nov	30	Supplies expense		540	195—	
		Supplies		120		195—
	30	Insurance expense		510	260—	
		prepaid insurance		130		260—
		Closing entries				
	30	Sales		410	1500—	
		Income summery		330		1500—
	30	Income summery		330	965—	
		Insurance expense		510		260—
		Misc expense		520		85—
		Rent expense		530		425—
		Supplies expense		540		195—
	30	Income summery		330	535—	
		A. Kellerman, Capital		310		535—
	30	A. Kellerman, Capital		310	350—	
		A. Kellerman, Drawing		320		350—

GENERAL LEDGER

ACCOUNT Cash **ACCOUNT NO.** 110

DATE		ITEM	POST. REF.	DEBIT	CREDIT	BALANCE DEBIT	BALANCE CREDIT
19-- Nov.	30	Balance	✓			3500 00	

ACCOUNT Supplies **ACCOUNT NO.** 120

DATE		ITEM	POST. REF.	DEBIT	CREDIT	BALANCE DEBIT	BALANCE CREDIT
19-- Nov.	30	Balance	✓			945 00	
	30		3		195—	750—	

ACCOUNT Prepaid Insurance **ACCOUNT NO.** 130

DATE		ITEM	POST. REF.	DEBIT	CREDIT	BALANCE DEBIT	BALANCE CREDIT
19-- Nov.	30	Balance	✓			540 00	
	30		3		260—	280—	

ACCOUNT Kern Supplies **ACCOUNT NO.** 210

DATE		ITEM	POST. REF.	DEBIT	CREDIT	BALANCE DEBIT	BALANCE CREDIT
19-- Nov.	30	Balance	✓				500 00

ACCOUNT Waite Supplies **ACCOUNT NO.** 220

DATE		ITEM	POST. REF.	DEBIT	CREDIT	BALANCE DEBIT	BALANCE CREDIT
19-- Nov.	30	Balance	✓				120 00

ACCOUNT A. Kellerman, Capital **ACCOUNT NO.** 310

DATE		ITEM	POST. REF.	DEBIT	CREDIT	BALANCE DEBIT	BALANCE CREDIT
19-- Nov.	30	Balance	✓				3725 00
	30		3		535—		3190—
	30		3	350—			[illegible] [illegible]

ACCOUNT A. Kellerman, Drawing **ACCOUNT NO.** 320

DATE		ITEM	POST. REF.	DEBIT	CREDIT	BALANCE DEBIT	BALANCE CREDIT
19-- Nov.	30	Balance	✓			350 00	
	30		3		350—		

[1–3]

GENERAL LEDGER

ACCOUNT Income Summary — ACCOUNT NO. 330

DATE		ITEM	POST. REF.	DEBIT	CREDIT	BALANCE DEBIT	BALANCE CREDIT
Nov.	30		3		1500—		1500—
	30		3	965—			535—
	30		3	535—			

ACCOUNT Sales — ACCOUNT NO. 410

DATE		ITEM	POST. REF.	DEBIT	CREDIT	BALANCE DEBIT	BALANCE CREDIT
19-- Nov.	30	Balance	✓				1 5 0 0 00
	30		3	1500—			

ACCOUNT Insurance Expense — ACCOUNT NO. 510

DATE		ITEM	POST. REF.	DEBIT	CREDIT	BALANCE DEBIT	BALANCE CREDIT
Nov.	30		3	260—		260—	
	30		3		260—		

ACCOUNT Miscellaneous Expense — ACCOUNT NO. 520

DATE		ITEM	POST. REF.	DEBIT	CREDIT	BALANCE DEBIT	BALANCE CREDIT
19-- Nov.	30	Balance	✓			8 5 00	
	30		3		85—		

ACCOUNT Rent Expense — ACCOUNT NO. 530

DATE		ITEM	POST. REF.	DEBIT	CREDIT	BALANCE DEBIT	BALANCE CREDIT
19-- Nov.	30	Balance	✓			4 2 5 00	
	30		3		425—		

ACCOUNT Supplies Expense — ACCOUNT NO. 540

DATE		ITEM	POST. REF.	DEBIT	CREDIT	BALANCE DEBIT	BALANCE CREDIT
Nov.	30		3	195—		195—	
	30		3		195—		

[3]

Kellerman Services'
Post Closing trial balance
November 30, 1994

ACCOUNT TITLE	DEBIT	CREDIT
Cash	3500 —	
Supplies	750 —	
Prepaid Insurance	280 —	
Kern Supplies		500 —
Waite Supplies		120 —
A. Kellerman, Capital		3910 —
totals	4530 —	4530 —

Extra form

ACCOUNT TITLE	DEBIT	CREDIT

Preparing a work sheet; journalizing adjusting and closing entries [1–3]

Reed Company
Work Sheet
For Month Ended December 31, 19--

	ACCOUNT TITLE	1 TRIAL BALANCE DEBIT	2 TRIAL BALANCE CREDIT	3 ADJUSTMENTS DEBIT	4 ADJUSTMENTS CREDIT	5 INCOME STATEMENT DEBIT	6 INCOME STATEMENT CREDIT	7 BALANCE SHEET DEBIT	8 BALANCE SHEET CREDIT	
1	Cash	8 900 00								1
2	Petty Cash	200 00								2
3	Supplies	1 600 00								3
4	Prepaid Insurance	1 200 00								4
5	Keller Supplies		400 00							5
6	Miller Office Supplies		330 00							6
7	Mitzy Hurlburt, Capital		11 900 00							7
8	Mitzy Hurlburt, Drawing	650 00								8
9	Income Summary									9
10	Sales		2 600 00							10
11	Advertising Expense	130 00								11
12	Insurance Expense									12
13	Miscellaneous Expense	200 00								13
14	Rent Expense	1 200 00								14
15	Repair Expense	780 00								15
16	Supplies Expense									16
17	Utilities Expense	370 00								17
18		15 230 00	15 230 00							18
19										19
20										20
21										21
22										22
23										23
24										24
25										25

[2, 3]

GENERAL JOURNAL

PAGE 3

DATE	ACCOUNT TITLE	DOC. NO.	POST. REF.	DEBIT	CREDIT

Perfect Score..... 39 Name ______________________

Deduct......... ___ Date ______________ Class ______________

Your Score..... ___ Checked by ______________________

STUDY GUIDE 10

UNIT A—Identifying Accounting Terms

DIRECTIONS: Select the one term in Column I that best fits each definition in Column II. Print the letter identifying your choice in the Answers column.

Column I

A. automated accounting
B. batch number
C. computer
D. computer program
E. computer programmer
F. control accounts
G. data
H. hardware
I. input
J. mainframe computer
K. manual accounting
L. menu
M. microcomputer
N. minicomputer
O. output
P. printout
Q. processing
R. run date
S. software
T. storage

Column II

Column II	Answers	For Scoring
0. Details or facts	G	**0.** ✓
1. A machine that accepts data, applies procedures, and produces results according to stored instructions		**1.**
2. Computer output in printed, human-readable form		**2.**
3. The date to be printed on reports prepared by a computer		**3.**
4. Information produced by a computer		**4.**
5. A set of instructions followed by a computer to process data		**5.**
6. Working with data according to precise instructions		**6.**
7. An accounting system in which data are recorded and reported mostly by hand		**7.**
8. A list of options from which an activity may be selected		**8.**
9. Data put into a computer		**9.**
10. Filing or holding data until it is needed		**10.**
11. A medium-sized computer with intermediate computing speed, storage capacity, and processing capability		**11.**
12. Programs used to direct the operations of a computer		**12.**
13. An accounting system in which data are recorded and reported mostly by using automated machines		**13.**
14. General ledger accounts that must be identified for special handling by computer software		**14.**
15. A person who prepares a computer program		**15.**
16. A small-sized computer with the slowest computing speed, smallest storage capacity, and the least processing capability		**16.**
17. The number assigned to a group of journal entries		**17.**
18. A large-sized computer with the greatest computing speed, largest storage capacity, and the most powerful processing capability		**18.**
19. Computer units		**19.**

UNIT B—Analyzing Concepts and Procedures for Starting An Automated Accounting System

DIRECTIONS: Place a check mark in the proper Answers column to show whether each of the following statements is true or false.

	True	False	For Scoring
0. Business owners and managers depend on accounting records and reports for effective decision making	✓		**0.** ✓
1. Accounting concepts vary with the procedures used			**1.**
2. In automated accounting, all procedures are done by machines			**2.**
3. The expectation that a business will make money and continue indefinitely is an application of the Going Concern accounting concept			**3.**
4. Both large and small businesses can make use of computers to record and report accounting data			**4.**
5. Using a computer changes accounting concepts			**5.**
6. Computer cost is based on the amount of data that can be processed and the processing speed			**6.**
7. A minicomputer was the first type of computer developed to process business data			**7.**
8. A microcomputer is used primarily by businesses who have the need for processing large amounts of data at very fast processing speeds			**8.**
9. Accuracy is more important in a manual accounting system than in an automated accounting system			**9.**
10. Automated accounting consists of three phases—input, processing, and storage			**10.**
11. A computer is divided into four separate units—central processing, input, output, and secondary storage			**11.**
12. Posting transaction data to general ledger accounts is an example of the storage phase of automated accounting			**12.**
13. The end result of processing data by a computer is the storage			**13.**
14. Operation of a computer keyboard is similar to operation of a typewriter keyboard			**14.**
15. Automated accounting requires a different chart of accounts numbering system than manual accounting			**15.**
16. Arranging accounts in a ledger, assigning account numbers, and keeping records current is file maintenance			**16.**
17. In automated accounting, the number of spaces that can be used for account numbers and account titles is unlimited			**17.**
18. A chart of accounts report is checked for accuracy by comparing the report with data recorded on a general ledger file maintenance input form			**18.**
19. A general ledger input form used in automated accounting resembles a journal used in manual accounting			**19.**
20. An opening balances report is assumed to be correct and needs no accuracy check			**20.**

Name ______________________ Date ________ Class ________

DRILL 10-D1, p. 213
[1–3]

Preparing a chart of accounts for automated accounting

1	2
Account Decriptions	**Account Number**
1. The first asset account.	110
2. The first liability account.	
3. The first owner's equity account.	
4. The first revenue account.	
5. The first expense account.	
6. The second asset account.	
7. The second liability account.	
8. The second owner's equity account.	
9. The second expense account.	
10. The third expense account.	

Analyzing steps for starting an automated accounting system

DRILL 10-D2, p. 214

1. ______________________________

2. ______________________________

3. ______________________________

4. ______________________________

5. ______________________________

6. ______________________________

7. ______________________________

8. ______________________________

Problem No. ____________

GENERAL LEDGER
FILE MAINTENANCE
Input Form

RUN DATE ___/___/___
MM DD YY

FORM GL-1

	1	2	
	ACCOUNT NUMBER	ACCOUNT TITLE	
1			1
2			2
3			3
4			4
5			5
6			6
7			7
8			8
9			9
10			10
11			11
12			12
13			13
14			14
15			15
16			16
17			17
18			18
19			19
20			20
21			21
22			22
23			23
24			24
25			25

Name ______________________ Date ________ Class ________

PROBLEM 10-2, p. 214
[1, 2]

Journalizing opening balances in an automated accounting system

RUN DATE ___/___/___ (MM DD YY)

BATCH NO. [ ]

GENERAL LEDGER
Input Form

Problem No. ________

FORM GL-2

	1 DAY	2 DOC. NO.	3 ACCOUNT NUMBER	4 DEBIT AMOUNT	5 CREDIT AMOUNT	
1						1
2						2
3						3
4						4
5						5
6						6
7						7
8						8
9						9
10						10
11						11
12						12
13						13
14						14
15						15
16						16
17						17
18						18
19						19
20						20
21						21
22						22
23						23
24						24
25						25
			BATCH TOTALS			

Problem No. ____________

RUN DATE ____/____/____
MM DD YY

GENERAL LEDGER
FILE MAINTENANCE
Input Form

FORM GL-1

	1	2	
	ACCOUNT NUMBER	ACCOUNT TITLE	
1			1
2			2
3			3
4			4
5			5
6			6
7			7
8			8
9			9
10			10
11			11
12			12
13			13
14			14
15			15
16			16
17			17
18			18
19			19
20			20
21			21
22			22
23			23
24			24
25			25

MASTERY PROBLEM 10-M, p. 215

[1]

Preparing a general ledger file maintenance input form and journalizing opening balances

Problem No. ____________

FORM GL-1

RUN DATE ___/___/___
MM DD YY

GENERAL LEDGER FILE MAINTENANCE Input Form

	1 ACCOUNT NUMBER	2 ACCOUNT TITLE	
1			1
2			2
3			3
4			4
5			5
6			6
7			7
8			8
9			9
10			10
11			11
12			12
13			13
14			14
15			15
16			16
17			17
18			18
19			19
20			20
21			21
22			22
23			23
24			24
25			25

[2, 3]

RUN DATE ____ / ____ / ____
MM DD YY

BATCH NO. [ ]

GENERAL LEDGER
Input Form

Problem No. ________

FORM GL-2

	1	2	3	4	5	
	DAY	DOC. NO.	ACCOUNT NUMBER	DEBIT AMOUNT	CREDIT AMOUNT	
1						1
2						2
3						3
4						4
5						5
6						6
7						7
8						8
9						9
10						10
11						11
12						12
13						13
14						14
15						15
16						16
17						17
18						18
19						19
20						20
21						21
22						22
23						23
24						24
25						25
			BATCH TOTALS			

Name ______________ Date ________ Class ______

CHALLENGE PROBLEM 10-C, p. 216
[1]

Preparing a general ledger file maintenance input form and journalizing opening balances

The solution to Challenge Problem 10-C is needed to complete Computer Application 1.

Problem No. ________

FORM GL-1

GENERAL LEDGER FILE MAINTENANCE Input Form

RUN DATE ___/___/___
MM DD YY

	1 ACCOUNT NUMBER	2 ACCOUNT TITLE	
1			1
2			2
3			3
4			4
5			5
6			6
7			7
8			8
9			9
10			10
11			11
12			12
13			13
14			14
15			15
16			16
17			17
18			18
19			19
20			20
21			21
22			22
23			23
24			24
25			25

[2, 3]

RUN DATE ____/____/____
MM DD YY

BATCH NO. [ ]

GENERAL LEDGER
Input Form

Problem No. ____________

FORM GL-2

	1 DAY	2 DOC. NO.	3 ACCOUNT NUMBER	4 DEBIT AMOUNT	5 CREDIT AMOUNT	
1						1
2						2
3						3
4						4
5						5
6						6
7						7
8						8
9						9
10						10
11						11
12						12
13						13
14						14
15						15
16						16
17						17
18						18
19						19
20						20
21						21
22						22
23						23
24						24
25						25
			BATCH TOTALS			

Perfect Score..... 35 Name ______________________

Deduct......... ___ Date ______________ Class ______________

Your Score..... ___ Checked by ______________________

STUDY GUIDE 11

UNIT A—Assigning Account Numbers to New Accounts

DIRECTIONS: Select the two-digit number in Column I required to complete each new account number for the accounts shown in Column II. Use the unused middle number method. Print the letter identifying your choice in the Answers column.

Column I

A. 11
B. 15
C. 19
D. 20
E. 21
F. 25
G. 30
H. 31
I. 35
J. 41
K. 45
L. 51
M. 55
N. 60

Column II		Answers	For Scoring
110	Petty Cash		
0. 1__	SUPPLIES—COMPUTER	B	**0.** ✓
120	Supplies—Office		
210	Butler Supply		
1. 2__	KRAMER ENTERPRISES		**1.**
220	Sussman Supply Company		
2. 2__	WATLEY COMPUTER SUPPLY		**2.**
530	Miscellaneous Expense		
3. 5__	RENT EXPENSE—BUILDING		**3.**
540	Rent Expense—Computer		
4. 5__	SUPPLIES EXPENSE—COMPUTER		**4.**
550	Supplies Expense—Office		
5. 5__	UTILITIES EXPENSE		**5.**

UNIT B—Examining Automated General Ledger Accounting Procedures

DIRECTIONS: For a business using an automated accounting system, determine how the procedures in Column II are completed. For each item in Column II, select the letter from Column I that identifies the way the procedure is completed. Print the letter identifying your choice in the Answers column.

Column I

A. manual operation
B. computer operation

Column II	Answers	For Scoring
0. Builds chart of accounts	A	**0.** ✓
1. Prepares general ledger file maintenance input form		**1.**
2. Processes chart of accounts		**2.**
3. Prepares chart of accounts report		**3.**
4. Prepares general ledger input form		**4.**
5. Prepares trial balance		**5.**
6. Processes journal entries		**6.**
7. Plans adjusting entries		**7.**
8. Prepares financial statements		**8.**
9. Posts closing entries		**9.**
10. Prepares post-closing trial balance		**10.**

UNIT C—Analyzing Concepts and Procedures for Using An Automated Accounting System

DIRECTIONS: Place a check mark in the proper Answers column to show whether each of the following statements is true or false.

Statement	True	False	For Scoring
0. Both large and small businesses make use of computers to record and report accounting data	✓		**0.** ✓
1. In automated accounting, a general ledger chart of accounts is stored on secondary computer storage			**1.**
2. File maintenance activities require that deletions and additions be recorded on a general ledger input form			**2.**
3. The word *Delete* is placed in parentheses on a general ledger file maintenance form to show that it is not to be entered into the computer			**3.**
4. In the unused middle number method, if no exact middle number is available, the nearest odd whole number is used			**4.**
5. Recording and reporting major expenses separately is an application of the accounting concept objective evidence			**5.**
6. Petlodge records transaction data on a general ledger input form daily			**6.**
7. The source document used to support the payment of an expense is a receipt			**7.**
8. Using a check to support a liability payment is an application of the accounting concept objective evidence			**8.**
9. A drawing account balance increases an owner's capital account balance			**9.**
10. An asset taken out of a business for an owner's personal use is recorded as a miscellaneous expense			**10.**
11. When additional cash is invested in a business, both the cash account balance and the capital account balance are increased			**11.**
12. A journal entries report is checked for accuracy by comparing the report with a general ledger input form			**12.**
13. The percentage relationship between one financial statement item and the total that includes that item is known as a relationship percentage			**13.**
14. In automated accounting, a journal entries report is used to plan adjusting entries			**14.**
15. Bringing certain general ledger accounts up to date at the end of an accounting period is an application of the accounting concept matching expenses with revenue			**15.**
16. When insurance premiums are paid, the expense account Insurance Expense is debited			**16.**
17. A balance sheet listing assets on the left and equities on the right is a report form of balance sheet			**17.**
18. A balance sheet listing the assets, liabilities, and capital vertically is an account form of balance sheet			**18.**
19. In Petlodge's automated accounting system, the computer software contains instructions for closing temporary accounts			**19.**
20. Accountants regularly use electronic spreadsheet for financial analysis			**20.**

Name ______________________ Date ________ Class ________

DRILL 11-D1, p. 239
[1, 2]

Adding new general ledger account numbers

1	2
New General Ledger Account Title	**Account Number Assigned**
Petty Cash	115
Supplies—Store	
Draper Enterprises	
Equipment Repair Expense	
Insurance Expense	
Rent Expense—Computer	
Supplies Expense—Store	
Utilities Expense	

Analyzing steps completed in an automated accounting system

DRILL 11-D2, p. 240

1. ______________________________

2. ______________________________

3. ______________________________

4. ______________________________

5. ______________________________

6. ______________________________

7. ______________________________

8. ______________________________

RUN DATE ____/____/____
MM DD YY

GENERAL LEDGER FILE MAINTENANCE
Input Form

Problem No. ________

FORM GL-1

	1 ACCOUNT NUMBER	2 ACCOUNT TITLE	
1			1
2			2
3			3
4			4
5			5
6			6
7			7
8			8
9			9
10			10
11			11
12			12
13			13
14			14
15			15
16			16
17			17
18			18
19			19
20			20
21			21
22			22
23			23
24			24
25			25

Name ________________ Date ________ Class ________

PROBLEM 11-2, p. 240
[1]

Journalizing transactions on a general ledger input form

RUN DATE ___/___/___
MM DD YY

BATCH NO. [ ]

GENERAL LEDGER
Input Form

Problem No. ________

FORM GL-2

	1	2	3	4	5	
	DAY	DOC. NO.	ACCOUNT NUMBER	DEBIT AMOUNT	CREDIT AMOUNT	
1						1
2						2
3						3
4						4
5						5
6						6
7						7
8						8
9						9
10						10
11						11
12						12
13						13
14						14
15						15
16						16
17						17
18						18
19						19
20						20
21						21
22						22
23						23
24						24
25						25
			BATCH TOTALS			

PROBLEM 11-2, concluded
[1, 2]

RUN DATE ____/____/____
MM DD YY

BATCH NO. [ ]

GENERAL LEDGER
Input Form

Problem No. ______

FORM GL-2

	1 DAY	2 DOC. NO.	3 ACCOUNT NUMBER	4 DEBIT AMOUNT	5 CREDIT AMOUNT	
1						1
2						2
3						3
4						4
5						5
6						6
25						25
			BATCH TOTALS			

Journalizing adjusting entries on a general ledger input form

PROBLEM 11-3, p. 241
[1, 2]

RUN DATE ____/____/____
MM DD YY

BATCH NO. [ ]

GENERAL LEDGER
Input Form

Problem No. ______

FORM GL-2

	1 DAY	2 DOC. NO.	3 ACCOUNT NUMBER	4 DEBIT AMOUNT	5 CREDIT AMOUNT	
1						1
2						2
3						3
4						4
5						5
6						6
25						25
			BATCH TOTALS			

Name ______________ Date ________ Class ________

MASTERY PROBLEM 11-M, p. 242
[1, 2]

Preparing input forms for an automated accounting system

Problem No. ________

FORM GL-1

RUN DATE ___/___/___
MM DD YY

GENERAL LEDGER FILE MAINTENANCE
Input Form

	1	2	
	ACCOUNT NUMBER	ACCOUNT TITLE	
1			1
2			2
3			3
4			4
5			5
6			6
7			7
8			8
9			9
10			10
11			11
12			12
13			13
14			14
15			15
16			16
17			17
18			18
19			19
20			20
21			21
22			22
23			23
24			24
25			25

[3, 4]

RUN DATE ___/___/___
MM DD YY

BATCH NO. [ ]

GENERAL LEDGER
Input Form

Problem No. ______

FORM GL-2

	1	2	3	4	5	
	DAY	DOC. NO.	ACCOUNT NUMBER	DEBIT AMOUNT	CREDIT AMOUNT	
1						1
2						2
3						3
4						4
5						5
6						6
7						7
8						8
9						9
10						10
11						11
12						12
13						13
14						14
15						15
16						16
17						17
18						18
19						19
20						20
21						21
22						22
23						23
24						24
25						25
			BATCH TOTALS			

Name ______________________ Date ________ Class ______

MASTERY PROBLEM 11-M, concluded
[5, 6]

RUN DATE ____/____/____
MM DD YY

BATCH NO. [ ]

GENERAL LEDGER
Input Form

Problem No. ________

FORM GL-2

	1	2	3	4	5	
	DAY	DOC. NO.	ACCOUNT NUMBER	DEBIT AMOUNT	CREDIT AMOUNT	
1						1
2						2
3						3
4						4
5						5
6						6
7						7
8						8
9						9
10						10
11						11
12						12
13						13
14						14
15						15
16						16
17						17
18						18
19						19
20						20
21						21
22						22
23						23
24						24
25						25
			BATCH TOTALS			

Preparing input forms for an automated accounting system

CHALLENGE PROBLEM 11-C, p. 243

[1, 2]

The solution to Challenge Problem 11-C is needed to complete Computer Application 2.

Problem No. ____________

FORM GL-1

RUN DATE ___/___/___
MM DD YY

GENERAL LEDGER FILE MAINTENANCE Input Form

	1 ACCOUNT NUMBER	2 ACCOUNT TITLE	
1			1
2			2
3			3
4			4
5			5
6			6
7			7
8			8
9			9
10			10
11			11
12			12
13			13
14			14
15			15
16			16
17			17
18			18
19			19
20			20
21			21
22			22
23			23
24			24
25			25

[3, 4]

RUN DATE ____/____/____
MM DD YY

BATCH NO. [ ]

Problem No. ________

FORM GL-2

GENERAL LEDGER
Input Form

	1	2	3	4	5	
	DAY	DOC. NO.	ACCOUNT NUMBER	DEBIT AMOUNT	CREDIT AMOUNT	
1						1
2						2
3						3
4						4
5						5
6						6
7						7
8						8
9						9
10						10
11						11
12						12
13						13
14						14
15						15
16						16
17						17
18						18
19						19
20						20
21						21
22						22
23						23
24						24
25						25
			BATCH TOTALS			

[5, 6]

RUN DATE ____/____/____
MM DD YY

Problem No. ____________

GENERAL LEDGER
Input Form

FORM GL-2

BATCH NO. [   ]

	1 DAY	2 DOC. NO.	3 ACCOUNT NUMBER	4 DEBIT AMOUNT	5 CREDIT AMOUNT	
1						1
2						2
3						3
4						4
5						5
6						6
7						7
8						8
9						9
10						10
11						11
12						12
13						13
14						14
15						15
16						16
17						17
18						18
19						19
20						20
21						21
22						22
23						23
24						24
25						25
			BATCH TOTALS			

Perfect Score..... 46 Name ____________________

Deduct......... ___ Date ______________ Class ______________

Your Score..... ___ Checked by ____________________

STUDY GUIDE 12

UNIT A—Identifying Accounting Terms

DIRECTIONS: Select the term in Column I that best fits each definition in Column II. Print the letter identifying your choice in the Answers column.

Column I

A. cash payments journal
B. correcting entry
C. cost of merchandise
D. general amount column
E. invoice
F. markup
G. merchandise
H. merchandising business
I. partner
J. partnership
K. purchase invoice
L. purchase on account
M. purchases journal
N. special amount column
O. special journal
P. terms of sale
Q. vendor

Column II

	Column II	Answers	For Scoring
0.	A journal used to record only one kind of transaction	O	**0.** ✓
1.	A journal amount column headed with an account title	N	**1.**
2.	The amount added to the cost of merchandise to establish the selling price	F	**2.**
3.	A business from which merchandise is purchased or supplies or other assets are bought	Q	**3.**
4.	Each member of a partnership	I	**4.**
5.	Goods that a merchandising business purchases to sell	G	**5.**
6.	A form describing the goods sold, the quantity, and the price	E	**6.**
7.	A business in which two or more persons combine their assets and skills	J	**7.**
8.	A business that purchases and sells goods	H	**8.**
9.	A journal amount column that is not headed with an account title	D	**9.**
10.	An agreement between a buyer and a seller about payment for merchandise	P	**10.**
11.	An invoice used as a source document for recording a purchase on account transaction	K	**11.**
12.	A journal entry made to correct an error in the ledger	B	**12.**
13.	A special journal used to record only cash payment transactions	A	**13.**
14.	A transaction in which the merchandise purchased is to be paid for later	L	**14.**
15.	The price a business pays for goods it purchases to sell	C	**15.**
16.	A special journal used to record only purchase on account transactions	M	**16.**

UNIT B—Analyzing Transactions Recorded in Special Journals

DIRECTIONS: In Answers Column 1, print the abbreviation for the journal in which each transaction is to be recorded. In Columns 2 and 3, print the letters identifying the accounts to be debited and credited for each transaction.

P—Purchases journal G—General journal CP—Cash payments journal

Account Title

A. Accounts Payable
B. Accounts Receivable
C. Advertising Expense
D. Cash
E. Miscellaneous Expense
F. Pat Hoyer, Capital
G. Pat Hoyer, Drawing
H. Purchases
I. Supplies—Office

Transaction	Answers 1 Journal	Answers 2 Debit	Answers 3 Credit	For Scoring 1 Journal	For Scoring 2 Debit	For Scoring 3 Credit
0–0–0. Paid cash for miscellaneous..........	CP	E	D	**0.** ✓	**0.** ✓	**0.** ✓
1–2–3. Paid cash for office supplies..........	G	I	D	**1.**	**2.**	**3.**
4–5–6. Purchased merchandise for cash..........	P	D	H	**4.**	**5.**	**6.**
7–8–9. Purchased merchandise on account..........	P	H	A	**7.**	**8.**	**9.**
10–11–12. Pat Hoyer, partner, withdrew cash for personal use..........	G	G	D	**10.**	**11.**	**12.**
13–14–15. Bought office supplies on account..........	P	I	A	**13.**	**14.**	**15.**
16–17–18. Paid cash on account.....	CP	A	D	**16.**	**17.**	**18.**
19–20–21. Paid cash for advertising.	CP	C	D	**19.**	**20.**	**21.**
22–23–24. Pat Hoyer, partner, withdrew merchandise for personal use..........	G	G	D	**22.**	**23.**	**24.**
25–26–27. Discovered that a transaction for office supplies bought last month was journalized and posted in error as a debit to Purchases instead of Supplies—Office..........	G	I	D	**25.**	**26.**	**27.**
28–29–30. Paid cash to replenish the petty cash fund: office supplies, advertising miscellaneous..........	G	I C E	D	**28.**	**29.**	**30.**

Analyzing transactions into debit and credit parts

The solution to Drill 12-D1 is needed to complete Drill 12-D2.

1.

Purchases	
900.00	

Accounts Payable	
	900.00

2.

3.

4.

5.

6.

7.

8.

9.

10.

11.

12.

13.

14.

15.

16.

Analyzing journal entries

DRILL 12-D2, p. 273

The solution to Drill 12-D1 is needed to complete Drill 12-D2.

Transaction	Purchases Journal	Cash Payments Journal				General Journal	
	Purchases Debit Accts. Pay. Credit	General		Accts. Pay. Debit	Cash Credit	Debit	Credit
		Debit	Credit				
1. Debit amount	900						
Credit amount	900						
2. Debit amount							
Credit amount							
3. Debit amount							
Credit amount							
4. Debit amount							
Credit amount							
5. Debit amount							
Credit amount							
6. Debit amount							
Credit amount							
7. Debit amount							
Credit amount							
8. Debit amount							
Credit amount							
9. Debit amount							
Credit amount							
10. Debit amount							
Credit amount							
11. Debit amount							
Credit amount							
12. Debit amount							
Credit amount							
13. Debit amount							
Credit amount							
14. Debit amount							
Credit amount							
15. Debit amount							
Credit amount							
16. Debit amount							
Credit amount							

Name ______________________ Date __________ Class __________

PROBLEM 12-1, p. 273

[1, 2]

Journalizing transactions in a purchases journal

PURCHASES JOURNAL

PAGE 9

DATE		ACCOUNT CREDITED	PURCH. NO.	POST. REF.	PURCHASES DR. ACCTS. PAY. CR.
1996 Sept.	1	Kemp Fashions	100		1350 —
	12	Bonner & Company	101		740 —
	23	Burton Fabrics	102		585 —
	29	Gifts, Inc.	103		635 —
	30	Total			3310 —

Journalizing transactions in a cash payments journal [1, 2]

CASH PAYMENTS JOURNAL

PAGE 18

	DATE		ACCOUNT TITLE	CK. NO.	POST. REF.	1 GENERAL DEBIT	2 GENERAL CREDIT	3 ACCOUNTS PAYABLE DEBIT	4 CASH CREDIT	
1	1996 Sept	1	Purchase	220		150 —			150 —	1
2		2	Supplies - Office	221		75 —			75 —	2
3		4	Supplies - Store	222		55 —			55 —	3
4		7	Purchase	223		120 —			120 —	4
5		8	Utilities expense	224		120 —			120 —	5
6		11	Purchase	225		110 —			110 —	6
7		12	Supplies - Office	226		60 —			60 —	7
8		14	Mary Demski, Drawing	227		1200 —			1200 —	8
9		14	Eileen Ivan, Drawing	228		1200 —			1200 —	9
10		18	Kemp Fashions	229		[illegible]		1350 —	1350 —	10
11		21	advertising expense	230		87 —			87 —	11
12		22	Bonner & Company	231				740 —	740 —	12
13		26	Burton Fabrics	232				585 —	585 —	13
14		30	Supplies - Office	233		103 —			305 —	14
15			Supplies - Store			51 —				15
16			advertising expense			88 —				16
17			Misc. expense			103 —				17
18		[illegible]	[illegible]							18
19		30	Pulver Supply	234		[illegible]		135 —	135 —	19
20		30	total			3482 —		2810 —	6292 —	20
21										21
22										22
23										23
24										24

Name ______________________ Date ________ Class ______ *PROBLEM 12-3, p. 274*

Journalizing transactions in a general journal

GENERAL JOURNAL

PAGE 9

DATE		ACCOUNT TITLE	DOC. NO.	POST. REF.	DEBIT	CREDIT
1994 Sept	7	Supplies-Store	M42		135 —	
		Accounts payable/Oliver Sup.		✓		135 —
	9	Supplies-Office	M43		85 —	
		Accounts payable/Lorand Supply		✓		85 —
	24	Mary Demski, Drawing	M44		100 —	
		Purchases				100 —
	25	Supplies-Office	M45		88 —	
		Purchases				88 —
	29	Eileen Ivan, Drawing	M46		120 —	
		Purchases				120 —

Journalizing purchases, cash payments, and other transactions

MASTERY PROBLEM 12-M, p. 274

[1, 2]

PURCHASES JOURNAL

PAGE 11

	DATE		ACCOUNT CREDITED	PURCH. NO.	POST. REF.	PURCHASES DR. ACCTS. PAY. CR.	
1	Nov. 1996	4	Quality Books	74		1450 —	1
2		14	Falk Book Company	75		1525 —	2
3		21	Voss Publishing	76		925 —	3
4		30	Total			3900 —	4
5							5
6							6
7							7
8							8
9							9
10							10
11							11
12							12
13							13
14							14

[1]

GENERAL JOURNAL

PAGE 11

	DATE		ACCOUNT TITLE	DOC. NO.	POST. REF.	DEBIT	CREDIT	
1	[illegible]		[illegible]					1
2	1996 Nov	7	Julia Steger, Drawing	M32		42 —		2
3			Purchases				42 —	3
4		10	Supplies - Store	M33		100 —		4
5			Accounts payable / Carson Supply		✓		100 —	5
6		16	Sylvia Prior, Drawing	M34		64 —		6
7			Purchases				64 —	7
8		17	Supplies - Store	M35		214 —		8
9			Accounts payable / Gray Supplies		✓		214 —	9
10		26	Supplies - Office	M36		94 —		10
11			Purchases				94 —	11
12		28	Supplies - Store	M37		118 —		12
13			Accounts payable / Carson Supply				118 —	13
14								14

[1, 3]

CASH PAYMENTS JOURNAL

PAGE 21

	DATE		ACCOUNT TITLE	CK. NO.	POST. REF.	1 GENERAL DEBIT	2 GENERAL CREDIT	3 ACCOUNTS PAYABLE DEBIT	4 CASH CREDIT	
1	19— Nov.	2	Rent expense	261		1250 —			1250 —	1
2		2	Sylvia Prior, Drawing	262		1500 —			1500 —	2
3		2	Vidia Steger, Drawing	263		1500 —			1500 —	3
4		3	Purchases	264		130 —			130 —	4
5		4	BFL Publishing	265				927 —	927 —	5
6		9	Utilities expense	267		154 —			154 —	6
7		5	Supplies-office	266		48 —			48 —	7
8		9	Quality Books	268		[illegible]		1235 —	1235 —	8
9		11	Matson Book Service	269				975 —	975 —	9
10		16	Supplies-store	270		62 —			62 —	10
11		18	Purchases	271		145 —			145 —	11
12		18	Supplies-office	272		73 —			302 —	12
13			Supplies-store			47 —				13
14			advertising expense			92 —				14
15			misc. expense			90 —				15
16		19	Quality Books	273				1450 —	1450 —	16
17		24	Falk Book Co.	274		[illegible]		1525 —	1525 —	17
18		30	Purchases	275		68 —			68 —	18
19		30	totals			5159 —		6105 —	11 264 —	19
20										20
21										21
22										22
23										23
24										24

GENERAL JOURNAL

PAGE 12

DATE		ACCOUNT TITLE	DOC. NO.	POST. REF.	DEBIT	CREDIT

Perfect Score..... 36 | Name ______________________

Deduct......... ___ | Date ______________ Class ______________

Your Score..... ___ | Checked by ______________________

STUDY GUIDE 13

UNIT A — Identifying Accounting Terms

DIRECTIONS: Select the term in Column I that best fits each definition in Column II. Print the letter identifying your choice in the Answers column.

Column I

A. cash receipts journal
B. cash sale
C. credit card sale
D. customer
E. partner
F. sale on account
G. sales invoice
H. sales journal
I. sales tax

Column II	Answers	For Scoring
0. Each member of a partnership	E	**0.** ✓
1. A sale for which cash will be received at a later date	F	**1.**
2. A tax on a sale of merchandise or services	I	**2.**
3. A person or business to whom merchandise or services are sold	D	**3.**
4. A sale in which cash is received for the total amount of the sale at the time of the transaction	B	**4.**
5. An invoice used as a source document for recording a sale on account	G	**5.**
6. A sale in which a credit card is used for the total amount of the sale at the time of the transaction	C	**6.**
7. A special journal used to record only sales on account transactions	H	**7.**
8. A special journal used to record only cash receipt transactions	A	**8.**

UNIT B—Analyzing Sales and Cash Receipts

DIRECTIONS: Place a check mark in the proper Answers column to show whether each of the following statements is true or false.

	Answers True	Answers False	For Scoring
0. Different accounting procedures are used for different sales tax rates		✓	**0.** ✓
1. Sales tax rates are usually stated as a percentage of sales	✓		**1.**
2. A sale of merchandise increases the revenue of a business	✓		**2.**
3. Recording revenue at the time of sale is an application of the accounting concept Objective Evidence		✓	**3.**
4. The account Sales has a debit balance		✓	**4.**
5. The amount of sales tax collected is a liability	✓		**5.**
6. The total price of goods sold plus the sales tax collected is recorded as a credit to sales		✓	**6.**
7. A sale on account is also known as a charge sale	✓		**7.**
8. Accounts Receivable is an asset account with a normal credit balance	✓		**8.**
9. A sales invoice is also known as a sales slip	✓		**9.**
10. The account Sales Tax Payable is increased by a credit	✓		**10.**
11. A journal is proved only at the end of a month		✓	**11.**

UNIT C—Using Columns in a Sales Journal and a Cash Receipts Journal

DIRECTIONS: The columns of the sales journal and the cash receipts journal below are identified with capital letters. For each item below, decide in which column each of the following items should be recorded. Print the letter identifying your choice in the Answers column.

SALES JOURNAL

PAGE

	DATE	ACCOUNT DEBITED	SALE NO.	POST. REF.	1 ACCOUNTS RECEIVABLE DEBIT	2 SALES CREDIT	3 SALES TAX PAYABLE CREDIT	
1	A	B	C	D	E	F	G	1

CASH RECEIPTS JOURNAL

PAGE

	DATE	ACCOUNT TITLE	DOC. NO.	POST. REF.	1 GENERAL DEBIT	2 GENERAL CREDIT	3 ACCOUNTS RECEIVABLE CREDIT	4 SALES CREDIT	5 SALES TAX PAYABLE CREDIT	6 CASH DEBIT	
1	H	I	J	K	L	M	N	O	P	Q	1

	Answers	For Scoring
A cash sales transaction is recorded by writing the		
0. date in	H	**0.** ✓
1. check mark in (to show that no account title needs to be written)	I	**1.**
2. cash register tape number in	J	**2.**
3. check mark in (to show that no individual amounts on this line need to be posted)	K	**3.**
4. debit amount in	Q	**4.**
5. credit amount in	O	**5.**
6. credit amount in	P	**6.**
A sale on account transaction is recorded by writing the		
7. date in	A	**7.**
8. customer name in	D	**8.**
9. sales invoice number	C	**9.**
10. debit amount in	B	**10.**
11. credit amount in	F	**11.**
12. credit amount in	G	**12.**
A cash received on account transaction is recorded by writing the		
13. date in	H	**13.**
14. customer name in	I	**14.**
15. receipt number in	J	**15.**
16. debit amount in	Q	**16.**
17. credit amount in	N	**17.**

Analyzing transactions into debit and credit parts

The solution to Drill 13-D1 is needed to complete Drill 13-D3.

1.

Cash	
1,575.00	

Sales	
	1,500.00

Sales Tax Payable	
	75.00

2.

3.

4.

5.

6.

Analyzing the effect of sales transactions on accounts

DRILL 13-D2, p. 287
[1, 2]

Cash	
(1) 2,862.00	

Sales	
	(1) 2,700.00

Accounts Receivable	

Sales Tax Payable	
	(1) 162.00

Analyzing journal entries

DRILL 13-D3, p. 288

The solution to Drill 13-D1 is needed to complete Drill 13-D3.

Trans.	Sales Journal			Cash Receipts Journal						
	Accts. Rec. Debit	Sales Credit	Sales Tax Pay. Credit	General Debit	General Credit	Accts. Rec. Credit	Sales Credit	Sales Tax Pay. Credit	Cash Debit
1.							1,500.00	75.00	1,575.00
2.									
3.									
4.									
5.									
6.									

Name ______________________ Date __________ Class __________

PROBLEM 13-1, p. 288
[1–3]

Journalizing transactions in a sales journal

SALES JOURNAL

PAGE 9

DATE		ACCOUNT DEBITED	SALE NO.	POST. REF.	1 ACCOUNTS RECEIVABLE DEBIT	2 SALES CREDIT	3 SALES TAX PAYABLE CREDIT
Sept	1	Valerie Seeley	66		52 —	50 —	2 —
	2	Jill Folker	67		130 —	125 —	5 —
	4	Jerome Hodges	68		88 40	85 —	3 40
	9	Anthony Zolte	69		119 60	115 —	4 60
	15	Beth Allen	70		119 60	115 —	4 60
	20	Jill Folker	71		78 —	75 —	3 —
	29	Karla Doyle	72		98 80	95 —	3 80
	31	Totals			686 40	560 —	26 40

PROBLEM 13-2, p. 288

Journalizing transactions in a cash receipts journal [1–4]

CASH RECEIPTS JOURNAL

PAGE 9

	DATE	ACCOUNT TITLE	DOC. NO.	POST. REF.	1 GENERAL DEBIT	2 GENERAL CREDIT	3 ACCOUNTS RECEIVABLE CREDIT	4 SALES CREDIT	5 SALES TAX PAYABLE CREDIT	6 CASH DEBIT	
1											1
2											2
3											3
4											4
5											5
6											6
7											7
8											8
9											9
10											10
11											11
12											12
13											13
14											14
15											15
16											16
17											17
18											18
19											19
20											20
21											21
22											22
23											23
24											24
25											25

Name ______________________ Date ________ Class ______

MASTERY PROBLEM 13-M, p. 289
[1, 2]

Journalizing sales and cash receipt transactions

SALES JOURNAL

PAGE 5

DATE		ACCOUNT DEBITED	SALE NO.	POST. REF.	1 ACCOUNTS RECEIVABLE DEBIT	2 SALES CREDIT	3 SALES TAX PAYABLE CREDIT
May	3	Susan Burton	23		57 75	55 —	2 75
	3	Lisa Bond	24		94 50	90 —	4 50
	6	Patrick Martin	25		117 60	112 —	5 60
	10	Sheila Newbern	26		172 20	164 —	8 20
	11	Kim Lee	27		45 15	43 —	2 15
	24	Thomas Coffey	28		91 35	87 —	4 35
	31	Roger Metcalf	29		143 85	137 —	6 85
					722 40	688 —	34 40

[1, 3, 4, 5]

CASH RECEIPTS JOURNAL

PAGE 8

	DATE		ACCOUNT TITLE	DOC. NO.	POST. REF.	1 GENERAL DEBIT	2 GENERAL CREDIT	3 ACCOUNTS RECEIVABLE CREDIT	4 SALES CREDIT	5 SALES TAX PAYABLE CREDIT	6 CASH DEBIT	
1	19-- May	5	Richard Kirby	R70				69 30			69 30	1
2		7	Thomas Coffey	R71				114 45				2
3		8	✓	T8	✓				2543 —	127 15	2670 15	3
4		13	Gene Lewis	R72				61 95			61 95	4
5		15	✓	T15	✓				2378 —	118 90	2496 90	5
6		17	Katherine Lynch	R73				142 80			142 80	6
7		20	Carl Thorpe	R74				91 35			91 35	7
8		22	✓	T22	✓				2493 —	124 65	2617 65	8
9		25	Susan Burton	R75				57 75			57 75	9
10		27	Patrick Martin	R76				117 60			117 60	10
11		29	✓	T29	✓				2173 —	108 65	2281 65	11
12		31	✓	T31	✓				512 —	25 60	537 60	12
13		31	Total					655 20	10099 —	504 95	11259 15	13
14												14
15												15
16												16
17												17
18												18
19												19
20												20
21												21
22												22
23												23
24												24
25												25

Name ______________________________ Date ________ Class ______

CHALLENGE PROBLEM 13-C, p. 290

[1, 2]

Journalizing transactions in special journals

SALES JOURNAL

PAGE 11

	DATE		ACCOUNT DEBITED	SALE NO.	POST. REF.	1 ACCOUNTS RECEIVABLE DEBIT	2 SALES CREDIT	3 SALES TAX PAYABLE CREDIT	
1									1
2									2
3									3
4									4
5									5
6									6
7									7
8									8
9									9
10									10
11									11
12									12
13									13
14									14

[1, 3]

PURCHASES JOURNAL

PAGE 11

	DATE		ACCOUNT CREDITED	PURCH. NO.	POST. REF.	PURCHASES DR. ACCTS. PAY. CR.	
1							1
2							2
3							3
4							4
5							5
6							6
7							7
8							8
9							9
10							10
11							11
12							12
13							13
14							14

CHALLENGE PROBLEM 13-C, continued

[1]

GENERAL JOURNAL

PAGE 6

DATE		ACCOUNT TITLE	DOC. NO.	POST. REF.	DEBIT	CREDIT

[1, 4, 6, 7]

CASH RECEIPTS JOURNAL

PAGE 19

	DATE	ACCOUNT TITLE	DOC. NO.	POST. REF.	1 GENERAL DEBIT	2 GENERAL CREDIT	3 ACCOUNTS RECEIVABLE CREDIT	4 SALES CREDIT	5 SALES TAX PAYABLE CREDIT	6 CASH DEBIT	
1											1
2											2
3											3
4											4
5											5
6											6
7											7
8											8
9											9
10											10
11											11
12											12
13											13
14											14
15											15
16											16
17											17
18											18
19											19
20											20
21											21
22											22
23											23
24											24
25											25

[1, 5, 6, 8]

CASH PAYMENTS JOURNAL

PAGE 20

	DATE	ACCOUNT TITLE	CK. NO.	POST. REF.	1 GENERAL DEBIT	2 GENERAL CREDIT	3 ACCOUNTS PAYABLE DEBIT	4 CASH CREDIT	
1									1
2									2
3									3
4									4
5									5
6									6
7									7
8									8
9									9
10									10
11									11
12									12
13									13
14									14
15									15
16									16
17									17
18									18
19									19
20									20
21									21
22									22
23									23
24									24

Perfect Score..... 25 Name ______________________

Deduct......... ___ Date ______________ Class ______________

Your Score..... ___ Checked by ______________________

STUDY GUIDE 14

UNIT A — Identifying Accounting Terms

DIRECTIONS: Select the one term in Column I that best fits each definition in Column II. Print the letter identifying your choice in the Answers column.

Column I	*Column II*	Answers	For Scoring
A. accounts payable ledger	**0.** A person or business to whom merchandise or services are sold................	D	**0.** ✓
B. accounts receivable ledger	**1.** A ledger that is summarized in a single general ledger account................		**1.**
C. controlling account	**2.** A listing of vendor accounts, account balances, and total amount due all vendors................		**2.**
D. customer	**3.** An account in a general ledger that summarizes all accounts in a subsidiary ledger................		**3.**
E. schedule of accounts payable	**4.** A subsidiary ledger containing only accounts for charge customers................		**4.**
F. subsidiary ledger	**5.** A subsidiary ledger containing only accounts for vendors from whom items are purchased or bought on account................		**5.**

UNIT B—Analyzing Posting from Special Journals

DIRECTIONS: Place a check mark in the proper Answers column to show whether each of the following statements is true or false.

	Answers True	Answers False	For Scoring
0. A journal provides a temporary record of transactions listed in chronological order................		✓	**0.** ✓
1. Transferring information from journal entries to ledger accounts is known as posting................			**1.**
2. When using an accounts payable ledger, the total amount owed to all vendors is summarized in a single general ledger account................			**2.**
3. A ledger that contains all accounts needed to prepare financial statements is known as a general ledger................			**3.**
4. A controlling account balance equals the total of all account balances in its related general ledger................			**4.**
5. A change in the balance of a vendor account also changes the balance of the controlling account, Accounts Payable................			**5.**
6. The heading of the balance column of an account in the accounts payable ledger is titled Debit Balance................			**6.**
7. Each transaction in a purchases journal is posted individually to a vendor account in the accounts payable ledger................			**7.**
8. The monthly total of a purchases journal is posted as a credit to Purchases................			**8.**
9. Each cash payment to a vendor is posted as a credit to an account in the accounts payable ledger................			**9.**
10. Each amount in the Debit column of a general journal is posted individually to an account in the accounts payable ledger................			**10.**

DIRECTIONS: For each of the following items, select the choice that best completes the statement. Print the letter identifying your choice in the Answers column.

Item	Answers	For Scoring
0. CarLand arranges the accounts in its accounts payable ledger in **(A)** address order **(B)** alphabetic order **(C)** geographic **(D)** none of these	B	**0.** ✓
1. Each account in the accounts payable ledger of CarLand has **(A)** two columns **(B)** three columns **(C)** four columns **(D)** none of these..........		**1.**
2. Each entry in the purchases journal is an amount that **(A)** is to be paid to a vendor **(B)** has been paid to a vendor **(C)** is to be collected from a customer **(D)** none of these		**2.**
3. Each entry in the purchases journal is **(A)** posted daily **(B)** posted often **(C)** posted at the end of a month **(D)** not posted..........		**3.**
4. A purchases journal is totaled and **(A)** posted daily **(B)** posted often **(C)** at the end of a month **(D)** not posted		**4.**
5. The Accounts Payable Debit column of a cash payments journal is totaled and **(A)** posted often **(B)** posted at the end of a month **(C)** not posted **(D)** none of these		**5.**
6. The separate amounts in the General Credit column of a cash payments journal are **(A)** posted individually **(B)** posted only as part of the column total **(C)** not posted **(D)** none of these		**6.**
7. The total of the Cash Credit column of a cash payments journal is **(A)** posted daily **(B)** posted weekly **(C)** posted at the end of a month **(D)** not posted		**7.**
8. Each account in the general ledger of CarLand has **(A)** one amount column **(B)** two amount columns **(C)** three amount columns **(D)** four amount columns............		**8.**
9. Entries in a general journal should be posted **(A)** only to the general ledger **(B)** only to the accounts payable ledger **(C)** to both the general and accounts payable ledgers **(D)** none of these............		**9.**
10. The totals of the Debit and Credit columns of a general journal are **(A)** posted daily **(B)** posted weekly **(C)** posted at the end of a month **(D)** not posted		**10.**

Name ______________________ Date ________ Class ______

DRILL 14-D1, p. 312
[1, 2]

Analyzing posting from purchases, cash payments, and general journals

Trans. No.	(A) Accounts affected	(B) Amounts posted individually to General Ledger	(B) Amounts posted individually to Accounts Payable Ledger	(D) Amounts not posted individually to any ledger
1.	Casa Enterprises		✓	
	Cash			✓
2.				
3.				
4.				
5.				
6.				
7.				
8.				
9.				

Opening accounts and posting from purchases, cash payments, and general journals

PROBLEM 14-1, p. 313
[3, 6]

PURCHASES JOURNAL

PAGE 9

DATE		ACCOUNT CREDITED	PURCH. NO.	POST. REF.	PURCHASES DR. ACCTS. PAY. CR.
19-- Sept.	4	Superior Carpeting	83		1680 00
	16	Crown Carpet Co.	84		3820 00
	22	V & P Carpet Co.	85		4500 00
	24	Marlow Industries	86		2830 00
	30	Total			

[4]

GENERAL JOURNAL

PAGE 9

DATE		ACCOUNT TITLE	DOC. NO.	POST. REF.	DEBIT	CREDIT
19-- Sept.	18	Miscellaneous Expense	M43		50 00	
		Prepaid Insurance				50 00
	21	Paul Sisco, Drawing	M44		960 00	
		Purchases				960 00
	23	Supplies—Office	M45		50 00	
		Accounts Payable/Superior Carpeting				50 00

[5, 7]

CASH PAYMENTS JOURNAL

PAGE 9

	DATE		ACCOUNT TITLE	CK. NO.	POST. REF.	1 GENERAL DEBIT	2 GENERAL CREDIT	3 ACCOUNTS PAYABLE DEBIT	4 CASH CREDIT	
1	19-- Sept.	1	Rent Expense	280		1000 00			1000 00	1
2		1	Diane Engler, Drawing	281		1000 00			1000 00	2
3		1	Paul Sisco, Drawing	282		1000 00			1000 00	3
4		3	Supplies—Office	283		80 00			80 00	4
5		7	Crown Carpet Co.	284				2575 00	2575 00	5
6		9	Marlow Industries	285				4220 00	4220 00	6
7		14	V & P Carpet Co.	286				3760 00	3760 00	7
8		24	Superior Carpeting	287				1680 00	1680 00	8
9		28	Supplies—Office	288		64 00			302 00	9
10			Supplies—Store			76 00				10
11			Advertising Expense			115 00				11
12			Miscellaneous Expense			47 00				12
13		30	Totals							13
14										14
15										15
16										16
17										17
18										18
19										19
20										20
21										21
22										22
23										23
24										24

GENERAL LEDGER

ACCOUNT ACCOUNT NO.

DATE		ITEM	POST. REF.	DEBIT	CREDIT	BALANCE DEBIT	BALANCE CREDIT

ACCOUNT ACCOUNT NO.

DATE		ITEM	POST. REF.	DEBIT	CREDIT	BALANCE DEBIT	BALANCE CREDIT

ACCOUNT ACCOUNT NO.

DATE		ITEM	POST. REF.	DEBIT	CREDIT	BALANCE DEBIT	BALANCE CREDIT

ACCOUNT ACCOUNT NO.

DATE		ITEM	POST. REF.	DEBIT	CREDIT	BALANCE DEBIT	BALANCE CREDIT

ACCOUNT ACCOUNT NO.

DATE		ITEM	POST. REF.	DEBIT	CREDIT	BALANCE DEBIT	BALANCE CREDIT

GENERAL LEDGER

ACCOUNT ACCOUNT NO.

DATE		ITEM	POST. REF.	DEBIT	CREDIT	BALANCE DEBIT	BALANCE CREDIT

ACCOUNT ACCOUNT NO.

DATE		ITEM	POST. REF.	DEBIT	CREDIT	BALANCE DEBIT	BALANCE CREDIT

ACCOUNT ACCOUNT NO.

DATE		ITEM	POST. REF.	DEBIT	CREDIT	BALANCE DEBIT	BALANCE CREDIT

ACCOUNT ACCOUNT NO.

DATE		ITEM	POST. REF.	DEBIT	CREDIT	BALANCE DEBIT	BALANCE CREDIT

ACCOUNT ACCOUNT NO.

DATE		ITEM	POST. REF.	DEBIT	CREDIT	BALANCE DEBIT	BALANCE CREDIT

ACCOUNT ACCOUNT NO.

DATE		ITEM	POST. REF.	DEBIT	CREDIT	BALANCE DEBIT	BALANCE CREDIT

Name ______________ Date ________ Class ________

PROBLEM 14-1, concluded
[2–5, 8]

ACCOUNTS PAYABLE LEDGER

VENDOR　　　　　　VENDOR NO.

DATE		ITEM	POST. REF.	DEBIT	CREDIT	CREDIT BALANCE

VENDOR　　　　　　VENDOR NO.

DATE		ITEM	POST. REF.	DEBIT	CREDIT	CREDIT BALANCE

VENDOR　　　　　　VENDOR NO.

DATE		ITEM	POST. REF.	DEBIT	CREDIT	CREDIT BALANCE

VENDOR　　　　　　VENDOR NO.

DATE		ITEM	POST. REF.	DEBIT	CREDIT	CREDIT BALANCE

[8]

Carpet Magic
Schedule of Accounts Payable
September 30, 1994

Crown Carpet Company	3,820 —
Marlow Industries	2,830 —
Superior Carpeting	50 —
V & P Carpet Company	4,500 —
Total accounts payable	11,200 —

[1, 4]

PURCHASES JOURNAL

PAGE 11

DATE		ACCOUNT CREDITED	PURCH. NO.	POST. REF.	PURCHASES DR. ACCTS. PAY. CR.
19-- Nov.	3	Clemco Leather Co.	73	220	1 136 00
	14	Blair Leather Products	74	210	2 690 00
	21	Rusch Leather Goods	75	240	3 720 00
	27	Norwood Supply	76	230	2 930 00
	30	Total			10 474 —
					(5110) (2110)

[2]

GENERAL JOURNAL

PAGE 11

DATE		ACCOUNT TITLE	DOC. NO.	POST. REF.	DEBIT	CREDIT
19-- Nov.	24	Amy Hymes, Drawing	M38	3120	138 00	
		Purchases		5110		138 00
	26	Supplies—Store	M39	1160	70 00	
		Accounts Payable/Norwood Supply		2110/230		70 00

[3, 5]

CASH PAYMENTS JOURNAL

PAGE 15

DATE		ACCOUNT TITLE	CK. NO.	POST. REF.	1 GENERAL DEBIT	2 GENERAL CREDIT	3 ACCOUNTS PAYABLE DEBIT	4 CASH CREDIT
19-- Nov.	2	Rent Expense	231		1 250 00			1 250 00
	2	Utilities Expense	232		173 00			173 00
	4	Norwood Supply	233				1 985 00	1 985 00
	6	Clemco Leather Co.	234				3 180 00	3 180 00
	9	Rusch Leather Goods	235				2 890 00	2 890 00
	13	Blair Leather Products	236				2 360 00	2 360 00
	13	Clemco Leather Co.	237				1 136 00	1 136 00
	16	Amy Hymes, Drawing	238		1 000 00			1 000 00
	16	Kara Morey, Drawing	239		1 000 00			1 000 00
	17	Miscellaneous Expense	240		80 00			80 00
	20	Advertising Expense	241		267 00			267 00
	26	Supplies—Office	242		83 00			83 00
	28	Supplies—Store	243		106 00			106 00
	30	Totals			3959		11551 —	15510 —
					(√)		(2110)	(1110)

[2–5]

GENERAL LEDGER

ACCOUNT Cash — ACCOUNT NO. 1110

DATE		ITEM	POST. REF.	DEBIT	CREDIT	BALANCE DEBIT	BALANCE CREDIT
19-- Nov.	1	Balance	✓			16 930 00	
	30		CP15		15510—	1420—	

ACCOUNT Supplies—Office — ACCOUNT NO. 1150

DATE		ITEM	POST. REF.	DEBIT	CREDIT	BALANCE DEBIT	BALANCE CREDIT
19-- Nov.	1	Balance	✓			2 960 00	
	26		CP15	83—		3043—	

ACCOUNT Supplies—Store — ACCOUNT NO. 1160

DATE		ITEM	POST. REF.	DEBIT	CREDIT	BALANCE DEBIT	BALANCE CREDIT
19-- Nov.	1	Balance	✓			3 420 00	
	26		G11	70—		3490—	
	28		CP15	106—		3596—	

ACCOUNT Accounts Payable — ACCOUNT NO. 2110

DATE		ITEM	POST. REF.	DEBIT	CREDIT	BALANCE DEBIT	BALANCE CREDIT
19-- Nov.	1	Balance	✓				10 415 00
	26		G11		70—		10485—
	30		P11		10476—		20961—
	30		CP15	11551—			9410—

ACCOUNT Amy Hymes, Drawing — ACCOUNT NO. 3120

DATE		ITEM	POST. REF.	DEBIT	CREDIT	BALANCE DEBIT	BALANCE CREDIT
19-- Nov.	1	Balance	✓			12 740 00	
	24		G11	138—		12878—	
	16		CP15	1000—		13878—	

[2–5]

GENERAL LEDGER

ACCOUNT Kara Morey, Drawing — ACCOUNT NO. 3140

DATE		ITEM	POST. REF.	DEBIT	CREDIT	BALANCE DEBIT	BALANCE CREDIT
19-- Nov.	1	Balance	✓			12 360 00	
	10		CP15	1000-		13360-	

ACCOUNT Purchases — ACCOUNT NO. 5110

DATE		ITEM	POST. REF.	DEBIT	CREDIT	BALANCE DEBIT	BALANCE CREDIT
19-- Nov.	1	Balance	✓			94 830 00	
	24		G11		138-	94692-	
	30		P11	10476-		84216-	

ACCOUNT Advertising Expense — ACCOUNT NO. 6110

DATE		ITEM	POST. REF.	DEBIT	CREDIT	BALANCE DEBIT	BALANCE CREDIT
19-- Nov.	1	Balance	✓			1 965 00	
	20		CP15	267-		2232-	

ACCOUNT Miscellaneous Expense — ACCOUNT NO. 6140

DATE		ITEM	POST. REF.	DEBIT	CREDIT	BALANCE DEBIT	BALANCE CREDIT
19-- Nov.	1	Balance	✓			1 138 00	
	17		CP15	80-		1218-	

ACCOUNT Rent Expense — ACCOUNT NO. 6160

DATE		ITEM	POST. REF.	DEBIT	CREDIT	BALANCE DEBIT	BALANCE CREDIT
19-- Nov.	1	Balance	✓			12 500 00	
	2		CP15	1250-		13750-	

ACCOUNT Utilities Expense — ACCOUNT NO. 6190

DATE		ITEM	POST. REF.	DEBIT	CREDIT	BALANCE DEBIT	BALANCE CREDIT
19-- Nov.	1	Balance	✓			1 730 00	
	2		CP15	173-		1903-	

[1–3, 6]

ACCOUNTS PAYABLE LEDGER

VENDOR Blair Leather Products **VENDOR NO.** 210

DATE		ITEM	POST. REF.	DEBIT	CREDIT	CREDIT BALANCE
19-- Nov.	1	Balance	✓			2360 00
	14		P11		2690 —	5050 —
	13		CP15	2360 —		2690 —

VENDOR Clemco Leather Co. **VENDOR NO.** 220

DATE		ITEM	POST. REF.	DEBIT	CREDIT	CREDIT BALANCE
19-- Nov.	1	Balance	✓			3180 00
	3		P11		1136 —	4316 —
	6		CP15	3180 —		1136 —
	13		CP15	1136 —		

VENDOR Norwood Supply **VENDOR NO.** 230

DATE		ITEM	POST. REF.	DEBIT	CREDIT	CREDIT BALANCE
19-- Nov.	1	Balance	✓			1985 00
	27		P11		2930 —	4915 —
	20		G11		70 —	4985 —
	4		CP15	1985 —		3000 —

VENDOR Rusch Leather Goods **VENDOR NO.** 240

DATE		ITEM	POST. REF.	DEBIT	CREDIT	CREDIT BALANCE
19-- Nov.	1	Balance	✓			2890 00
	21		P11		3720 —	6610 —
	9		CP15	2890 —		3720 —

[6]

Anton Leather Goods
Schedule of Accounts payable
November 30, 1996

Blair Leather Products	2690 —
Norwood Supply	3000 —
Rusch Leather Goods	~~6610~~
	3720 —
totals of accounts Payable	9410 —

[1, 4]

PURCHASES JOURNAL

PAGE 11

DATE		ACCOUNT CREDITED	PURCH. NO.	POST. REF.	PURCHASES DR. ACCTS. PAY. CR.
19-- Nov.	2	Kendall Picture Frames	82		1 160 00
	5	Canton Photo Products	83		1 820 00
	19	Foto Factory	84		3 680 00
	26	Kendall Picture Frames	85		2 130 00
	30	Total			

[2]

GENERAL JOURNAL

PAGE 11

DATE		ACCOUNT TITLE	DOC. NO.	POST. REF.	DEBIT	CREDIT
19-- Nov.	6	Julie Kemp, Drawing	M41		340 00	
		Purchases				340 00
	9	Supplies—Store	M42		619 00	
		Accounts Payable/Sunset Supply				619 00
	20	Supplies—Office	M43		90 00	
		Supplies—Store				90 00

[3, 5]

CASH PAYMENTS JOURNAL

PAGE 11

	DATE		ACCOUNT TITLE	CK. NO.	POST. REF.	1 GENERAL DEBIT	2 GENERAL CREDIT	3 ACCOUNTS PAYABLE DEBIT	4 CASH CREDIT	
1	19-- Nov.	2	Rent Expense	235		1 300 00			1 300 00	1
2		4	Kendall Picture Frames	236				2 980 00	2 980 00	2
3		5	Foto Factory	237				4 310 00	4 310 00	3
4		12	Supplies—Office	238		115 00			115 00	4
5		13	Canton Photo Products	239				3 740 00	3 740 00	5
6		16	Julie Kemp, Drawing	240		1 500 00			1 500 00	6
7		16	Todd Kemp, Drawing	241		1 500 00			1 500 00	7
8		20	Advertising Expense	242		315 00			315 00	8
9		24	Sunset Supply	243				980 00	980 00	9
10		28	Supplies—Office	244		66 00			303 00	10
11			Supplies—Store			73 00				11
12			Advertising Expense			110 00				12
13			Miscellaneous Expense			54 00				13
14		30	Totals							14
15										15
16										16
17										17
18										18
19										19
20										20
21										21
22										22
23										23
24										24
25										25

[2–5]

GENERAL LEDGER

ACCOUNT Cash — ACCOUNT NO. 1110

DATE		ITEM	POST. REF.	DEBIT	CREDIT	BALANCE DEBIT	BALANCE CREDIT
19-- Nov.	1	Balance	✓			21 480 00	

ACCOUNT Supplies—Office — ACCOUNT NO. 1150

DATE		ITEM	POST. REF.	DEBIT	CREDIT	BALANCE DEBIT	BALANCE CREDIT
19-- Nov.	1	Balance	✓			3 960 00	

ACCOUNT Supplies—Store — ACCOUNT NO. 1160

DATE		ITEM	POST. REF.	DEBIT	CREDIT	BALANCE DEBIT	BALANCE CREDIT
19-- Nov.	1	Balance	✓			4 290 00	

ACCOUNT Accounts Payable — ACCOUNT NO. 2110

DATE		ITEM	POST. REF.	DEBIT	CREDIT	BALANCE DEBIT	BALANCE CREDIT
19-- Nov.	1	Balance	✓				12 010 00

ACCOUNT Julie Kemp, Drawing — ACCOUNT NO. 3120

DATE		ITEM	POST. REF.	DEBIT	CREDIT	BALANCE DEBIT	BALANCE CREDIT
19-- Nov.	1	Balance	✓			15 000 00	

[2–5]

GENERAL LEDGER

ACCOUNT Todd Kemp, Drawing — ACCOUNT NO. 3140

DATE		ITEM	POST. REF.	DEBIT	CREDIT	BALANCE DEBIT	BALANCE CREDIT
19-- Nov.	1	Balance	✓			15 310 00	

ACCOUNT Purchases — ACCOUNT NO. 5110

DATE		ITEM	POST. REF.	DEBIT	CREDIT	BALANCE DEBIT	BALANCE CREDIT
19-- Nov.	1	Balance	✓			126 360 00	

ACCOUNT Advertising Expense — ACCOUNT NO. 6110

DATE		ITEM	POST. REF.	DEBIT	CREDIT	BALANCE DEBIT	BALANCE CREDIT
19-- Nov.	1	Balance	✓			1 930 00	

ACCOUNT Miscellaneous Expense — ACCOUNT NO. 6140

DATE		ITEM	POST. REF.	DEBIT	CREDIT	BALANCE DEBIT	BALANCE CREDIT
19-- Nov.	1	Balance	✓			1 320 00	

ACCOUNT Rent Expense — ACCOUNT NO. 6160

DATE		ITEM	POST. REF.	DEBIT	CREDIT	BALANCE DEBIT	BALANCE CREDIT
19-- Nov.	1	Balance	✓			13 000 00	

Name ______________________ Date ________ Class ________

CHALLENGE PROBLEM 14-C, continued
[1–3, 6]

ACCOUNTS PAYABLE LEDGER

VENDOR Canton Photo Products — VENDOR NO. 210

DATE		ITEM	POST. REF.	DEBIT	CREDIT	CREDIT BALANCE
19-- Nov.	1	Balance	✓			3 740 00

VENDOR Foto Factory — VENDOR NO. 220

DATE		ITEM	POST. REF.	DEBIT	CREDIT	CREDIT BALANCE
19-- Nov.	1	Balance	✓			4 310 00

VENDOR Kendall Picture Frames — VENDOR NO. 230

DATE		ITEM	POST. REF.	DEBIT	CREDIT	CREDIT BALANCE
19-- Nov.	1	Balance	✓			2 980 00

VENDOR Sunset Supply — VENDOR NO. 240

DATE		ITEM	POST. REF.	DEBIT	CREDIT	CREDIT BALANCE
19-- Nov.	1	Balance	✓			980 00

[6]

Extra form

Perfect Score..... 30 Name ____________________

Deduct......... ___ Date ______________ Class ______________

Your Score..... ___ Checked by ____________________

STUDY GUIDE 15

UNIT A—Analyzing Posting and an Accounts Receivable Ledger

DIRECTIONS: For each of the following items, select the choice that best completes the statement. Print the letter identifying your choice in the Answers column.

	Answers	For Scoring
0. The separate amounts in the Accounts Receivable Debit column of a sales journal are **(A)** not posted **(B)** posted individually **(C)** posted only as a part of the column total **(D)** none of these	B	**0.** ✓
1. The separate amounts in the Sales Credit column of a sales journal are **(A)** not posted **(B)** posted individually **(C)** posted only as part of the column total **(D)** none of these		**1.**
2. The separate amounts in the General Debit column of a cash receipts journal are **(A)** not posted **(B)** posted individually **(C)** posted only as part of the column total **(D)** none of these		**2.**
3. The separate amounts in the Sales Tax Payable Credit column of a cash receipts journal are **(A)** not posted **(B)** posted individually **(C)** posted only as part of the column total **(D)** none of these		**3.**
4. Each account in the accounts receivable ledger of the OffiCenter has **(A)** two amount columns **(B)** three amount columns **(C)** four amount columns **(D)** none of these		**4.**
5. Each entry in the Accounts Receivable Debit column of a sales journal is an amount that **(A)** is to be paid to a vendor **(B)** has been collected from a customer **(C)** is to be collected from a customer **(D)** none of these		**5.**
6. Each entry in the Accounts Receivable Credit column of a cash receipts journal is an amount that **(A)** is to be paid to a vendor **(B)** has been collected from a customer **(C)** is to be collected from a customer **(D)** none of these		**6.**
7. Completion of posting an individual amount from the sales journal is indicated by **(A)** writing the subsidiary ledger account number in the Post. Ref. column **(B)** writing the general ledger account number in the Post. Ref. column **(C)** writing the general ledger account number under the column total **(D)** none of these		**7.**
8. Completion of posting a column total from the cash receipts journal is indicated by **(A)** writing the subsidiary ledger account number under the column total **(B)** writing the general ledger account number in the Post. Ref. column **(C)** writing the general ledger account number under the column total **(D)** none of these		**8.**
9. Completion of posting an individual amount from the General Debit column of a cash receipts journal is indicated by **(A)** writing the subsidiary ledger account number in the Post. Ref. column **(B)** writing the general ledger account number in the Post. Ref. column **(C)** writing the general ledger account number under the column total **(D)** none of these		**9.**
10. The accounts receivable ledger contains an account for each **(A)** cash customer **(B)** customer who will pay later **(C)** vendor **(D)** none of these		**10.**
11. The total of the Accounts Receivable Debit column of a sales journal is **(A)** not posted **(B)** posted weekly **(C)** posted daily **(D)** none of these		**11.**
12. The total of the General Debit column of a cash receipts journal is **(A)** not posted **(B)** posted weekly **(C)** posted daily **(D)** none of these............		**12.**
13. The accuracy of posting to the accounts receivable ledger is proved by preparing a **(A)** post-closing trial balance **(B)** cash proof **(C)** trial balance **(D)** schedule of accounts receivable		**13.**
14. Individual amounts in a sales journal should be posted **(A)** only to the general ledger **(B)** only to the accounts receivable ledger **(C)** to both the accounts receivable and general ledger **(D)** none of these		**14.**

UNIT B — Analyzing Posting from a Sales and a Cash Receipts Journal

DIRECTIONS: Place a check mark in the proper Answers column to show whether each of the following statements is true or false.

	Answers		For Scoring
	True	False	
0. One of the monthly totals of a sales journal is posted as a credit to Sales............	✓		**0.** ✓
1. One of the monthly totals of a sales journal is posted as a credit to Accounts Receivable............			**1.**
2. One of the monthly totals of a sales journal is posted as a debit to Sales Tax Payable............			**2.**
3. The amount of sales tax is posted to the general ledger account Sales Tax Payable each time a cash sale occurs............			**3.**
4. Each amount in the Accounts Receivable Credit column of a cash receipts journal is posted individually to the account of the customer named in the Account Title column			**4.**
5. Each amount in the General Credit column of a cash receipts journal is posted individually to the accounts receivable ledger account named in the Account Title column............			**5.**
6. The balance column of an account in the accounts receivable ledger is titled Accounts Receivable Credit			**6.**
7. A listing of customer accounts, account balances, and total amount due from all customers is a schedule of accounts receivable			**7.**
8. Amounts recorded in special amount columns are posted to the general ledger daily............			**8.**
9. The totals of the General columns of a cash receipts journal are usually posted only at the end of a month			**9.**
10. Items affecting general ledger account balances need to be posted more frequently than items affecting subsidiary ledger account balances			**10.**
11. The accounts receivable ledger is proved by completing a trial balance..			**11.**
12. The general ledger controlling account for customers is Accounts Payable............			**12.**
13. Completion of posting special column monthly totals of the cash receipts journal is indicated by writing the general ledger account number below the column total............			**13.**
14. Completion of posting General column monthly totals of the cash receipts journal is indicated by writing the general ledger account number below the column total............			**14.**
15. A change in the balance of a customer's account also changes the balance of the controlling account, Accounts Receivable............			**15.**
16. The best order to post special journals is (1) sales, (2) purchases, (3) general, (4) cash receipts, and (5) cash payments............			**16.**

Name ______________________ Date ________ Class ________

DRILL 15-D1, p. 329
[1, 2]

Analyzing posting transactions from sales and cash receipts journals

Trans. No.	(A) Accounts affected	(B) Amounts posted individually to: General Ledger	(C) Amounts posted individually to: Accounts Receivable Ledger	(D) Amounts not posted individually to any ledger
1.	Accounts Receivable			✓
	Allison Hartley		✓	
	Sales			✓
	Sales Tax Payable			✓
2.				
3.				
4.				
5.				
6.				

Opening accounts and posting from sales and cash receipts journals

PROBLEM 15-1, p. 330
[3, 5]

SALES JOURNAL

PAGE 11

	DATE		ACCOUNT DEBITED	SALE NO.	POST. REF.	1 ACCOUNTS RECEIVABLE DEBIT	2 SALES CREDIT	3 SALES TAX PAYABLE CREDIT	
1	19-- Nov.	4	Deborah Carson	35	110	146 28	138 00	8 28	1
2		17	Nell Lehr	36	130	185 50	175 00	10 50	2
3		29	Cecil Gleim	37	120	200 34	189 00	11 34	3
4		30	Totals			532 12	502 —	30 12	4
5						(1130)	(4110)	(2130)	5

[4, 6]

CASH RECEIPTS JOURNAL

PAGE 15

	DATE		ACCOUNT TITLE	DOC. NO.	POST. REF.	1 GENERAL DEBIT	2 GENERAL CREDIT	3 ACCOUNTS RECEIVABLE CREDIT	4 SALES CREDIT	5 SALES TAX PAYABLE CREDIT	6 CASH DEBIT	
1	19-- Nov.	3	Cecil Gleim	R56	120			367 50			367 50	1
2		5	✓	T5					2350 00	141 00	2491 00	2
3		12	✓	T12					2548 00	152 88	2700 88	3
4		15	James Salerno	R57	140			271 50			271 50	4
5		19	✓	T19					2436 00	146 16	2582 16	5
6		24	Nell Lehr	R58	130			213 00			213 00	6
7		26	✓	T26					2688 00	161 28	2849 28	7
8		30	✓	T31					2646 00	158 76	2804 76	8
9		30	Totals					852 —	12668 —	760 08	14280 08	9
10								(1130)	(4110)	(2130)	(1110)	10

CASH RECEIPTS JOURNAL

PAGE

	DATE	ACCOUNT TITLE	DOC. NO.	POST. REF.	1 GENERAL DEBIT	2 GENERAL CREDIT	3 ACCOUNTS RECEIVABLE CREDIT	4 SALES CREDIT	5 SALES TAX PAYABLE CREDIT	6 CASH DEBIT	
1											1
2											2
3											3
4											4
5											5
6											6
7											7
8											8
9											9
10											10
11											11
12											12
13											13
14											14
15											15
16											16
17											17
18											18
19											19
20											20
21											21
22											22
23											23
24											24
25											25

Name ______________________ Date ________ Class ________

PROBLEM 15-1, continued
[1, 5, 6]

GENERAL LEDGER

ACCOUNT Cash ACCOUNT NO. 1110

DATE		ITEM	POST. REF.	DEBIT	CREDIT	BALANCE DEBIT	BALANCE CREDIT
1996 Nov.	1	Balance	✓			7280 —	
	30		CR15	14280 00		21560 00	

ACCOUNT Accounts receivable ACCOUNT NO. 1130

DATE		ITEM	POST. REF.	DEBIT	CREDIT	BALANCE DEBIT	BALANCE CREDIT
1996 Nov.	1	Balance	✓			852 —	
	30		S11	532 12		1384 12	
	30		CR15		852 —	532 12	

ACCOUNT Sales tax payable ACCOUNT NO. 2130

DATE		ITEM	POST. REF.	DEBIT	CREDIT	BALANCE DEBIT	BALANCE CREDIT
1996 Nov.	1	Balance	✓				603 —
	30		S11		[illegible]		633 12
	[illegible]		[illegible]		30 12		[illegible]
	30		CR15		760 08		1393 20

ACCOUNT Sales ACCOUNT NO. 4110

DATE		ITEM	POST. REF.	DEBIT	CREDIT	BALANCE DEBIT	BALANCE CREDIT
1996 Nov.	30		S11		502 —		502 —
	30		CR15		12668 —		13170 —

ACCOUNTS RECEIVABLE LEDGER

CUSTOMER Deborah Carson CUSTOMER NO. 110

DATE		ITEM	POST. REF.	DEBIT	CREDIT	DEBIT BALANCE
1996 Nov.	4		S11	146 28		146 28

CUSTOMER Cecil Gleim CUSTOMER NO. 120

DATE		ITEM	POST. REF.	DEBIT	CREDIT	DEBIT BALANCE
1996 Nov.	1	Balance	✓			367 50
	29		S11	200 34		567 84
	3		CR15		367 50	200 34

CUSTOMER Nell Lehr CUSTOMER NO. 130

DATE		ITEM	POST. REF.	DEBIT	CREDIT	DEBIT BALANCE
1996 Nov.	1	Balance	✓			213 —
	17		S11	185 50		398 50
	24		CR15		213 —	185 50

CUSTOMER James Solerno CUSTOMER NO. 140

DATE		ITEM	POST. REF.	DEBIT	CREDIT	DEBIT BALANCE
1996 Nov.	1	Balance	✓			271 50
	15		CR15		271 50	——

Name ______________________ Date ________ Class ________

PROBLEM 15-1, concluded

[7]

Specialty Supplies
Schedule of accounts Receivable
November 30, 1996

Deborah Carson	146 28
Cecil Gleim	200 34
Nell Lehr	185 50
Total accounts receivable	532 12

Extra form

SALES JOURNAL

PAGE

DATE		ACCOUNT DEBITED	SALE NO.	POST. REF.	1 ACCOUNTS RECEIVABLE DEBIT	2 SALES CREDIT	3 SALES TAX PAYABLE CREDIT

Name ______________________ Date ________ Class ________

MASTERY PROBLEM 15-M, p. 330
[1, 3]

Posting from sales and cash receipts journals

SALES JOURNAL

PAGE 12

	DATE		ACCOUNT DEBITED	SALE NO.	POST. REF.	1 ACCOUNTS RECEIVABLE DEBIT	2 SALES CREDIT	3 SALES TAX PAYABLE CREDIT	
1	19-- Dec.	9	Belle Chilton	64	110	133 56	126 00	7 56	1
2		15	Rick Farrell	65	120	118 72	112 00	6 72	2
3		17	Dawn Nichols	66	130	192 92	182 00	10 92	3
4		28	Rick Farrell	67	120	127 20	120 00	7 20	4
5		31	Totals			572 40	540 —	32 40	5
6						(1130)	(4110)	(2140)	6

[2, 4]

CASH RECEIPTS JOURNAL

PAGE 17

	DATE		ACCOUNT TITLE	DOC. NO.	POST. REF.	1 GENERAL DEBIT	2 GENERAL CREDIT	3 ACCOUNTS RECEIVABLE CREDIT	4 SALES CREDIT	5 SALES TAX PAYABLE CREDIT	6 CASH DEBIT	
1	19-- Dec.	5	✓	T5					2 300 00	138 00	2 438 00	1
2		7	Nancy Unruh	R96	140			88 00			88 00	2
3		12	✓	T12					3 164 00	189 84	3 353 84	3
4		19	✓	T19					3 374 00	202 44	3 576 44	4
5		23	Dawn Nichols	R97	130			110 25			110 25	5
6		24	Belle Chilton	R98	110			176 00			176 00	6
7		26	✓	T26					3 332 00	199 92	3 531 92	7
8		31	✓	T31					2 044 00	122 64	2 166 64	8
9		31	Totals					374 25	14 214 —	852 84	15 441 09	9
10								(1130)	(4110)	(2140)	(1110)	10

[3, 4]

GENERAL LEDGER

ACCOUNT Cash — ACCOUNT NO. 1110

DATE		ITEM	POST. REF.	DEBIT	CREDIT	BALANCE DEBIT	BALANCE CREDIT
19-- Dec.	1	Balance	✓			9 2 4 0 00	
	31		CR17	15441 09		24681 09	

ACCOUNT Accounts Receivable — ACCOUNT NO. 1130

DATE		ITEM	POST. REF.	DEBIT	CREDIT	BALANCE DEBIT	BALANCE CREDIT
19-- Dec.	1	Balance	✓			3 7 4 25	
	31		S12	572 40		946 65	
	31		CR17		374 25	572 40	

ACCOUNT Sales Tax Payable — ACCOUNT NO. 2140

DATE		ITEM	POST. REF.	DEBIT	CREDIT	BALANCE DEBIT	BALANCE CREDIT
19-- Dec.	1	Balance	✓				6 8 9 15
	31		S12		32 40		721 55
	31		CR17		852 84		1574 39

ACCOUNT Sales — ACCOUNT NO. 4110

DATE		ITEM	POST. REF.	DEBIT	CREDIT	BALANCE DEBIT	BALANCE CREDIT
1990 Dec	31		S12		540 —		540 —
	31		CR17		14 214 —		14 754 —

ACCOUNTS RECEIVABLE LEDGER

CUSTOMER Belle Chilton — CUSTOMER NO. 110

DATE		ITEM	POST. REF.	DEBIT	CREDIT	DEBIT BALANCE
19-- Dec.	1	Balance	✓			176 00
	9		S12	133 50		309 50
	24		CR17		176 —	133 50

CUSTOMER Rick Farrell — CUSTOMER NO. 120

DATE		ITEM	POST. REF.	DEBIT	CREDIT	DEBIT BALANCE
1990 Nov	15		S12	118 72		118 72
	28		S12	127 20		245 92

CUSTOMER Dawn Nichols — CUSTOMER NO. 130

DATE		ITEM	POST. REF.	DEBIT	CREDIT	DEBIT BALANCE
19-- Dec.	1	Balance	✓			110 25
	17		S12	192 92		303 17
	23		CR17		110 25	192 92

CUSTOMER Nancy Unruh — CUSTOMER NO. 140

DATE		ITEM	POST. REF.	DEBIT	CREDIT	DEBIT BALANCE
19-- Dec.	1	Balance	✓			88 00
	7		CR17		88 —	———

[5]

Roland's Shoes
Schedule of Accounts Receivable
December 31, 1996

Belle Chilton		133 50
Rick Farrell		245 92
Dawn Nichols		192 92
Total Accounts Receivable		572 40

Extra form

CHALLENGE PROBLEM 15-C, p. 331
[1, 2]

SALES JOURNAL

PAGE 11

	DATE	ACCOUNT DEBITED	SALE NO.	POST. REF.	1 ACCOUNTS RECEIVABLE DEBIT	2 SALES CREDIT	3 SALES TAX PAYABLE CREDIT	
1								1
2								2
3								3
4								4
5								5
6								6
7								7
8								8
9								9
10								10
11								11
12								12
13								13
14								14
15								15
16								16
17								17
18								18
19								19
20								20
21								21
22								22
23								23
24								24
25								25
26								26
27								27
28								28
29								29
30								30
31								31
32								32

[1, 3]

PURCHASES JOURNAL

PAGE 11

DATE		ACCOUNT CREDITED	PURCH. NO.	POST. REF.	PURCHASES DR. ACCTS. PAY. CR.

[1]

GENERAL JOURNAL

PAGE 11

DATE		ACCOUNT TITLE	DOC. NO.	POST. REF.	DEBIT	CREDIT

[1, 4–6]

CASH RECEIPTS JOURNAL

PAGE 11

	DATE	ACCOUNT TITLE	DOC. NO.	POST. REF.	1 GENERAL DEBIT	2 GENERAL CREDIT	3 ACCOUNTS RECEIVABLE CREDIT	4 SALES CREDIT	5 SALES TAX PAYABLE CREDIT	6 CASH DEBIT	
1											1
2											2
3											3
4											4
5											5
6											6
7											7
8											8
9											9
10											10
11											11
12											12
13											13
14											14
15											15
16											16
17											17
18											18
19											19
20											20
21											21
22											22
23											23
24											24
25											25

[1, 4, 5, 7]

CASH PAYMENTS JOURNAL

PAGE 21

	DATE	ACCOUNT TITLE	CK. NO.	POST. REF.	1 GENERAL DEBIT	2 GENERAL CREDIT	3 ACCOUNTS PAYABLE DEBIT	4 CASH CREDIT	
1									1
2									2
3									3
4									4
5									5
6									6
7									7
8									8
9									9
10									10
11									11
12									12
13									13
14									14
15									15
16									16
17									17
18									18
19									19
20									20
21									21
22									22
23									23
24									24

GENERAL LEDGER

ACCOUNT Cash — ACCOUNT NO. 1110

DATE		ITEM	POST. REF.	DEBIT	CREDIT	BALANCE DEBIT	BALANCE CREDIT
19-- Nov.	1	Balance	✓			16 850 00	

ACCOUNT Accounts Receivable — ACCOUNT NO. 1130

DATE		ITEM	POST. REF.	DEBIT	CREDIT	BALANCE DEBIT	BALANCE CREDIT
19-- Nov.	1	Balance	✓			2 867 30	

ACCOUNT Supplies—Office — ACCOUNT NO. 1150

DATE		ITEM	POST. REF.	DEBIT	CREDIT	BALANCE DEBIT	BALANCE CREDIT
19-- Nov.	1	Balance	✓			2 635 00	

ACCOUNT Supplies—Store — ACCOUNT NO. 1160

DATE		ITEM	POST. REF.	DEBIT	CREDIT	BALANCE DEBIT	BALANCE CREDIT
19-- Nov.	1	Balance	✓			2 160 00	

CHALLENGE PROBLEM 15-C, continued
[1–3, 5–7]

GENERAL LEDGER

ACCOUNT Accounts Payable — ACCOUNT NO. 2110

DATE		ITEM	POST. REF.	DEBIT	CREDIT	BALANCE DEBIT	BALANCE CREDIT
19-- Nov.	1	Balance	✓				8 023 00

ACCOUNT Sales Tax Payable — ACCOUNT NO. 2120

DATE		ITEM	POST. REF.	DEBIT	CREDIT	BALANCE DEBIT	BALANCE CREDIT
19-- Nov.	1	Balance	✓				1 312 00

ACCOUNT Maria Adolfo, Drawing — ACCOUNT NO. 3120

DATE		ITEM	POST. REF.	DEBIT	CREDIT	BALANCE DEBIT	BALANCE CREDIT
19-- Nov.	1	Balance	✓			12 800 00	

ACCOUNT Lawrence Phipps, Drawing — ACCOUNT NO. 3140

DATE		ITEM	POST. REF.	DEBIT	CREDIT	BALANCE DEBIT	BALANCE CREDIT
19-- Nov.	1	Balance	✓			12 540 00	

ACCOUNT Sales — ACCOUNT NO. 4110

DATE		ITEM	POST. REF.	DEBIT	CREDIT	BALANCE DEBIT	BALANCE CREDIT
19-- Nov.	1	Balance	✓				218 749 00

GENERAL LEDGER

ACCOUNT Purchases ACCOUNT NO. 5110

DATE		ITEM	POST. REF.	DEBIT	CREDIT	BALANCE DEBIT	BALANCE CREDIT
19-- Nov.	1	Balance	✓			112 500 00	

ACCOUNT Advertising Expense ACCOUNT NO. 6110

DATE		ITEM	POST. REF.	DEBIT	CREDIT	BALANCE DEBIT	BALANCE CREDIT
19-- Nov.	1	Balance	✓			2 940 00	

ACCOUNT Miscellaneous Expense ACCOUNT NO. 6140

DATE		ITEM	POST. REF.	DEBIT	CREDIT	BALANCE DEBIT	BALANCE CREDIT
19-- Nov.	1	Balance	✓			1 410 00	

ACCOUNT Rent Expense ACCOUNT NO. 6160

DATE		ITEM	POST. REF.	DEBIT	CREDIT	BALANCE DEBIT	BALANCE CREDIT
19-- Nov.	1	Balance	✓			9 500 00	

ACCOUNT Utilities Expense ACCOUNT NO. 6190

DATE		ITEM	POST. REF.	DEBIT	CREDIT	BALANCE DEBIT	BALANCE CREDIT
19-- Nov.	1	Balance	✓			1 785 00	

[1, 8]

ACCOUNTS PAYABLE LEDGER

VENDOR Artex Golf Products — VENDOR NO. 210

DATE		ITEM	POST. REF.	DEBIT	CREDIT	CREDIT BALANCE
19-- Nov.	1	Balance	✓			2 430 00

VENDOR Ecola Golf Equipment — VENDOR NO. 220

DATE		ITEM	POST. REF.	DEBIT	CREDIT	CREDIT BALANCE
19-- Nov.	1	Balance	✓			1 965 00

VENDOR Garcia Supply — VENDOR NO. 230

DATE		ITEM	POST. REF.	DEBIT	CREDIT	CREDIT BALANCE

VENDOR Patton Golf Co. — VENDOR NO. 240

DATE		ITEM	POST. REF.	DEBIT	CREDIT	CREDIT BALANCE
19-- Nov.	1	Balance	✓			948 00

VENDOR Valiant Golf Co. — VENDOR NO. 250

DATE		ITEM	POST. REF.	DEBIT	CREDIT	CREDIT BALANCE
19-- Nov.	1	Balance	✓			2 680 00

[1, 8]

ACCOUNTS RECEIVABLE LEDGER

CUSTOMER William Backus **CUSTOMER NO.** 110

DATE		ITEM	POST. REF.	DEBIT	CREDIT	DEBIT BALANCE
19-- Nov.	1	Balance	✓			795 00

CUSTOMER Linda Boge **CUSTOMER NO.** 120

DATE		ITEM	POST. REF.	DEBIT	CREDIT	DEBIT BALANCE
19-- Nov.	1	Balance	✓			678 40

CUSTOMER Jonathan Dunbar **CUSTOMER NO.** 130

DATE		ITEM	POST. REF.	DEBIT	CREDIT	DEBIT BALANCE

CUSTOMER James Patco **CUSTOMER NO.** 140

DATE		ITEM	POST. REF.	DEBIT	CREDIT	DEBIT BALANCE
19-- Nov.	1	Balance	✓			1 160 70

CUSTOMER Bertha Welsh **CUSTOMER NO.** 150

DATE		ITEM	POST. REF.	DEBIT	CREDIT	DEBIT BALANCE
19-- Nov.	1	Balance	✓			233 20

[8]

[8]

Perfect Score..... 45 Name ______________________

Deduct......... ___ Date ______________ Class ______________

Your Score..... ___ Checked by ______________________

STUDY GUIDE 16

UNIT A—Analyzing Payroll Records

DIRECTIONS: Place a check mark in either the True or False Answers column to show whether each of the following statements is true or false.

	Answers: True	Answers: False	For Scoring
0. A pay period may be weekly	✓		**0.** ✓
1. The federal social security program provides disability insurance benefits for spouses of qualified employees			**1.**
2. Any employee can be exempt, upon request, from having federal income tax withheld			**2.**
3. Records pertaining to social security tax payments and deductions should be retained for four years			**3.**
4. Every employee must have a social security card			**4.**
5. A married person supporting a spouse usually has less federal income tax withheld than a single person with the same earnings			**5.**
6. One withholding allowance can be claimed for each person supported by the employee to a maximum of 8 allowances			**6.**
7. Federal law requires that each employer have on file a properly completed Form W-4, Employee's Withholding Allowance Certificate, for each employee			**7.**
8. Some employees are exempt from FICA taxes			**8.**
9. Most employees will have received their social security number as a child			**9.**
10. Federal income tax is withheld from employee earnings only in states that have state income tax			**10.**
11. Taxes withheld from employees represent an asset to an employer until the taxes are paid to the federal or state government			**11.**
12. Some employees are exempt from having federal income tax withheld from their salaries			**12.**
13. FICA tax is paid by both the employer and the employee			**13.**
14. The FICA tax rate increases as an employee's salary rate increases			**14.**
15. The amount of FICA tax withheld is figured on employee net pay			**15.**
16. All deductions from employee wages are recorded in a payroll register			**16.**
17. Most of the information in the payroll register is taken from the payroll check stub			**17.**
18. All salaries paid to an employee, regardless of the amount, are subject to FICA taxes			**18.**
19. Federal unemployment tax is paid entirely by the employee			**19.**
20. Payments to partners of a company are included on the payroll register			**20.**
21. Total earnings are sometimes referred to as gross earnings and gross pay			**21.**
22. The columns of the employee earnings record consist of the columns in a payroll register and an accumulated earnings column			**22.**
23. Employers frequently use time cards as the basic source of data to prepare a payroll			**23.**
24. An individual employee earnings record is used as the source document to prepare the payroll check			**24.**
25. All information about a payroll is recorded on a payroll register			**25.**
26. An important purpose of pegboard payroll is to record information on several forms with one writing			**26.**

UNIT B — Identifying Accounting Terms

DIRECTIONS: Select the one term in Column I that best fits each definition in Column II. Print the letter identifying your choice in the Answers column.

Column I

A. employee earnings record
B. federal unemployment tax
C. FICA tax
D. Medicare
E. net pay
F. pay period
G. payroll
H. payroll register
I. payroll taxes
J. pegboard
K. salary
L. state unemployment tax
M. tax base
N. total earnings
O. withholding allowance

Column II

		Answers	For Scoring
0.	Taxes based on the payroll of a business	I	**0.** ✓
1.	A business form used to record details affecting payments made to an employee		**1.**
2.	A business form used to record payroll information		**2.**
3.	The total earnings paid to an employee after payroll taxes and other deductions		**3.**
4.	The period covered by a salary payment		**4.**
5.	A special device used to write the same information at one time on several forms		**5.**
6.	A federal tax paid by employees and employers for old-age, survivors, disability, and hospitalization insurance		**6.**
7.	The money paid for employee services		**7.**
8.	The federal health insurance program for people who have reached retirement age		**8.**
9.	A federal tax used for state and federal administrative expenses of the unemployment program		**9.**
10.	A deduction from total earnings for each person legally supported by a taxpayer		**10.**
11.	The total pay due for a pay period before deductions		**11.**
12.	The total amount earned by all employees for a pay period		**12.**
13.	The maximum amount of earnings on which a tax is calculated		**13.**
14.	A state tax used to pay benefits to unemployed workers		**14.**

UNIT C—Analyzing Payroll Procedures

DIRECTIONS: For each of the following items, select the choice that best completes the statement. Print the letter identifying your choice in the Answers column.

0. Employee total earnings are figured as **(A)** total hours × total rate **(B)** regular hours × regular rate, plus overtime hours × overtime rate **(C)** regular hours × regular rate, plus overtime hours × 1.5 × overtime rate **(D)** total hours × total rate, plus overtime hours × overtime rate
Answers: B — For Scoring: **0.** ✓

1. Information contained on a Form W-4, Employee's Withholding Allowance Certificate, includes the employee **(A)** name, address, marital status, and wage rate **(B)** name, social security number, wage rate, and place of employment **(C)** social security number, allowances claimed, and marital status **(D)** name, wage rate, and total hours
For Scoring: **1.**

2. Employers must pay the following payroll taxes: **(A)** FICA and federal unemployment tax **(B)** FICA and federal income tax **(C)** federal and state income tax **(D)** FICA and federal and state income tax
For Scoring: **2.**

3. Information needed to determine the employee FICA tax withholding for a pay period is **(A)** total earnings and FICA tax rate **(B)** total earnings and accumulated earnings **(C)** total earnings, number of withholding allowances, and FICA tax rate **(D)** total earnings, accumulated earnings, and FICA tax rate and tax base
For Scoring: **3.**

4. The accumulated earnings column of an employee's earnings record shows accumulated earnings for the **(A)** year **(B)** month **(C)** employee's total employment with the business **(D)** quarter
For Scoring: **4.**

5. A separate payroll checking account is used primarily to **(A)** simplify the payroll accounting system **(B)** help reduce the cost of preparing a payroll **(C)** eliminate employee earnings records **(D)** provide additional protection and control of individual payroll checks
For Scoring: **5.**

Figuring employee earnings

Employee Number	Hours Worked		Regular Rate	Earnings		Total Earnings
	Regular	Overtime		Regular	Overtime	
1	40	1	$6.00	240.00	9.00	249
2	40	5	9.00	360.00	67.50	427.50
3	30	0	6.50	195.00	—	195.00
4	25	0	7.75	193.75	—	193.75
5	40	4	8.50	340.00	12.75	352.75
6	35	0	7.00	245.00	—	245.00

Determining payroll tax withholdings

DRILL 16-D2, p. 374
[1, 2]

Employee		Marital Status	Number of Withholding Allowances	Total Earnings	Federal Income Tax Withholding	FICA Tax Withholding
No.	Name					
2	Adams, Winston	M	2	$870.00		
6	Forte, Peter	M	3	780.00		
3	Gable, Joanne	S	1	670.00		
1	Jenkins, Mary	M	5	760.00		
8	Little, Edward	S	1	650.00		
7	Nelson, Janice	S	2	710.00		
4	Pate, Kim	S	1	640.00		
5	Sanders, Michael	M	3	890.00		

Completing payroll time cards [1, 2]

EMPLOYEE NO. 14

NAME Patricia Franklin

PERIOD ENDING June 15, 19--

	MORNING		AFTERNOON		OVERTIME		HOURS	
	IN	OUT	IN	OUT	IN	OUT	REG	OT
2	759	1201	1256	501			8	
3	757	1202	1257	502			8	
4	756	1201	1258	504	701	802	8	1
5	802	1204	101	506			8	
6	756	1203	1259	500			8	
9	759	1200	1259	459	559	731	8	1.5
10	800	1200	1258	501			8	
11	759	1202	1257	506			8	
12	756	1159	1256	502	558	732	8	1.5
13	757	1203	1257	501			8	

	HOURS	RATE	AMOUNT
REGULAR	80	8.40	672.00
OVERTIME	4	12.60	50.40
TOTAL HOURS	84	TOTAL EARNINGS	722.40

EMPLOYEE NO. 11

NAME Charles Lambert

PERIOD ENDING June 15, 19--

	MORNING		AFTERNOON		OVERTIME		HOURS	
	IN	OUT	IN	OUT	IN	OUT	REG	OT
2	757	1201	1259	502			8	
3	757	1202	1258	501			8	
4	756	1204	100	501	556	659	8	1
5	757	1205	1259	500			8	
6	759	1205	100	502			8	
9	757	1204	1259	505			8	
10	758	1205	1256	504	600	731	8	1.5
11	756	1202	1257	502			8	
12	756	1201	1259	501	700	932	8	2.5
13	757	1200	101	500			8	

	HOURS	RATE	AMOUNT
REGULAR	80	7.00	560.00
OVERTIME	5	10.50	52.50
TOTAL HOURS	85	TOTAL EARNINGS	612.50

EMPLOYEE NO. 16

NAME Faye Little

PERIOD ENDING June 15, 19--

	MORNING		AFTERNOON		OVERTIME		HOURS	
	IN	OUT	IN	OUT	IN	OUT	REG	OT
2	758	1202	1259	503			8	
3	757	1203	100	500	702	832	8	1.5
4	800	1200	1259	500			8	
5	759	1201	1258	504			8	
6	759	1202	1255	503			8	
9	758	1201	1256	502			8	
10	756	1200	1257	501			8	
11	757	1202	1257	458			8	
12	758	1200	1259	501			8	
13	759	1204	1259	500			8	

	HOURS	RATE	AMOUNT
REGULAR	80	6.60	528.00
OVERTIME	1.5	9.90	14.85
TOTAL HOURS	81.5	TOTAL EARNINGS	542.85

PROBLEM 16-1, p. 374

Name ____________ Date ________ Class ______ *PROBLEM 16-2, p. 375*

Preparing a semimonthly payroll [1–3]

PAYROLL REGISTER

SEMIMONTHLY PERIOD ENDED ____________ DATE OF PAYMENT ____________

	EMPL. NO.	EMPLOYEE'S NAME	MARITAL STATUS	NO. OF ALLOWANCES	EARNINGS 1 REGULAR	EARNINGS 2 OVERTIME	EARNINGS 3 TOTAL	DEDUCTIONS 4 FEDERAL INCOME TAX	DEDUCTIONS 5 FICA TAX	DEDUCTIONS 6 HEALTH INSURANCE	DEDUCTIONS 7 OTHER	DEDUCTIONS 8 TOTAL	9 NET PAY	CHECK NO.	
1	2	Agne, Roberta	S	1	704 00	36 00				28 00	B 10 00				1
2	10	Beville, Michael	M	3	424 00					45 00					2
3	9	Day, Mellisa	M	2	739 20	63 00				36 00	B 5 00				3
4	3	Finley, Lisa	M	2	560 00					36 00	B 5 00				4
5	6	Gunter, Jill	S	1	484 00	33 00									5
6	11	Locke, Alan	S	1	589 60										6
7	1	O'Neal, Barton	S	2	756 80	64 50				28 00					7
8	5	Soehn, Lucille	M	4	809 60					45 00	B 25 00				8
9	4	Webb, Ronald	M	3	686 40	23 40				45 00					9
10	7	Wyatt, Pamela	S	1	809 40	41 40					B 10 00				10
11	8	Yang, Kim	M	2	598 40					28 00					11
12	12	Zucconi, Robert	S	1	572 00	19 50					B 5 00				12
13															13
14															14
15															15
16															16
17															17
18															18
19															19
20															20
21															21
22															22

OTHER DEDUCTIONS: B—U.S. SAVINGS BONDS; UW—UNITED WAY

No. 630

Date ______ 19 ______ $ ______

To ______

For ______

Bal. Bro't For'd	
Amt. Deposited	
Total	
Amt. This Check	
Bal. Car'd For'd	

GENERAL ACCOUNT — No. **630** — 66-877/530

CITY HARDWARE COMPANY

______ 19 ______

Pay to the order of ______ $ ______

______ Dollars

FOR CLASSROOM USE ONLY

PEOPLES BANK AND TRUST
Charlotte, NC 28206-8444

⑆053008774⑆ 196⑈ 2236⑈ 42⑈

Check No. **765**

PERIOD ENDING	
EARNINGS	$
REG.	$
O.T.	$
DEDUCTIONS	$
INC. TAX	$
FICA TAX	$
GROUP INS.	$
HEALTH INS.	$
OTHER	$
NET PAY	$

PAYROLL ACCOUNT — 66-877/530

______ 19 ______

No. **765**

Pay to the order of ______ $ ______

______ Dollars

FOR CLASSROOM USE ONLY

PEOPLES BANK AND TRUST
Charlotte, NC 28206-8444

CITY HARDWARE COMPANY

⑆053008774⑆ 196⑈ 2236⑈ 44⑈

Check No. **769**

PERIOD ENDING	
EARNINGS	$
REG.	$
O.T.	$
DEDUCTIONS	$
INC. TAX	$
FICA TAX	$
GROUP INS.	$
HEALTH INS.	$
OTHER	$
NET PAY	$

PAYROLL ACCOUNT — 66-877/530

______ 19 ______

No. **769**

Pay to the order of ______ $ ______

______ Dollars

FOR CLASSROOM USE ONLY

PEOPLES BANK AND TRUST
Charlotte, NC 28206-8444

CITY HARDWARE COMPANY

⑆053008774⑆ 196⑈ 2236⑈ 44⑈

Preparing an employee earnings record [1, 2]

EARNINGS RECORD FOR QUARTER ENDED ____________

EMPLOYEE NO. 32   Hammond (LAST NAME)   Derrick (FIRST)   ___ (MIDDLE INITIAL)   MARITAL STATUS M   WITHHOLDING ALLOWANCES 2

RATE OF PAY 14.00 PER HR.   SOCIAL SECURITY NO. 218-78-2104   POSITION Service manager

PAY PERIOD		EARNINGS			DEDUCTIONS					NET PAY	ACCUMULATED EARNINGS
		1	2	3	4	5	6	7	8	9	10
NO.	ENDED	REGULAR	OVERTIME	TOTAL	FEDERAL INCOME TAX	FICA TAX	HEALTH INSURANCE	OTHER	TOTAL		7,928.—
1	4/15	1,232.00	105.00	1,337.00	156.—	106.96	40.—	B 10.—	312.96	1,024.04	9,205.—
2	4/30	1,120.00	63.00	1,183.00	135.—	94.64	40.—	10.—	279.64	903.36	10,448.—
3	5/15	1,232.00		1,232.00	141.—	98.56	40.—	10.—	289.56	942.44	11,680.—
4	5/31	952.00		952.00	99.—	76.16	40.—	10.—	225.16	726.84	12,632.—
5	6/15	1,232.00	147.00	1,379.00	162.—	110.32	40.—	10.—	322.32	1,056.68	14,011.—
6	6/30	1,120.00		1,120.00	126.—	89.60	40.—	10.—	265.60	854.40	15,131.—
7		6,888.—	315.—	7,203.—	819.—	576.24	240.—	60.—	1,095.24	5,507.76	
QUARTERLY TOTALS											

OTHER DEDUCTIONS: B—U.S. SAVINGS BONDS; UW—UNITED WAY

Preparing a semimonthly payroll [1–3]

PAYROLL REGISTER

SEMIMONTHLY PERIOD ENDED | DATE OF PAYMENT

	EMPL. NO.	EMPLOYEE'S NAME	MARITAL STATUS	NO. OF ALLOWANCES	EARNINGS REGULAR	EARNINGS OVERTIME	EARNINGS TOTAL	DEDUCTIONS FEDERAL INCOME TAX	DEDUCTIONS FICA TAX	DEDUCTIONS HEALTH INSURANCE	DEDUCTIONS OTHER	DEDUCTIONS TOTAL	NET PAY	CK. NO.	
1	3	Abney, Patricia	M	2	512 00	12 80	524 80	30 —	41 98	30 —	10 —	117 98	406 82		1
2	6	Blanks, Wilma	S	1	576 00	21 60	597 60	70 —	47 81			117 81	479 79		2
3	8	Fitts, Deborah	M	3	624 00	11 70	635 70	39 —	50 86	38 —	5 —	132 86	502 84		3
4	1	Greer, Daniel	M	2	399 00	34 20	433 20	22 —	34 66	30 —	5 —	91 66	341 54		4
5	5	Habig, Vincent	S	1	672 00		672 —	82 —	53 76			135 76	536 24		5
6	9	Jones, Phyllis	M	2	608 00	79 80	687 80	60 —	55 02	30 —	10 —	155 02	532 78		6
7	10	Malloy, Timothy	S	2	544 00	10 20	554 20	52 —	44 34	30 —	10 —	136 34	417 86		7
8	2	Paxton, Alice	M	4	496 00		496 —	6 —	39 68	44 —		89 68	585 68		8
9	4	Tait, Michelle	S	1	640 00	36 00	676 —	82 —	54 08			136 08	539 92		9
10	7	Walzak, Thomas	S	1	472 00		472 —	53 —	37 76		15 —	105 76	366 24		10
11							5749 30	502 —	459 95	202 —	55 —	1218 05	4530 35		11
12															12
13															13
14															14
15															15
16															16
17															17
18															18
19															19
20															20
21															21
22															22

OTHER DEDUCTIONS: B—U.S. SAVINGS BONDS; UW—UNITED WAY

MASTERY PROBLEM 16-M, p. 376

[2, 3]

No. **872**

Date ______ 19 ______ $ ______

To ______________________

For ______________________

Bal. Bro't For'd

Amt. Deposited

Total

Amt. This Check

Bal. Car'd For'd

GENERAL ACCOUNT

No. **872**

8–8335/430

MERCER COMPANY

______________ 19 ______

Pay to the order of ______________________ $ ______

______________________ Dollars

FOR CLASSROOM USE ONLY

FIRST SECURITY BANK OF PITTSBURGH
Pittsburgh, PA 15210-3402

⑆043083356⑆ 00597216 4⑈

Check No. **426**

PERIOD ENDING

EARNINGS $

REG. $

O.T. $

DEDUCTIONS $

INC. TAX $

FICA TAX $

GROUP INS. $

HEALTH INS. $

OTHER $

NET PAY $

PAYROLL ACCOUNT

8–8335/430

______________ 19 ______

No. **426**

Pay to the order of ______________________ $ ______

______________________ Dollars

FOR CLASSROOM USE ONLY

FIRST SECURITY BANK OF PITTSBURGH
Pittsburgh, PA 15210-3402

MERCER COMPANY

⑆043083356⑆ 00597216 5⑈

Check No. **431**

PERIOD ENDING

EARNINGS $

REG. $

O.T. $

DEDUCTIONS $

INC. TAX $

FICA TAX $

GROUP INS. $

HEALTH INS. $

OTHER $

NET PAY $

PAYROLL ACCOUNT

8–8335/430

______________ 19 ______

No. **431**

Pay to the order of ______________________ $ ______

______________________ Dollars

FOR CLASSROOM USE ONLY

FIRST SECURITY BANK OF PITTSBURGH
Pittsburgh, PA 15210-3402

MERCER COMPANY

⑆043083356⑆ 00597216 5⑈

PAYROLL REGISTER

SEMIMONTHLY PERIOD ENDED

DATE OF PAYMENT

	EMPL. NO.	EMPLOYEE'S NAME	MARITAL STATUS	NO. OF ALLOWANCES	1 EARNINGS REGULAR	2 EARNINGS INCENTIVE	3 EARNINGS TOTAL	4 DEDUCTIONS FEDERAL INCOME TAX	5 DEDUCTIONS FICA TAX	6 DEDUCTIONS HEALTH INSURANCE	7 DEDUCTIONS OTHER	8 DEDUCTIONS TOTAL	9 NET PAY	CHECK NO.	
1	C2	Simpson, Alan	S	1											1
2	C4	Creek, Janice	M	1											2
3	C8	Pate, Marie	M	2											3
4	A1	Meese, Frank	S	1											4
5	A6	Harris, Kevin	M	3											5
6	A7	Martin, Angela	S	1											6
7	F5	Quinn, Karen	M	2											7
8	F3	Raines, Jon	M	2											8
9															9
10															10
11															11
12															12
13															13
14															14
15															15
16															16
17															17
18															18
19															19
20															20
21															21
22															22

OTHER DEDUCTIONS: B—U.S. SAVINGS BONDS; UW—UNITED WAY

Perfect Score..... 35 Name ______________________

Deduct......... ___ Date ______________ Class ______________

Your Score..... ___ Checked by ______________________

STUDY GUIDE 17

UNIT A—Analyzing Payroll Records

DIRECTIONS: For each of the following items, select the choice that best completes the statement. Print the letter identifying your choice in the Answers column.

0. The payroll tax paid only by the employee is **(A)** federal income tax **(B)** FICA tax **(C)** federal unemployment tax **(D)** state unemployment tax...

1. At the end of each year, an employer must give each employee a form **(A)** W-4 **(B)** W-3 **(C)** W-2 **(D)** 941 ....

2. Employers with more than 250 employees may report information about withholding taxes to the federal government on **(A)** Form W-4 **(B)** Form W-2 **(C)** a company letterhead **(D)** computer files........

3. The payroll tax paid by both the employee and the employer is **(A)** federal income tax **(B)** FICA tax **(C)** federal unemployment tax **(D)** state unemployment tax ....

4. When a semimonthly payroll is paid, the credit to Cash is equal to the **(A)** total earnings of all employees **(B)** total deductions for income tax and FICA tax **(C)** total deductions **(D)** net pay of all employees ....

5. FICA taxes withheld from employee wages and employer FICA taxes owed should be posted to **(A)** the same liability account **(B)** separate asset accounts **(C)** separate liability accounts **(D)** the same asset account ....

6. FICA taxes are paid **(A)** by employers only **(B)** by employees only **(C)** more by the employer than the employee **(D)** equally by both the employer and the employee........

7. The total of the Net Pay column of the payroll register is credited to a(an) **(A)** revenue account **(B)** expense account **(C)** asset account **(D)** liability account ....

8. The total of the Federal Income Tax column of a payroll register is credited to a(an) **(A)** revenue account **(B)** expense account **(C)** asset account **(D)** liability account........

9. The total of the FICA tax column of a payroll register is credited to a(an) **(A)** liability account **(B)** expense account **(C)** asset account **(D)** revenue account ....

10. A business' payroll taxes for a pay period are debited to a(an) **(A)** asset account **(B)** liability account **(C)** revenue account **(D)** expense account...

11. Payroll information for each employee is recorded in a payroll register at the end of each **(A)** pay period **(B)** month **(C)** year **(D)** week ....

12. To record the employer payroll taxes expense, CarLand credits the following accounts: **(A)** FICA Tax Expense, Unemployment Tax Payable—Federal **(B)** Payroll Taxes Expense, FICA Tax Payable, Unemployment Tax Payable—State **(C)** FICA Tax Payable, Unemployment Tax Payable—State, Unemployment Tax Payable—Federal **(D)** Payroll Taxes Expense, Federal Income Tax Payable........

13. Payroll taxes are posted to the **(A)** payroll register **(B)** journal **(C)** general ledger accounts **(D)** expense journal........

14. An application of the accounting concept Objective Evidence is **(A)** using a memorandum as the basis for journalizing payroll taxes expense **(B)** sending Form W-2 to an employee **(C)** completing Form 941 **(D)** none of these.....

15. The information used to determine if an employee earnings exceed the tax base for unemployment taxes is found on the **(A)** payroll register **(B)** Form W-4 **(C)** employee earnings record **(D)** Form 941 ....

Answers	For Scoring
A	0. ✓
	1.
	2.
	3.
	4.
	5.
	6.
	7.
	8.
	9.
	10.
	11.
	12.
	13.
	14.
	15.

UNIT B—Analyzing Transactions Affecting Payroll

DIRECTIONS: Analyze each of the following transactions into debit and credit parts. Print the letters identifying your choices in the proper Answers column.

Account Title

A. Cash
B. Employee Income Tax Payable
C. FICA Tax Payable
D. Payroll Taxes Expense
E. Salary Expense
F. Unemployment Tax Payable—Federal
G. Unemployment Tax Payable—State
H. U.S. Savings Bonds Payable

Transaction	Answers Debit	Answers Credit	For Scoring Debit	For Scoring Credit
0–0. Paid cash for federal unemployment tax liability............	F	A	**0.** ✓	**0.** ✓
1–2. Recorded employer payroll taxes..............................			**1.**	**2.**
3–4. Paid cash for liability for employee income tax and FICA tax..........................			**3.**	**4.**
5–6. Paid cash for state unemployment tax liability.................			**5.**	**6.**
7–8. Paid cash for semimonthly payroll less deductions for employee income tax, FICA tax, and U.S. Savings Bonds.........			**7.**	**8.**

UNIT C—Analyzing Form W-2

DIRECTIONS: Analyze the following statements about a Form W-2, Wage and Tax Statement. Use the Form W-2 at the right to answer the specific questions about Mr. Turner. Place a check mark in the proper Answers column to show whether each of the following statements is true or false.

1 Control number 22222 OMB No 1545 0008

2 Employer's name, address, and ZIP code
CarLand
1374 Parklane
Rockville, RI 02873-4121

6 Statutory employee ☐ Deceased ☐ Pension plan ☐ Legal rep ☐ 942 emp ☐ Subtotal ☐ Deferred compensation ☐ Void ☐

7 Allocated tips | 8 Advance EIC payment

9 Federal income tax withheld 1,032.00 | 10 Wages, tips, other compensation 18,192.00

3 Employer's identification number 31-0429632 | 4 Employer's state I D number

11 Social security tax withheld 1,455.36 | 12 Social security wages 18,192.00

5 Employee's social security number 450-70-6432

13 Social security tips | 14 Nonqualified plans

19 Employee's name, address and ZIP code
Patrick S. Turner
1625 Northland Drive
Rockville, RI 02873-5073

15 Dependent care benefits | 16 Fringe benefits incl in Box 10

17 | 18 Other

20 | 21 | 22 | 23

24 State income tax | 25 State wages, tips, etc | 26 Name of state | 27 Local income tax | 28 Local wages, tips, etc | 29 Name of locality

Copy A For Social Security Administration — Dept. of the Treasury—Internal Revenue Service

Form **W-2 Wage and Tax Statement 19 --**

Statement	Answers True	Answers False	For Scoring
0. Patrick Turner's total salary for 1988 from CarLand are more than his total FICA salary for 1988....................		✓	**0.** ✓
1. CarLand withheld state income tax from Patrick Turner's salary.........			**1.**
2. If Mr. Turner had city income tax withheld from his pay, it would be listed on his W-2 form....................			**2.**
3. This Form W-2 indicates whether Patrick Turner had more than one employer during 1988....................			**3.**
4. This Form W-2 shows Patrick Turner's net pay from CarLand for the entire year....................			**4.**
5. The amount withheld for Mr. Turner's FICA tax was more than the amount withheld for his federal income tax....................			**5.**
6. If an employee works for several employers during the year, that employee must receive a Form W-2 from each employer			**6.**
7. When Patrick Turner files his federal income tax return, he must attach Copy B of his Form W-2 to his return....................			**7.**
8. This Form W-2 shows the total amount withheld from Mr. Turner's earnings by CarLand for his FICA tax....................			**8.**
9. An employer is required to provide employees with a Form W-2 no later than January 31 of the year following the one for which the report has been completed....................			**9.**
10. CarLand did not pay Federal Unemployment Tax on part of Mr. Turner's salary....................			**10.**
11. All deductions from Mr. Turner's salary are shown on his Form W-2.....			**11.**
12. An employees' social security number must be shown on all copies of his or her Form W-2....................			**12.**

Name ______________________ Date ________ Class ______

DRILL 17-D1, p. 397
[1, 2]

Analyzing payroll transactions

Business A

Business C

Business B

Business D

Calculating employer payroll taxes

DRILL 17-D2, p. 397
[1, 2]

Employee Name	Accumulated Earnings, April 30	Total Earnings for May 1–15 Pay Period	Unemployment Taxable Earnings
Blette, Kathryn	$ 4,689.00	$ 586.00	______
Easton, Phillip	3,882.50	427.00	______
Goodpaster, Sandra	8,450.00	1,045.00	______
Lake, Margaret	5,725.90	827.75	______
Raymond, Peter	7,329.00	945.60	______
Saenz, Raul	10,426.00	1,236.00	______
Williams, Patricia	4,107.25	518.50	______
	Totals	______	______
FICA Tax Payable		______	
Unemployment Tax Payable—Federal		______	
Unemployment Tax Payable—State		______	

Journalizing and posting payment of semimonthly payrolls

PROBLEM 17-1, p. 397
[2]

GENERAL LEDGER

ACCOUNT Employee Income Tax Payable — ACCOUNT NO. 2120

DATE		ITEM	POST. REF.	DEBIT	CREDIT	BALANCE DEBIT	BALANCE CREDIT
1997 Aug	15		CP17		514 —		514 —
	31		CP17		437 —		951 —

ACCOUNT FICA Tax Payable — ACCOUNT NO. 2130

DATE		ITEM	POST. REF.	DEBIT	CREDIT	BALANCE DEBIT	BALANCE CREDIT
1997 Aug	15		CP17		293 60		293 60
	31		CP17		254 40		548 —
	15		G18		293 60		841 60
	31		G18		254 40		1096 —

The general ledger accounts prepared in Problem 17-1 are needed to complete Problem 17-2.

[2]

GENERAL LEDGER

ACCOUNT Unemployment Tax Payable—Federal ACCOUNT NO. 2150

DATE		ITEM	POST. REF.	DEBIT	CREDIT	BALANCE DEBIT	BALANCE CREDIT
1997 Aug.	15		G18		$16 20		16 20
~~	1 ~~		~~G18~~		~~109 89~~		
	31		G18		13 36		29 14

ACCOUNT Unemployment Tax Payable—State ACCOUNT NO. 2160

DATE		ITEM	POST. REF.	DEBIT	CREDIT	BALANCE DEBIT	BALANCE CREDIT
1997 Aug.	15		G18		109 89		109 89
	31		G18		9010 —		9127 89

ACCOUNT U.S. Savings Bonds Payable ACCOUNT NO. 2180

DATE		ITEM	POST. REF.	DEBIT	CREDIT	BALANCE DEBIT	BALANCE CREDIT
1997 Aug.	15		CP17		90 —		90 —
	31		CP17		15 —		105 —

ACCOUNT Payroll Taxes Expense ACCOUNT NO. 6150

DATE		ITEM	POST. REF.	DEBIT	CREDIT	BALANCE DEBIT	BALANCE CREDIT
19-- Aug.	1	Balance	✓			4 9 3 9 23	
	15		G18	419 77		5359 —	
	31		G18	9299 12		14650 12	

ACCOUNT Salary Expense ACCOUNT NO. 6170

DATE		ITEM	POST. REF.	DEBIT	CREDIT	BALANCE DEBIT	BALANCE CREDIT
19-- Aug.	1	Balance	✓			38 6 0 9 00	
	15		CP17	3670 —		42279 —	
	31		CP17	3180 —		45459 —	

The general ledger accounts prepared in Problem 17-1 are needed to complete Problem 17-2.

[1, 2]

CASH PAYMENTS JOURNAL

PAGE 17

	DATE		ACCOUNT TITLE	CK. NO.	POST. REF.	1 GENERAL DEBIT	2 GENERAL CREDIT	3 ACCOUNTS PAYABLE DEBIT	4 CASH CREDIT	
1	1997 Aug.	15	Salary expense	756	6170	3670 —			2772 40	1
2			employee income tax payable		2120		514 —			2
3			fica tax payable		2130		293 60			3
4			U.S. savings bonds payable		2180		90 —			4
5		31	Salary expense	768	6170	3180 —			2413 60	5
6			employee income tax payable		2120		437 —			6
7			fica tax payable		2130		254 40			7
8			U.S. Savings bonds payable		2180		75 —			8
9										9
10										10
11										11
12										12
13										13
14										14
15										15
16										16
17										17
18										18
19										19
20										20
21										21
22										22
23										23
24										24
25										25

Name ______________________ Date ________ Class ________

PROBLEM 17-2, p. 398
[1–3, 5, 6]

Calculating, journalizing, and posting employer payroll taxes

The general ledger accounts prepared in Problem 17-1 are needed to complete Problem 17-2.

Employee Name	Accumulated Earnings, July 31	Total Earnings for August 1–15 Pay Period	Unemployment Taxable Earnings August 15	Accumulated Earnings, August 15	Total Earnings for August 16–31 Pay Period	Unemployment Taxable Earnings August 31
Carson, Michael	$ 4,634.00	$767.50	767.50	5401.50	$634.50	634.50
Franks, Janice	5,623.50	430.00	430.00	6053.50	324.50	324.50
Hester, Mary	12,230.00	924.00	-0-	13154.00	874.00	-0-
Marchese, Thomas	2,346.50	213.00	213.00	2559.50	138.00	138.00
Pait, Kim	3,243.00	624.50	624.50	3867.50	573.00	573.00
Toler, Troy	10,532.00	711.00	-0-	11243.00	636.00	-0-
	Totals	3670.00	2035.00	Totals	3180.00	1670.00

FICA Tax Payable	293.60	FICA Tax Payable	254.40
Unemployment Tax Payable—Federal	16.28	Unemployment Tax Payable—Federal	13.36
Unemployment Tax Payable—State	109.89	Unemployment Tax Payable—State	9018.00

[3, 4, 6, 7]

GENERAL JOURNAL

PAGE 18

DATE		ACCOUNT TITLE	DOC. NO.	POST. REF.	DEBIT	CREDIT
1993 Aug.	15	Payroll tax expense	MT	6150	419 77	
		FICA tax payable		2130		293 60
		Unemployment tax pay. f		2150		16 28
		Unemployment tax pay. s		2160		109 89
	31	Payroll tax expense		6150	9299 12	
		FICA tax payable		2130		254 40
		Unemployment tax pay. fed		2150		13 36
		Unemployment tax pay. state		2160		9018 —

Form **941** (Rev. April 19--) Department of the Treasury Internal Revenue Service

Employer's Quarterly Federal Tax Return

4142 ▶ **For Paperwork Reduction Act Notice, see page 2.**

Please type or print.

Your name, address, employer identification number, and calendar quarter of return. (If not correct, please change.) ▶

Name (as distinguished from trade name) | Date quarter ended

Trade name, if any | Employer identification number

Address and ZIP code

OMB No. 1545-0029
Expires: 8-31--

T
FF
FD
FP
I
T

If address is different from prior return, check here ▶ ☐

IRS Use

1 1 1 1 1 1 1 1 1 1 2 3 3 3 3 3 3 4 4 4

5 5 5 6 7 8 8 8 8 8 8 9 9 9 10 10 10 10 10 10 10 10 10 10

If you are not liable for returns in the future, check here . . . ▶ ☐ Date final wages paid . . . . ▶

	Complete for First Quarter Only		
1a	Number of employees (except household) employed in the pay period that includes March 12th . ▶	1a	
b	If you are a subsidiary corporation AND your parent corporation files a consolidated Form 1120, enter parent corporation employer identification number (EIN) . . ▶ 1b –		
2	Total wages and tips subject to withholding, plus other compensation . . . . ▶	2	
3	Total income tax withheld from wages, tips, pensions, annuities, sick pay, gambling, etc. . . . ▶	3	
4	Adjustment of withheld income tax for preceding quarters of calendar year (see instructions) . . ▶	4	
5	Adjusted total of income tax withheld	5	
6	Taxable social security wages paid . . . . . $ ______ × 16% (.16) .	6	
7a	Taxable tips reported . . . . $ ______ × 16% (.16) .	7a	
b	Taxable hospital insurance wages paid . . . . $ ______ × 2.9% (.029) .	7b	
8	Total social security taxes (add lines 6, 7a, and 7b)	8	
9	Adjustment of social security taxes (see instructions for required explanation)	9	
10	Adjusted total of social security taxes (see instructions) . . . . ▶	10	
11	Backup withholding (see instructions)	11	
12	Adjustment of backup withholding tax for preceding quarters of calendar year . . . . . ▶	12	
13	Adjusted total of backup withholding	13	
14	Total taxes (add lines 5, 10, and 13)	14	
15	Advance earned income credit (EIC) payments, if any . . . . ▶	15	
16	Net taxes (subtract line 15 from line 14). **This must equal line IV below** (plus line IV of Schedule A (Form 941) if you have treated backup withholding as a separate liability).	16	
17	Total deposits for quarter, including overpayment applied from a prior quarter, from your records . ▶	17	
18	Balance due (subtract line 17 from line 16). This should be less than $500. Pay to IRS . . . . ▶	18	
19	If line 17 is more than line 16, enter overpayment here ▶ $ ______ and check if to be: ☐ Applied to next return **OR** ☐ Refunded.		

Record of Federal Tax Liability (Complete if line 16 is $500 or more.) See the instructions under rule 4 for details before checking these boxes.

Check only if you made eighth-monthly deposits using the 95% rule ▶ ☐ Check only if you are a first time 3-banking-day depositor ▶ ☐

Date wages paid	Tax liability ▼ *Do NOT Show Federal Tax Deposits Below* ▼ First month of quarter		Second month of quarter		Third month of quarter	
1st through 3rd	A		I		Q	
4th through 7th	B		J		R	
8th through 11th	C		K		S	
12th through 15th	D		L		T	
16th through 19th	E		M		U	
20th through 22nd	F		N		V	
23rd through 25th	G		O		W	
26th through the last	H		P		X	
Total liability for month	*I*		*II*		*III*	
IV Total for quarter (add lines *I*, *II*, and *III*). **This must equal line 16 above** . . . . ▶						

▶ **Do NOT** Show Federal Tax Deposits Here ▶

Under penalties of perjury, I declare that I have examined this return, including accompanying schedules and statements, and to the best of my knowledge and belief, it is true, correct, and complete.

Signature ▶ **Title** ▶ **Date** ▶

[1]

CASH PAYMENTS JOURNAL

PAGE 1

	DATE	ACCOUNT TITLE	CK. NO.	POST. REF.	1 GENERAL DEBIT	2 GENERAL CREDIT	3 ACCOUNTS PAYABLE DEBIT	4 CASH CREDIT	
1									1
2									2
3									3
4									4
5									5
6									6
7									7
8									8
9									9
10									10
11									11
12									12
13									13
14									14
15									15
16									16
17									17
18									18
19									19
20									20
21									21
22									22
23									23
24									24
25									25

[1, 2]

CASH PAYMENTS JOURNAL

PAGE 2

	DATE		ACCOUNT TITLE	CK. NO.	POST. REF.	1 GENERAL DEBIT	2 GENERAL CREDIT	3 ACCOUNTS PAYABLE DEBIT	4 CASH CREDIT	
1										1
2										2
3										3
4										4
5										5
6										6
7										7
8										8
9										9
10										10
11										11
12										12
13										13
14										14
15										15
16										16
17										17
18										18
19										19
20										20
21										21
22										22
23										23
24										24
25										25

[1]

GENERAL LEDGER

ACCOUNT Employee Income Tax Payable ACCOUNT NO. 2120

DATE		ITEM	POST. REF.	DEBIT	CREDIT	BALANCE DEBIT	BALANCE CREDIT
19-- Jan.	1	Balance	✓				1 215 00

ACCOUNT FICA Tax Payable ACCOUNT NO. 2130

DATE		ITEM	POST. REF.	DEBIT	CREDIT	BALANCE DEBIT	BALANCE CREDIT
19-- Jan.	1	Balance	✓				1 342 68

ACCOUNT Unemployment Tax Payable—Federal ACCOUNT NO. 2150

DATE		ITEM	POST. REF.	DEBIT	CREDIT	BALANCE DEBIT	BALANCE CREDIT
19-- Jan.	1	Balance	✓				83 62

CHALLENGE PROBLEM 17-C, concluded

[1]

GENERAL LEDGER

ACCOUNT Unemployment Tax Payable—State ACCOUNT NO. 2160

DATE		ITEM	POST. REF.	DEBIT	CREDIT	BALANCE DEBIT	BALANCE CREDIT
19-- Jan.	1	Balance	✓				564 45

ACCOUNT U.S. Savings Bonds Payable ACCOUNT NO. 2180

DATE		ITEM	POST. REF.	DEBIT	CREDIT	BALANCE DEBIT	BALANCE CREDIT
19-- Jan.	1	Balance	✓				300 00

ACCOUNT Payroll Taxes Expense ACCOUNT NO. 6150

DATE		ITEM	POST. REF.	DEBIT	CREDIT	BALANCE DEBIT	BALANCE CREDIT

ACCOUNT Salary Expense ACCOUNT NO. 6170

DATE		ITEM	POST. REF.	DEBIT	CREDIT	BALANCE DEBIT	BALANCE CREDIT

Name ______________________ Date ________ Class ______

REINFORCEMENT ACTIVITY 2
PART A–p. 402
[1, 5, 6, 9, 10, 12]

AN ACCOUNTING CYCLE FOR A PARTNERSHIP: JOURNALIZING AND POSTING TRANSACTIONS

The ledgers used in Reinforcement Activity 2, Part A, will be needed to complete Part B.

GENERAL LEDGER

ACCOUNT Cash — ACCOUNT NO. 1110

DATE		ITEM	POST. REF.	DEBIT	CREDIT	BALANCE DEBIT	BALANCE CREDIT
19-- Dec.	1	Balance	✓			19 450 00	

ACCOUNT Petty Cash — ACCOUNT NO. 1120

DATE		ITEM	POST. REF.	DEBIT	CREDIT	BALANCE DEBIT	BALANCE CREDIT
19-- Jan.	1	Balance	✓			500 00	

ACCOUNT Accounts Receivable — ACCOUNT NO. 1130

DATE		ITEM	POST. REF.	DEBIT	CREDIT	BALANCE DEBIT	BALANCE CREDIT
19-- Dec.	1	Balance	✓			1 388 60	

ACCOUNT Merchandise Inventory — ACCOUNT NO. 1140

DATE		ITEM	POST. REF.	DEBIT	CREDIT	BALANCE DEBIT	BALANCE CREDIT
19-- Jan.	1	Balance	✓			215 600 00	

ACCOUNT Supplies—Office — ACCOUNT NO. 1145

DATE		ITEM	POST. REF.	DEBIT	CREDIT	BALANCE DEBIT	BALANCE CREDIT
19-- Dec.	1	Balance	✓			3 690 00	

GENERAL LEDGER

[1, 5, 6, 9, 10, 12]

ACCOUNT Supplies—Store ACCOUNT NO. 1150

DATE		ITEM	POST. REF.	DEBIT	CREDIT	BALANCE DEBIT	BALANCE CREDIT
19-- Dec.	1	Balance	✓			4 3 8 0 00	

ACCOUNT Prepaid Insurance ACCOUNT NO. 1160

DATE		ITEM	POST. REF.	DEBIT	CREDIT	BALANCE DEBIT	BALANCE CREDIT
19-- Dec.	1	Balance	✓			1 8 2 0 00	

ACCOUNT Accounts Payable ACCOUNT NO. 2110

DATE		ITEM	POST. REF.	DEBIT	CREDIT	BALANCE DEBIT	BALANCE CREDIT
19-- Dec.	1	Balance	✓				4 3 6 0 00

ACCOUNT Employee Income Tax Payable ACCOUNT NO. 2120

DATE		ITEM	POST. REF.	DEBIT	CREDIT	BALANCE DEBIT	BALANCE CREDIT

ACCOUNT FICA Tax Payable ACCOUNT NO. 2130

DATE		ITEM	POST. REF.	DEBIT	CREDIT	BALANCE DEBIT	BALANCE CREDIT

ACCOUNT Sales Tax Payable ACCOUNT NO. 2140

DATE		ITEM	POST. REF.	DEBIT	CREDIT	BALANCE DEBIT	BALANCE CREDIT
19-- Dec.	1	Balance	✓				1 6 2 1 00

Name ______________________ Date ________ Class ______

REINFORCEMENT ACTIVITY 2
PART A–continued
[1, 5, 6, 9, 10, 12]

GENERAL LEDGER

ACCOUNT Unemployment Tax Payable—Federal ACCOUNT NO. 2150

DATE		ITEM	POST. REF.	DEBIT	CREDIT	BALANCE DEBIT	BALANCE CREDIT
19-- Dec.	1	Balance	✓				35 20

ACCOUNT Unemployment Tax Payable—State ACCOUNT NO. 2160

DATE		ITEM	POST. REF.	DEBIT	CREDIT	BALANCE DEBIT	BALANCE CREDIT
19-- Dec.	1	Balance	✓				237 60

ACCOUNT Health Insurance Premiums Payable ACCOUNT NO. 2170

DATE		ITEM	POST. REF.	DEBIT	CREDIT	BALANCE DEBIT	BALANCE CREDIT
19-- Dec.	1	Balance	✓				568 00

ACCOUNT U.S. Savings Bonds Payable ACCOUNT NO. 2180

DATE		ITEM	POST. REF.	DEBIT	CREDIT	BALANCE DEBIT	BALANCE CREDIT
19-- Dec.	1	Balance	✓				50 00

ACCOUNT United Way Donations Payable ACCOUNT NO. 2190

DATE		ITEM	POST. REF.	DEBIT	CREDIT	BALANCE DEBIT	BALANCE CREDIT
19-- Dec.	1	Balance	✓				120 00

ACCOUNT Tara Bruski, Capital ACCOUNT NO. 3110

DATE		ITEM	POST. REF.	DEBIT	CREDIT	BALANCE DEBIT	BALANCE CREDIT
19-- Jan.	1	Balance	✓				94 882 60

[1, 5, 6, 9, 10, 12]

GENERAL LEDGER

ACCOUNT Tara Bruski, Drawing — **ACCOUNT NO.** 3120

DATE		ITEM	POST. REF.	DEBIT	CREDIT	BALANCE DEBIT	BALANCE CREDIT
19-- Dec.	1	Balance	✓			13 200 00	

ACCOUNT James Myler, Capital — **ACCOUNT NO.** 3130

DATE		ITEM	POST. REF.	DEBIT	CREDIT	BALANCE DEBIT	BALANCE CREDIT
19-- Jan.	1	Balance	✓				94 139 40

ACCOUNT James Myler, Drawing — **ACCOUNT NO.** 3140

DATE		ITEM	POST. REF.	DEBIT	CREDIT	BALANCE DEBIT	BALANCE CREDIT
19-- Dec.	1	Balance	✓			13 450 00	

ACCOUNT Income Summary — **ACCOUNT NO.** 3150

DATE		ITEM	POST. REF.	DEBIT	CREDIT	BALANCE DEBIT	BALANCE CREDIT

ACCOUNT Sales — **ACCOUNT NO.** 4110

DATE		ITEM	POST. REF.	DEBIT	CREDIT	BALANCE DEBIT	BALANCE CREDIT
19-- Dec.	1	Balance	✓				275 620 00

ACCOUNT Purchases — **ACCOUNT NO.** 5110

DATE		ITEM	POST. REF.	DEBIT	CREDIT	BALANCE DEBIT	BALANCE CREDIT
19-- Dec.	1	Balance	✓			115 760 00	

Name ______________ Date ________ Class ______

REINFORCEMENT ACTIVITY 2
PART A–continued
[1, 5, 6, 9, 10, 12]

GENERAL LEDGER

ACCOUNT Advertising Expense — ACCOUNT NO. 6110

DATE		ITEM	POST. REF.	DEBIT	CREDIT	BALANCE DEBIT	BALANCE CREDIT
19-- Dec.	1	Balance	✓			4 230 00	

ACCOUNT Credit Card Fee Expense — ACCOUNT NO. 6120

DATE		ITEM	POST. REF.	DEBIT	CREDIT	BALANCE DEBIT	BALANCE CREDIT
19-- Dec.	1	Balance	✓			2 910 00	

ACCOUNT Insurance Expense — ACCOUNT NO. 6130

DATE		ITEM	POST. REF.	DEBIT	CREDIT	BALANCE DEBIT	BALANCE CREDIT

ACCOUNT Miscellaneous Expense — ACCOUNT NO. 6140

DATE		ITEM	POST. REF.	DEBIT	CREDIT	BALANCE DEBIT	BALANCE CREDIT
19-- Dec.	1	Balance	✓			1 685 00	

ACCOUNT Payroll Taxes Expense — ACCOUNT NO. 6150

DATE		ITEM	POST. REF.	DEBIT	CREDIT	BALANCE DEBIT	BALANCE CREDIT
19-- Dec.	1	Balance	✓			5 670 20	

GENERAL LEDGER

ACCOUNT Rent Expense — ACCOUNT NO. 6160

DATE		ITEM	POST. REF.	DEBIT	CREDIT	BALANCE DEBIT	BALANCE CREDIT
19-- Dec.	1	Balance	✓			13 2 0 0 00	

ACCOUNT Salary Expense — ACCOUNT NO. 6170

DATE		ITEM	POST. REF.	DEBIT	CREDIT	BALANCE DEBIT	BALANCE CREDIT
19-- Dec.	1	Balance	✓			51 9 4 0 00	

ACCOUNT Supplies Expense—Office — ACCOUNT NO. 6175

DATE		ITEM	POST. REF.	DEBIT	CREDIT	BALANCE DEBIT	BALANCE CREDIT

ACCOUNT Supplies Expense—Store — ACCOUNT NO. 6180

DATE		ITEM	POST. REF.	DEBIT	CREDIT	BALANCE DEBIT	BALANCE CREDIT

ACCOUNT Utilities Expense — ACCOUNT NO. 6190

DATE		ITEM	POST. REF.	DEBIT	CREDIT	BALANCE DEBIT	BALANCE CREDIT
19-- Dec.	1	Balance	✓			2 7 6 0 00	

Name ______________ Date ________ Class ________

REINFORCEMENT ACTIVITY 2
PART A–continued

ACCOUNTS PAYABLE LEDGER [1, 11]

VENDOR A & B Optical Co. VENDOR NO. 210

DATE		ITEM	POST. REF.	DEBIT	CREDIT	CREDIT BALANCE
19-- Dec.	1	Balance	✓			1 0 6 0 40

VENDOR Central Office Supply VENDOR NO. 220

DATE		ITEM	POST. REF.	DEBIT	CREDIT	CREDIT BALANCE

VENDOR Kosh Optical Lab VENDOR NO. 230

DATE		ITEM	POST. REF.	DEBIT	CREDIT	CREDIT BALANCE
19-- Dec.	1	Balance	✓			9 7 5 80

VENDOR Optical Imports VENDOR NO. 240

DATE		ITEM	POST. REF.	DEBIT	CREDIT	CREDIT BALANCE
19-- Dec.	1	Balance	✓			1 8 4 0 00

VENDOR Trend Optics Co. VENDOR NO. 250

DATE		ITEM	POST. REF.	DEBIT	CREDIT	CREDIT BALANCE
19-- Dec.	1	Balance	✓			4 8 3 80

VENDOR Weaver Supply VENDOR NO. 260

DATE		ITEM	POST. REF.	DEBIT	CREDIT	CREDIT BALANCE

[1, 11]

ACCOUNTS RECEIVABLE LEDGER

CUSTOMER Theresa Abbey — CUSTOMER NO. 110

DATE		ITEM	POST. REF.	DEBIT	CREDIT	DEBIT BALANCE

CUSTOMER Nancy Bonner — CUSTOMER NO. 120

DATE		ITEM	POST. REF.	DEBIT	CREDIT	DEBIT BALANCE
19-- Dec.	1	Balance	✓			344 50

CUSTOMER Jonathan Doran — CUSTOMER NO. 130

DATE		ITEM	POST. REF.	DEBIT	CREDIT	DEBIT BALANCE

CUSTOMER Irma Iznaga — CUSTOMER NO. 140

DATE		ITEM	POST. REF.	DEBIT	CREDIT	DEBIT BALANCE
19-- Dec.	1	Balance	✓			683 70

CUSTOMER Brian Patco — CUSTOMER NO. 150

DATE		ITEM	POST. REF.	DEBIT	CREDIT	DEBIT BALANCE

CUSTOMER Norman Witte — CUSTOMER NO. 160

DATE		ITEM	POST. REF.	DEBIT	CREDIT	DEBIT BALANCE
19-- Dec.	1	Balance	✓			360 40

[1, 5]

SALES JOURNAL

PAGE 12

	DATE		ACCOUNT DEBITED	SALE NO.	POST. REF.	1 ACCOUNTS RECEIVABLE DEBIT	2 SALES CREDIT	3 SALES TAX PAYABLE CREDIT	
1									1
2									2
3									3
4									4
5									5
6									6
7									7
8									8
9									9
10									10
11									11
12									12
13									13
14									14

[1, 6]

PURCHASES JOURNAL

PAGE 12

	DATE		ACCOUNT CREDITED	PURCH. NO.	POST. REF.	PURCHASES DR. ACCTS. PAY. CR.	
1							1
2							2
3							3
4							4
5							5
6							6
7							7
8							8
9							9
10							10
11							11
12							12

[1]

GENERAL JOURNAL

PAGE 12

DATE		ACCOUNT TITLE	DOC. NO.	POST. REF.	DEBIT	CREDIT

[1, 7–9]

CASH RECEIPTS JOURNAL

PAGE 12

	DATE	ACCOUNT TITLE	DOC. NO.	POST. REF.	1 GENERAL DEBIT	2 GENERAL CREDIT	3 ACCOUNTS RECEIVABLE CREDIT	4 SALES CREDIT	5 SALES TAX PAYABLE CREDIT	6 CASH DEBIT	
1											1
2											2
3											3
4											4
5											5
6											6
7											7
8											8
9											9
10											10
11											11
12											12
13											13
14											14
15											15
16											16
17											17
18											18
19											19
20											20
21											21
22											22
23											23
24											24
25											25

[1-3]

CASH PAYMENTS JOURNAL

PAGE 23

	DATE	ACCOUNT TITLE	CK. NO.	POST. REF.	1 GENERAL DEBIT	2 GENERAL CREDIT	3 ACCOUNTS PAYABLE DEBIT	4 CASH CREDIT	
1									1
2									2
3									3
4									4
5									5
6									6
7									7
8									8
9									9
10									10
11									11
12									12
13									13
14									14
15									15
16									16
17									17
18									18
19									19
20									20
21									21
22									22
23									23
24									24

[3, 4, 7, 8, 10]

CASH PAYMENTS JOURNAL

PAGE 24

	DATE	ACCOUNT TITLE	CK. NO.	POST. REF.	1 GENERAL DEBIT	2 GENERAL CREDIT	3 ACCOUNTS PAYABLE DEBIT	4 CASH CREDIT	
1									1
2									2
3									3
4									4
5									5
6									6
7									7
8									8
9									9
10									10
11									11
12									12
13									13
14									14
15									15
16									16
17									17
18									18
19									19
20									20
21									21
22									22
23									23
24									24

[11]

Perfect Score..... 40	Name ______	
Deduct........ ___	Date ______	Class ______
Your Score..... ___	Checked by ______	

STUDY GUIDE 18

UNIT A—Analyzing Adjustments on a Work Sheet

DIRECTIONS: For each of the following items, select the choice that best completes the statement. Print the letter identifying your choice in the Answers column.

	Answers	For Scoring
0. The two accounts used to adjust the Office Supplies account are **(A)** Supplies—Office and Income Summary **(B)** Supplies—Office and Supplies Expense—Office **(C)** Supplies Expense—Office and Income Summary **(D)** Supplies and Purchases	B	**0.** ✓
1. The Merchandise Inventory amount in a work sheet's Trial Balance Debit column represents the merchandise inventory **(A)** at the beginning of a fiscal period **(B)** purchased during a fiscal period **(C)** available during a fiscal period **(D)** at the end of a fiscal period		**1.**
2. The two accounts used to adjust the Merchandise Inventory account are **(A)** Merchandise Inventory and Purchases **(B)** Merchandise Inventory and Income Summary **(C)** Merchandise Inventory and Supplies **(D)** none of the above		**2.**
3. The Income Summary amount in a work sheet's Adjustments Debit column represents the **(A)** increase in Merchandise Inventory **(B)** decrease in Merchandise Inventory **(C)** beginning Merchandise Inventory **(D)** ending Merchandise Inventory		**3.**
4. The Income Summary amount in a work sheet's Adjustments Credit column represents the **(A)** increase in Merchandise Inventory **(B)** decrease in Merchandise Inventory **(C)** beginning Merchandise Inventory **(D)** ending Merchandise Inventory		**4.**
5. The Supplies—Office amount in a work sheet's Trial Balance Debit column represents the value of supplies **(A)** at the beginning of a fiscal period **(B)** used during a fiscal period **(C)** bought during a fiscal period **(D)** available during a fiscal period		**5.**
6. Recording expenses in the accounting period in which the expenses contribute to earning revenue is an application of the accounting concept **(A)** consistent reporting **(B)** historical cost **(C)** matching expenses with revenue **(D)** adequate disclosure		**6.**
7. The portion of the insurance premiums that has expired during a fiscal period is classified as **(A)** a liability **(B)** an asset **(C)** capital **(D)** an expense		**7.**
8. The two accounts used to adjust the Prepaid Insurance account are **(A)** Prepaid Insurance and Insurance Expense **(B)** Insurance Expense and Income Summary **(C)** Prepaid Insurance and Income Summary **(D)** none of the above		**8.**

UNIT B—Analyzing Work Sheet Extensions

DIRECTIONS: For each account listed below, place a check mark in the column to which amounts are extended on a work sheet.

Account	Income Statement Debit	Income Statement Credit	Balance Sheet Debit	Balance Sheet Credit	For Scoring
0. Cash			✓		**0.** ✓
1. Petty Cash					**1.**
2. Accounts Receivable					**2.**
3. Merchandise Inventory					**3.**
4. Supplies—Office					**4.**
5. Supplies—Store					**5.**
6. Prepaid Insurance					**6.**
7. Accounts Payable					**7.**
8. Employee Income Tax Payable					**8.**
9. FICA Tax Payable					**9.**
10. Sales Tax Payable					**10.**
11. Unemployment Tax Payable—Federal					**11.**
12. Unemployment Tax Payable—State					**12.**
13. Health Insurance Premium Payable					**13.**
14. U.S. Savings Bonds Payable					**14.**
15. United Way Donations Payable					**15.**
16. Susan Archer, Capital					**16.**
17. Susan Archer, Drawing					**17.**
18. Hubert Marsh, Capital					**18.**
19. Hubert Marsh, Drawing					**19.**
20. Income Summary (Ending inventory smaller than beginning inventory)					**20.**
21. Sales					**21.**
22. Purchases					**22.**
23. Advertising Expense					**23.**
24. Credit Card Fee Expense					**24.**
25. Insurance Expense					**25.**
26. Miscellaneous Expense					**26.**
27. Payroll Taxes Expense					**27.**
28. Rent Expense					**28.**
29. Salary Expense					**29.**
30. Supplies Expense—Office					**30.**
31. Supplies Expense—Store					**31.**
32. Utilities Expense					**32.**

Name ________________ Date ________ Class ________ *DRILL 18-D1, p. 428*

Analyzing adjusting entries

1	2	3	4	5
Business	**Adjustment Number**	**Accounts Affected**	**Adjustment Column**	
			Debit	**Credit**
A	1.	Income Summary	$14,000.00	
		Merchandise Inventory		$14,000.00
	2.			
	3.			
	4.			
B	1.			
	2.			
	3.			
	4.			
C	1.			
	2.			
	3.			
	4.			

Extending balance sheet and income statement items [1–3]

Madison Enterprises

Work Sheet

For Year Ended December 31, 19--

	ACCOUNT TITLE	1 TRIAL BALANCE DEBIT	2 TRIAL BALANCE CREDIT	3 ADJUSTMENTS DEBIT	4 ADJUSTMENTS CREDIT	5 INCOME STATEMENT DEBIT	6 INCOME STATEMENT CREDIT	7 BALANCE SHEET DEBIT	8 BALANCE SHEET CREDIT	
1	Cash	21 770 00								1
2	Petty Cash	500 00								2
3	Accounts Receivable	8 911 00								3
4	Merchandise Inventory	211 870 00			(a) 12 408 00					4
5	Supplies—Office	5 076 00			(b) 3 704 00					5
6	Supplies—Store	5 430 00			(c) 3 065 00					6
7	Prepaid Insurance	4 620 00			(d) 2 520 00					7
8	Accounts Payable		8 950 00							8
9	Sales Tax Payable		1 654 00							9
10	Diane Casey, Capital		98 230 00							10
11	Diane Casey, Drawing	17 108 00								11
12	Julia Gibbs, Capital		98 764 00							12
13	Julia Gibbs, Drawing	17 482 00								13
14	Income Summary			(a) 12 408 00						14
15	Sales		263 700 00							15
16	Purchases	148 800 00								16
17	Advertising Expense	5 170 00								17
18	Credit Card Fee Expense	2 720 00								18
19	Insurance Expense			(d) 2 520 00						19
20	Miscellaneous Expense	2 051 00								20
21	Rent Expense	16 800 00								21
22	Supplies Expense—Office			(b) 3 704 00						22
23	Supplies Expense—Store			(c) 3 065 00						23
24	Utilities Expense	2 990 00								24
25		471 298 00	471 298 00	21 697 00	21 697 00					25
26										26
27										27
28										27
29										29
30										30
31										31
32										32

Completing a work sheet **[1–3]**

Eastside Supply
Work Sheet
For Year Ended December 31, 19--

	ACCOUNT TITLE	1 TRIAL BALANCE DEBIT	2 TRIAL BALANCE CREDIT	3 ADJUSTMENTS DEBIT	4 ADJUSTMENTS CREDIT	5 INCOME STATEMENT DEBIT	6 INCOME STATEMENT CREDIT	7 BALANCE SHEET DEBIT	8 BALANCE SHEET CREDIT	
1	Cash	22 460 00								1
2	Petty Cash	500 00								2
3	Accounts Receivable	9 195 00								3
4	Merchandise Inventory	218 600 00								4
5	Supplies — Office	5 230 00								5
6	Supplies — Store	5 610 00								6
7	Prepaid Insurance	4 515 00								7
8	Accounts Payable		9 235 00							8
9	Sales Tax Payable		1 145 00							9
10	Pablo Sanchez, Capital		81 236 00							10
11	Pablo Sanchez, Drawing	14 640 00								11
12	Carmen Zapata, Capital		81 778 00							12
13	Carmen Zapata, Drawing	14 820 00								13
14	Income Summary									14
15	Sales		274 900 00							15
16	Purchases	123 705 00								16
17	Advertising Expense	5 335 00								17
18	Credit Card Fee Expense	2 810 00								18
19	Insurance Expense									19
20	Miscellaneous Expense	2 134 00								20
21	Rent Expense	15 600 00								21
22	Supplies Expense—Office									22
23	Supplies Expense—Store									23
24	Utilities Expense	3 140 00								24
25		448 294 00	448 294 00							25
26										26
27										27
28										28
29										29
30										30
31										31
32										32

Completing a work sheet **[1–3]**

PROBLEM 18-2, p. 431

Jomar
Work Sheet
For Year Ended December 31, 19--

	ACCOUNT TITLE	1 TRIAL BALANCE DEBIT	2 TRIAL BALANCE CREDIT	3 ADJUSTMENTS DEBIT	4 ADJUSTMENTS CREDIT	5 INCOME STATEMENT DEBIT	6 INCOME STATEMENT CREDIT	7 BALANCE SHEET DEBIT	8 BALANCE SHEET CREDIT	
1	Cash	22,100.00								1
2	Petty Cash	300.00								2
3	Accounts Receivable	9,620.00								3
4	Merchandise Inventory	243,600.00								4
5	Supplies—Office	5,730.00								5
6	Supplies—Store	5,380.00								6
7	Prepaid Insurance	5,060.00								7
8	Accounts Payable		9,864.00							8
9	Sales Tax Payable		916.00							9
10	Lidia Jomar, Capital		151,850.00							10
11	Lidia Jomar, Drawing	12,860.00								11
12	Philip Jomar, Capital		150,894.00							12
13	Philip Jomar, Drawing	12,674.00								13
14	Income Summary									14
15	Sales		183,110.00							15
16	Purchases	147,150.00								16
17	Advertising Expense	5,820.00								17
18	Credit Card Fee Expense	1,615.00								18
19	Insurance Expense									19
20	Miscellaneous Expense	2,285.00								20
21	Rent Expense	19,200.00								21
22	Supplies Expense—Office									22
23	Supplies Expense—Store									23
24	Utilities Expense	3,240.00								24
25		496,634.00	496,634.00							25
26										26
27										27
28										28
29										29
30										30
31										31
32										32

Completing a work sheet **[1–3]**

Marine Supply

Work Sheet

For Year Ended December 31, 19--

	ACCOUNT TITLE	1 TRIAL BALANCE DEBIT	2 TRIAL BALANCE CREDIT	3 ADJUSTMENTS DEBIT	4 ADJUSTMENTS CREDIT	5 INCOME STATEMENT DEBIT	6 INCOME STATEMENT CREDIT	7 BALANCE SHEET DEBIT	8 BALANCE SHEET CREDIT	
1	Cash	23 740 00								1
2	Petty Cash	500 00								2
3	Accounts Receivable	10 200 00								3
4	Merchandise Inventory	185 300 00								4
5	Supplies — Office	5 585 00								5
6	Supplies — Store	5 735 00								6
7	Prepaid Insurance	4 275 00								7
8	Accounts Payable		9 680 00							8
9	Sales Tax Payable		1 376 00							9
10	Mark Edwards, Capital		88 740 00							10
11	Mark Edwards, Drawing	18 380 00								11
12	David Parker, Capital		89 459 00							12
13	David Parker, Drawing	18 610 00								13
14	Income Summary									14
15	Sales		275 300 00							15
16	Purchases	161 290 00								16
17	Advertising Expense	5 920 00								17
18	Credit Card Fee Expense	2 735 00								18
19	Insurance Expense									19
20	Miscellaneous Expense	2 365 00								20
21	Rent Expense	16 800 00								21
22	Supplies Expense—Office									22
23	Supplies Expense—Store									23
24	Utilities Expense	3 120 00								24
25		464 555 00	464 555 00							25
26										26
27										27
28										28
29										29
30										30
31										31
32										32

Ultimate

Work

For Year Ended

	ACCOUNT TITLE	1 TRIAL BALANCE DEBIT	2 TRIAL BALANCE CREDIT	3 ADJUSTMENTS DEBIT	4 ADJUSTMENTS CREDIT	
1	Cash	25340 00				1
2	Petty Cash	500 00				2
3	Accounts Receivable	9485 00				3
4	Merchandise Inventory	215870 00				4
5	Supplies—Office	5130 00				5
6	Supplies—Store	5335 00				6
7	Prepaid Insurance	3960 00				7
8	Accounts Payable		10320 00			8
9	Sales Tax Payable		810 00			9
10	Debra Brown, Capital		109635 00			10
11	Debra Brown, Drawing	18340 00				11
12	Richard Leyba, Capital		108845 00			12
13	Richard Leyba, Drawing	18560 00				13
14	Income Summary					14
15	Sales		192380 00			15
16	Purchases	86570 00				16
17	Advertising Expense	6140 00				17
18	Credit Card Fee Expense	2385 00				18
19	Insurance Expense					19
20	Miscellaneous Expense	2530 00				20
21	Rent Expense	18600 00				21
22	Supplies Expense—Office					22
23	Supplies Expense—Store					23
24	Utilities Expense	3245 00				24
25		421990 00	421990 00			25
26						26
27						27
28						28
29						29
30						30
31						31
32						32

Fashion

Sheet

December 31, 19--

	5	6	7	8	9	10	
	ADJUSTED TRIAL BALANCE		INCOME STATEMENT		BALANCE SHEET		
	DEBIT	CREDIT	DEBIT	CREDIT	DEBIT	CREDIT	
1							1
2							2
3							3
4							4
5							5
6							6
7							7
8							8
9							9
10							10
11							11
12							12
13							13
14							14
15							15
16							16
17							17
18							18
19							19
20							20
21							21
22							22
23							23
24							24
25							25
26							26
27							27
28							28
29							29
30							30
31							31
32							32

	ACCOUNT TITLE	TRIAL BALANCE 1 DEBIT	TRIAL BALANCE 2 CREDIT	ADJUSTMENTS 3 DEBIT	ADJUSTMENTS 4 CREDIT	INCOME STATEMENT 5 DEBIT	INCOME STATEMENT 6 CREDIT	BALANCE SHEET 7 DEBIT	BALANCE SHEET 8 CREDIT	
1										1
2										2
3										3
4										4
5										5
6										6
7										7
8										8
9										9
10										10
11										11
12										12
13										13
14										14
15										15
16										16
17										17
18										18
19										19
20										20
21										21
22										22
23										23
24										24
25										25
26										26
27										27
28										28
29										29
30										30
31										31
32										32

Perfect Score..... 45 Name ______________________

Deduct......... ___ Date __________ Class __________

Your Score..... ___ Checked by ______________________

STUDY GUIDE 19

UNIT A—Identifying Accounting Terms

DIRECTIONS: Select the one term in Column I that best fits each definition in Column II. Print the letter identifying your choice in the Answers column.

Column I

A. cost of merchandise sold
B. distribution of net income statement
C. gross profit on sales
D. merchandise inventory
E. owners' equity statement
F. supporting schedule

Column II	Answers	For Scoring
0. The amount of goods on hand for sale to customers	D	**0.** ✓
1. The revenue remaining after cost of merchandise sold has been deducted		**1.**
2. A report prepared to give details about an item on a principal financial statement		**2.**
3. The total original price of all merchandise sold during a fiscal period		**3.**
4. A financial statement that summarizes the changes in owners' equity during a fiscal period		**4.**
5. A partnership financial statement showing net income or loss distribution to partners		**5.**

UNIT B—Classifying Accounts

DIRECTIONS: Decide the classification for each item below. Print the letter identifying your choice in the Answers column.

Account Classifications

A—Assets
CM—Cost of Merchandise
E—Expense
L—Liability
O—Owners' equity
N—Not an account
R—Revenue

	Answers	For Scoring
0. Supplies Expense—Office	E	**0.** ✓
1. Purchases		**1.**
2. Revenue		**2.**
3. Net Income		**3.**
4. Gross Profit		**4.**
5. Insurance Expense		**5.**
6. Merchandise Inventory		**6.**
7. Supplies—Store		**7.**
8. Kay Myer, Capital		**8.**
9. Kay Myer, Drawing		**9.**
10. Salary Expense		**10.**

	Answers	For Scoring
11. Sales		**11.**
12. Cash		**12.**
13. Cost of Merchandise Sold		**13.**
14. Sales Tax Payable		**14.**
15. Accounts Receivable		**15.**
16. Income Summary		**16.**
17. Rent Expense		**17.**
18. Accounts Payable		**18.**
19. Prepaid Insurance		**19.**
20. FICA Tax Payable		**20.**

UNIT C—Analyzing Financial Statements for a Merchandise Business

DIRECTIONS: Place a check mark in the proper Answers column to show whether each of the following statements is true or false.

	Answers True	Answers False	For Scoring
0. Financial statements provide the primary source of information needed by owners and managers to make decisions on the future activity of a business	✓		**0.** ✓
1. Reporting financial information the same way from one fiscal period to the next is an application of the accounting concept Adequate Disclosure			**1.**
2. Three financial statements are used to report the financial condition and progress of a business organized as a partnership			**2.**
3. An income statement is used to report a business' financial progress			**3.**
4. An income statement can be compared to a previous balance sheet to determine reasons for increases or decreases in net income			**4.**
5. Information from a completed work sheet is used to prepare an income statement			**5.**
6. An income statement for a merchandising business has four main sections			**6.**
7. For a merchandising business, every sales dollar reported on the income statement includes three components			**7.**
8. The percentage relationship between one financial statement item and the total that includes that item is known as a component percentage			**8.**
9. Increasing sales revenue while keeping cost of merchandise sold the same will increase gross profit on sales			**9.**
10. When a business' expenses are greater than the gross profit on sales, the difference is known as a net loss			**10.**
11. A separate financial statement may be prepared to show the distribution of net income or loss to partners			**11.**
12. A financial statement that reports changes in owners' equity is sometimes known as a supporting schedule			**12.**
13. The owners' equity of a business is affected when a business earns an income or incurs a loss			**13.**
14. Data needed to prepare the liabilities section of a balance sheet are obtained from a work sheet's Balance Sheet Credit column			**14.**
15. Net income is shown on the last line of a balance sheet			**15.**
16. The information on an owners' equity statement may be included as part of a balance sheet			**16.**
17. The data for the revenue section of the income statement are obtained from the work sheet's Income Statement Debit column			**17.**
18. Revenue less cost of merchandise sold equals net income			**18.**
19. Total expenses on an income statement are deducted from the gross profit on sales to find net income			**19.**
20. Partners' salaries are listed in the Expenses section of an income statement			**20.**

Name ______________________ Date __________ Class ________ *DRILL 19-D1, p. 454*

Figuring the cost of merchandise sold

Business	Account Title	Trial Balance Debit	Income Statement Debit	Balance Sheet Debit	Cost of Merchandise Sold
A	Merchandise Inventory	$118,000.00		$124,000.00	
	Purchases		$23,800.00		________
B	Merchandise Inventory	$174,000.00		$192,000.00	
	Purchases		$38,200.00		________
C	Merchandise Inventory	$152,000.00		$144,000.00	
	Purchases		$29,400.00		________

Figuring net income or loss *DRILL 19-D2, p. 454*

Business	Account Title	Trial Balance Debit	Income Statement		Balance Sheet Debit	Net Income (+) or Net Loss (−)
			Debit	Credit		
A	Merchandise Inventory	$225,000.00			$214,000.00	
	Sales			$162,400.00		
	Purchases		$64,600.00			
	Total Expenses		42,300.00			________
B	Merchandise Inventory	$186,400.00			$198,000.00	
	Sales			$122,000.00		
	Purchases		$82,000.00			
	Total Expenses		53,800.00			________
C	Merchandise Inventory	$210,000.00			$202,600.00	
	Sales			$135,400.00		
	Purchases		$58,800.00			
	Total Expenses		29,600.00			________

Figuring component percentages

DRILL 19-D3, p. 454

1	2	3	4
Business	**Component**	**Amount**	**Percentage**
A	Sales	$186,000.00	
	Cost of Merchandise Sold	91,000.00	
	Gross Profit on Sales	95,000.00	
	Total Expenses	41,000.00	
	Net Income	54,000.00	
B	Sales	$164,000.00	
	Cost of Merchandise Sold	78,000.00	
	Gross Profit on Sales	86,000.00	
	Total Expenses	48,000.00	
	Net Income	38,000.00	
C	Sales	$226,000.00	
	Cost of Merchandise Sold	121,000.00	
	Gross Profit on Sales	105,000.00	
	Total Expenses	68,000.00	
	Net Income	37,000.00	

Figuring the distribution of net income or loss

DRILL 19-D4, p. 455
[1, 2]

Business	**Partner**	**Agreement on Sharing Income or Loss**	**[1] $64,000.00 net income**	**[2] $8,000.00 net loss**
A	**1**	50.0% of income or loss		
	2	50.0% of income or loss		
B	**1**	40.0% of income or loss		
	2	60.0% of income or loss		
C	**1**	25.0% of income or loss		
	2	30.0% of income or loss		
	3	45.0% of income or loss		

Preparing financial statements **[1–4]**

Midwest Supply
Work Sheet
For Year Ended December 31, 19--

	ACCOUNT TITLE	1 TRIAL BALANCE DEBIT	2 TRIAL BALANCE CREDIT	3 ADJUSTMENTS DEBIT	4 ADJUSTMENTS CREDIT	5 INCOME STATEMENT DEBIT	6 INCOME STATEMENT CREDIT	7 BALANCE SHEET DEBIT	8 BALANCE SHEET CREDIT	
1	Cash	18 940 00						18 940 00		1
2	Petty Cash	300 00						300 00		2
3	Accounts Receivable	9 685 00						9 685 00		3
4	Merchandise Inventory	224 860 00			(a) 8 530 00			216 330 00		4
5	Supplies—Office	4 935 00			(b) 3 110 00			1 825 00		5
6	Supplies—Store	5 210 00			(c) 2 740 00			2 470 00		6
7	Prepaid Insurance	4 275 00			(d) 2 700 00			1 575 00		7
8	Accounts Payable		8 830 00						8 830 00	8
9	Sales Tax Payable		845 20						845 20	9
10	Elsa Angulo, Capital		102 648 20						102 648 20	10
11	Elsa Angulo, Drawing	14 835 00						14 835 00		11
12	Jorge Munoz, Capital		101 716 60						101 716 60	12
13	Jorge Munoz, Drawing	14 920 00						14 920 00		13
14	Income Summary			(a) 8 530 00		8 530 00				14
15	Sales		202 850 00				202 850 00			15
16	Purchases	91 280 00				91 280 00				16
17	Advertising Expense	5 160 00				5 160 00				17
18	Credit Card Fee Expense	2 045 00				2 045 00				18
19	Insurance Expense			(d) 2 700 00		2 700 00				19
20	Miscellaneous Expense	2 490 00				2 490 00				20
21	Rent Expense	15 600 00				15 600 00				21
22	Supplies Expense—Office			(b) 3 110 00		3 110 00				22
23	Supplies Expense—Store			(c) 2 740 00		2 740 00				23
24	Utilities Expense	2 355 00				2 355 00				24
25		416 890 00	416 890 00	17 080 00	17 080 00	136 010 00	202 850 00	280 880 00	214 040 00	25
26	Net Income					66 840 00			66 840 00	26
27						202 850 00	202 850 00	280 880 00	280 880 00	27

PROBLEM 19-1, continued
[1, 2]

			% OF SALES

[2, 3]

[3, 4]

PROBLEM 19-1, concluded

[4]

[1, 2]

Preparing a distribution of net income statement and an owners' equity statement (net income)

[2]

Name ______________________________ Date ________ Class ______

MASTERY PROBLEM 19-M, p. 456
[1, 2]

Preparing financial statements

			% OF SALES

[2, 3]

[3, 4]

[4]

Preparing financial statements (unequal distribution of net income; additional investment)

CHALLENGE PROBLEM 19-C, p. 457

[1, 2]

[2]

Perfect Score..... 42 Name ______________________

Deduct......... ___ Date ______________ Class ______________

Your Score..... ___ Checked by ______________________

STUDY GUIDE 20

UNIT A—Analyzing Accounts Affected by Adjusting and Closing Entries

DIRECTIONS: For each adjusting or closing entry described, decide which accounts are debited and credited. Print the letter identifying your choice in the proper Answers column.

A. Advertising Expense
B. Jane Carey, Capital
C. Jane Carey, Drawing
D. Income Summary
E. Insurance Expense
F. Merchandise Inventory
G. Prepaid Insurance
H. Purchases
I. Sales
J. Supplies—Office
K. Supplies Expense—Office
L. John Vogel, Capital
M. John Vogel, Drawing

		Accounts to be Debited	Accounts to be Credited	For Scoring Debit	For Scoring Credit
0–0.	Adjusting entry for office supplies ..	K	J	**0.** ✓	**0.** ✓
1–2.	Adjusting entry for prepaid insurance			**1.**	**2.**
3–4.	Adjusting entry for a decrease in merchandise inventory			**3.**	**4.**
5–6.	Closing entry for the sales account ..			**5.**	**6.**
7–8.	Closing entry for the purchases account			**7.**	**8.**
9–10.	Adjusting entry for an increase in merchandise inventory			**9.**	**10.**
11–12.	Closing entry for the advertising expense account			**11.**	**12.**
13–14.	Closing entry for the office supplies expense account			**13.**	**14.**
15–16.	Closing entry for the insurance expense account			**15.**	**16.**
17–18.	Closing entry for the income summary with a net income			**17.**	**18.**
19–20.	Closing entry for the income summary with a net loss			**19.**	**20.**
21–22.	Closing entry for the partners' drawing accounts			**21.**	**22.**

UNIT B—Examining Adjusting and Closing Entries

DIRECTIONS: Place a check mark in the proper Answers column to show whether each of the following statements is true or false.

	Answers: True	Answers: False	For Scoring
0. General ledger account balances are changed only by posting journal entries	✓		**0.** ✓
1. Adjusting entries bring subsidiary ledger accounts up to date			**1.**
2. Closing entries prepare temporary accounts for the next fiscal period			**2.**
3. The Income Statement columns of a work sheet contain the information needed to journalize adjusting entries			**3.**
4. The Trial Balance columns of a work sheet and a distribution of net income statement contain the information needed to journalize closing entries			**4.**
5. Adjusting entries are recorded in a journal on the next line following the last daily transaction			**5.**
6. Adjusting entries are entered in the General Debit and Credit columns of a journal			**6.**
7. A memorandum is used as the source document for adjusting entries			**7.**
8. After posting the merchandise inventory adjusting entry, the merchandise inventory account has a zero balance			**8.**
9. An office supplies adjustment includes a debit to Supplies Expense—Office and a credit to Supplies—Office			**9.**
10. Temporary accounts are closed at the end of a fiscal period to prepare the general ledger for the next fiscal period			**10.**
11. A temporary account is closed by transferring its balance out of the account			**11.**
12. Revenue accounts are transferred to the credit side of the income summary account			**12.**
13. Closing the revenue account at the end of a fiscal period is an application of the accounting concept Matching Expenses with Revenue			**13.**
14. Expense accounts are closed by debiting the expense accounts and crediting Income Summary			**14.**
15. The income summary account is closed into the capital accounts			**15.**
16. A closing entry is made to close the drawing accounts into the Income Summary			**16.**
17. After all closing entries are posted, the income statement accounts are the only general ledger accounts that have balances			**17.**
18. After all closing entries are posted, the balance of the partners' capital accounts equal the amounts reported in the owners' section of the balance sheet			**18.**
19. After all closing entries are posted, the income statement accounts are the only general ledger accounts that have balances			**19.**
20. The purpose of the post-closing trial balance is to prove the general ledger equality of debits and credits			**20.**

Name ______________________ Date ________ Class ______

DRILL 20-D1, p. 478
[1, 2]

Analyzing adjusting entries

Drill 20-D2 is on page 272.

DRILL 20-D3, p. 480
[1, 2]

Analyzing closing entries

Analyzing adjusting entries [1, 2]

Business 1

Business 2

Business 3

Name ____________________ Date ________ Class ________

PROBLEM 20-1, p. 481
[1–4]

Journalizing and posting adjusting and closing entries; preparing a post-closing trial balance

GENERAL JOURNAL

PAGE 25

DATE		ACCOUNT TITLE	DOC. NO.	POST. REF.	DEBIT	CREDIT

GENERAL LEDGER

ACCOUNT Cash — ACCOUNT NO. 1110

DATE		ITEM	POST. REF.	DEBIT	CREDIT	BALANCE DEBIT	BALANCE CREDIT
19-- Dec.	31	Balance	✓			19 460 00	

ACCOUNT Petty Cash — ACCOUNT NO. 1120

DATE		ITEM	POST. REF.	DEBIT	CREDIT	BALANCE DEBIT	BALANCE CREDIT
19-- Dec.	31	Balance	✓			500 00	

ACCOUNT Accounts Receivable — ACCOUNT NO. 1130

DATE		ITEM	POST. REF.	DEBIT	CREDIT	BALANCE DEBIT	BALANCE CREDIT
19-- Dec.	31	Balance	✓			8 860 00	

ACCOUNT Merchandise Inventory — ACCOUNT NO. 1140

DATE		ITEM	POST. REF.	DEBIT	CREDIT	BALANCE DEBIT	BALANCE CREDIT
19-- Jan.	1	Balance	✓			296 830 00	

ACCOUNT Supplies—Office — ACCOUNT NO. 1145

DATE		ITEM	POST. REF.	DEBIT	CREDIT	BALANCE DEBIT	BALANCE CREDIT
19-- Dec.	31	Balance	✓			4 710 00	

ACCOUNT Supplies—Store — ACCOUNT NO. 1150

DATE		ITEM	POST. REF.	DEBIT	CREDIT	BALANCE DEBIT	BALANCE CREDIT
19-- Dec.	31	Balance	✓			4 580 00	

ACCOUNT Prepaid Insurance — ACCOUNT NO. 1160

DATE		ITEM	POST. REF.	DEBIT	CREDIT	BALANCE DEBIT	BALANCE CREDIT
19-- Dec.	31	Balance	✓			3 740 00	

GENERAL LEDGER

ACCOUNT Accounts Payable — ACCOUNT NO. 2110

DATE		ITEM	POST. REF.	DEBIT	CREDIT	BALANCE DEBIT	BALANCE CREDIT
19-- Dec.	31	Balance	✓				9 2 3 0 00

ACCOUNT Employee Income Tax Payable — ACCOUNT NO. 2120

DATE		ITEM	POST. REF.	DEBIT	CREDIT	BALANCE DEBIT	BALANCE CREDIT
19-- Dec.	31	Balance	✓				4 3 0 00

ACCOUNT FICA Tax Payable — ACCOUNT NO. 2130

DATE		ITEM	POST. REF.	DEBIT	CREDIT	BALANCE DEBIT	BALANCE CREDIT
19-- Dec.	31	Balance	✓				7 8 5 00

ACCOUNT Sales Tax Payable — ACCOUNT NO. 2140

DATE		ITEM	POST. REF.	DEBIT	CREDIT	BALANCE DEBIT	BALANCE CREDIT
19-- Dec.	31	Balance	✓				1 5 8 0 00

ACCOUNT Unemployment Tax Payable—Federal — ACCOUNT NO. 2150

DATE		ITEM	POST. REF.	DEBIT	CREDIT	BALANCE DEBIT	BALANCE CREDIT
19-- Dec.	31	Balance	✓				3 8 40

ACCOUNT Unemployment Tax Payable—State — ACCOUNT NO. 2160

DATE		ITEM	POST. REF.	DEBIT	CREDIT	BALANCE DEBIT	BALANCE CREDIT
19-- Dec.	31	Balance	✓				2 5 9 20

ACCOUNT Paula Chaney, Capital — ACCOUNT NO. 3110

DATE		ITEM	POST. REF.	DEBIT	CREDIT	BALANCE DEBIT	BALANCE CREDIT
19-- Dec.	31	Balance	✓				130 1 0 9 40

GENERAL LEDGER

ACCOUNT Paula Chaney, Drawing — ACCOUNT NO. 3120

DATE		ITEM	POST. REF.	DEBIT	CREDIT	BALANCE DEBIT	BALANCE CREDIT
19-- Dec.	31	Balance	✓			14 580 00	

ACCOUNT Scott Chaney, Capital — ACCOUNT NO. 3130

DATE		ITEM	POST. REF.	DEBIT	CREDIT	BALANCE DEBIT	BALANCE CREDIT
19-- Dec.	31	Balance	✓				128 008 00

ACCOUNT Scott Chaney, Drawing — ACCOUNT NO. 3140

DATE		ITEM	POST. REF.	DEBIT	CREDIT	BALANCE DEBIT	BALANCE CREDIT
19-- Dec.	31	Balance	✓			14 720 00	

ACCOUNT Income Summary — ACCOUNT NO. 3150

DATE		ITEM	POST. REF.	DEBIT	CREDIT	BALANCE DEBIT	BALANCE CREDIT

ACCOUNT Sales — ACCOUNT NO. 4110

DATE		ITEM	POST. REF.	DEBIT	CREDIT	BALANCE DEBIT	BALANCE CREDIT
19-- Dec.	31	Balance	✓				316 000 00

ACCOUNT Purchases — ACCOUNT NO. 5110

DATE		ITEM	POST. REF.	DEBIT	CREDIT	BALANCE DEBIT	BALANCE CREDIT
19-- Dec.	31	Balance	✓			126 450 00	

GENERAL LEDGER

ACCOUNT Advertising Expense ACCOUNT NO. 6110

DATE		ITEM	POST. REF.	DEBIT	CREDIT	BALANCE DEBIT	BALANCE CREDIT
19-- Dec.	31	Balance	✓			4 7 2 0 00	

ACCOUNT Credit Card Fee Expense ACCOUNT NO. 6120

DATE		ITEM	POST. REF.	DEBIT	CREDIT	BALANCE DEBIT	BALANCE CREDIT
19-- Dec.	31	Balance	✓			3 2 6 0 00	

ACCOUNT Insurance Expense ACCOUNT NO. 6130

DATE		ITEM	POST. REF.	DEBIT	CREDIT	BALANCE DEBIT	BALANCE CREDIT

ACCOUNT Miscellaneous Expense ACCOUNT NO. 6140

DATE		ITEM	POST. REF.	DEBIT	CREDIT	BALANCE DEBIT	BALANCE CREDIT
19-- Dec.	31	Balance	✓			1 9 3 0 00	

ACCOUNT Payroll Taxes Expense ACCOUNT NO. 6150

DATE		ITEM	POST. REF.	DEBIT	CREDIT	BALANCE DEBIT	BALANCE CREDIT
19-- Dec.	31	Balance	✓			6 7 7 3 00	

ACCOUNT Rent Expense ACCOUNT NO. 6160

DATE		ITEM	POST. REF.	DEBIT	CREDIT	BALANCE DEBIT	BALANCE CREDIT
19-- Dec.	31	Balance	✓			15 6 0 0 00	

ACCOUNT Salary Expense ACCOUNT NO. 6170

DATE		ITEM	POST. REF.	DEBIT	CREDIT	BALANCE DEBIT	BALANCE CREDIT
19-- Dec.	31	Balance	✓			56 7 8 7 00	

PROBLEM 20-1, concluded

[2, 4, 5]

GENERAL LEDGER

ACCOUNT Supplies Expense—Office ACCOUNT NO. 6175

DATE		ITEM	POST. REF.	DEBIT	CREDIT	BALANCE DEBIT	BALANCE CREDIT

ACCOUNT Supplies Expense—Store ACCOUNT NO. 6180

DATE		ITEM	POST. REF.	DEBIT	CREDIT	BALANCE DEBIT	BALANCE CREDIT

ACCOUNT Utilities Expense ACCOUNT NO. 6190

DATE		ITEM	POST. REF.	DEBIT	CREDIT	BALANCE DEBIT	BALANCE CREDIT
19-- Dec.	31	Balance	✓			2 9 4 0 00	

[5]

ACCOUNT TITLE	DEBIT	CREDIT

Name ______________________ Date ________ Class ______

MASTERY PROBLEM 20-M, p. 482
[1–4]

Journalizing and posting adjusting and closing entries; preparing a post-closing trial balance

GENERAL JOURNAL

PAGE 25

DATE		ACCOUNT TITLE	DOC. NO.	POST. REF.	DEBIT	CREDIT

[2, 4, 5]

GENERAL LEDGER

ACCOUNT Cash — ACCOUNT NO. 1110

DATE		ITEM	POST. REF.	DEBIT	CREDIT	BALANCE DEBIT	BALANCE CREDIT
19-- Dec.	31	Balance	✓			22 580 00	

ACCOUNT Petty Cash — ACCOUNT NO. 1120

DATE		ITEM	POST. REF.	DEBIT	CREDIT	BALANCE DEBIT	BALANCE CREDIT
19-- Dec.	31	Balance	✓			500 00	

ACCOUNT Accounts Receivable — ACCOUNT NO. 1130

DATE		ITEM	POST. REF.	DEBIT	CREDIT	BALANCE DEBIT	BALANCE CREDIT
19-- Dec.	31	Balance	✓			8 630 00	

ACCOUNT Merchandise Inventory — ACCOUNT NO. 1140

DATE		ITEM	POST. REF.	DEBIT	CREDIT	BALANCE DEBIT	BALANCE CREDIT
19-- Jan.	1	Balance	✓			288 640 00	

ACCOUNT Supplies—Office — ACCOUNT NO. 1145

DATE		ITEM	POST. REF.	DEBIT	CREDIT	BALANCE DEBIT	BALANCE CREDIT
19-- Dec.	31	Balance	✓			4 830 00	

ACCOUNT Supplies—Store — ACCOUNT NO. 1150

DATE		ITEM	POST. REF.	DEBIT	CREDIT	BALANCE DEBIT	BALANCE CREDIT
19-- Dec.	31	Balance	✓			4 280 00	

ACCOUNT Prepaid Insurance — ACCOUNT NO. 1160

DATE		ITEM	POST. REF.	DEBIT	CREDIT	BALANCE DEBIT	BALANCE CREDIT
19-- Dec.	31	Balance	✓			3 030 00	

Name ______________________ Date ________ Class ________

MASTERY PROBLEM 20-M, continued
[2, 4, 5]

GENERAL LEDGER

ACCOUNT Accounts Payable — ACCOUNT NO. 2110

DATE		ITEM	POST. REF.	DEBIT	CREDIT	BALANCE DEBIT	BALANCE CREDIT
19-- Dec.	31	Balance	✓				7 830 00

ACCOUNT Employee Income Tax Payable — ACCOUNT NO. 2120

DATE		ITEM	POST. REF.	DEBIT	CREDIT	BALANCE DEBIT	BALANCE CREDIT
19-- Dec.	31	Balance	✓				435 00

ACCOUNT FICA Tax Payable — ACCOUNT NO. 2130

DATE		ITEM	POST. REF.	DEBIT	CREDIT	BALANCE DEBIT	BALANCE CREDIT
19-- Dec.	31	Balance	✓				825 00

ACCOUNT Sales Tax Payable — ACCOUNT NO. 2140

DATE		ITEM	POST. REF.	DEBIT	CREDIT	BALANCE DEBIT	BALANCE CREDIT
19-- Dec.	31	Balance	✓				1 630 00

ACCOUNT Unemployment Tax Payable—Federal — ACCOUNT NO. 2150

DATE		ITEM	POST. REF.	DEBIT	CREDIT	BALANCE DEBIT	BALANCE CREDIT
19-- Dec.	31	Balance	✓				39 60

ACCOUNT Unemployment Tax Payable—State — ACCOUNT NO. 2160

DATE		ITEM	POST. REF.	DEBIT	CREDIT	BALANCE DEBIT	BALANCE CREDIT
19-- Dec.	31	Balance	✓				267 30

ACCOUNT Marcus Florie, Capital — ACCOUNT NO. 3110

DATE		ITEM	POST. REF.	DEBIT	CREDIT	BALANCE DEBIT	BALANCE CREDIT
19-- Dec.	31	Balance	✓				130 525 10

MASTERY PROBLEM 20-M, continued
[2, 4, 5]

GENERAL LEDGER

ACCOUNT Marcus Florie, Drawing — ACCOUNT NO. 3120

DATE		ITEM	POST. REF.	DEBIT	CREDIT	BALANCE DEBIT	BALANCE CREDIT
19-- Dec.	31	Balance	✓			18 2 3 0 00	

ACCOUNT Karen Rader, Capital — ACCOUNT NO. 3130

DATE		ITEM	POST. REF.	DEBIT	CREDIT	BALANCE DEBIT	BALANCE CREDIT
19-- Dec.	31	Balance	✓				128 3 2 2 00

ACCOUNT Karen Rader, Drawing — ACCOUNT NO. 3140

DATE		ITEM	POST. REF.	DEBIT	CREDIT	BALANCE DEBIT	BALANCE CREDIT
19-- Dec.	31	Balance	✓			18 7 1 0 00	

ACCOUNT Income Summary — ACCOUNT NO. 3150

DATE		ITEM	POST. REF.	DEBIT	CREDIT	BALANCE DEBIT	BALANCE CREDIT

ACCOUNT Sales — ACCOUNT NO. 4110

DATE		ITEM	POST. REF.	DEBIT	CREDIT	BALANCE DEBIT	BALANCE CREDIT
19-- Dec.	31	Balance	✓				325 6 3 0 00

ACCOUNT Purchases — ACCOUNT NO. 5110

DATE		ITEM	POST. REF.	DEBIT	CREDIT	BALANCE DEBIT	BALANCE CREDIT
19-- Dec.	31	Balance	✓			130 4 5 0 00	

ACCOUNT Advertising Expense — ACCOUNT NO. 6110

DATE		ITEM	POST. REF.	DEBIT	CREDIT	BALANCE DEBIT	BALANCE CREDIT
19-- Dec.	31	Balance	✓			5 1 8 0 00	

GENERAL LEDGER

ACCOUNT Credit Card Fee Expense — ACCOUNT NO. 6120

DATE		ITEM	POST. REF.	DEBIT	CREDIT	BALANCE DEBIT	BALANCE CREDIT
19-- Dec.	31	Balance	✓			3 420 00	

ACCOUNT Insurance Expense — ACCOUNT NO. 6130

DATE		ITEM	POST. REF.	DEBIT	CREDIT	BALANCE DEBIT	BALANCE CREDIT

ACCOUNT Miscellaneous Expense — ACCOUNT NO. 6140

DATE		ITEM	POST. REF.	DEBIT	CREDIT	BALANCE DEBIT	BALANCE CREDIT
19-- Dec.	31	Balance	✓			2 060 00	

ACCOUNT Payroll Taxes Expense — ACCOUNT NO. 6150

DATE		ITEM	POST. REF.	DEBIT	CREDIT	BALANCE DEBIT	BALANCE CREDIT
19-- Dec.	31	Balance	✓			7 124 00	

ACCOUNT Rent Expense — ACCOUNT NO. 6160

DATE		ITEM	POST. REF.	DEBIT	CREDIT	BALANCE DEBIT	BALANCE CREDIT
19-- Dec.	31	Balance	✓			15 600 00	

ACCOUNT Salary Expense — ACCOUNT NO. 6170

DATE		ITEM	POST. REF.	DEBIT	CREDIT	BALANCE DEBIT	BALANCE CREDIT
19-- Dec.	31	Balance	✓			59 360 00	

ACCOUNT Supplies Expense—Office — ACCOUNT NO. 6175

DATE		ITEM	POST. REF.	DEBIT	CREDIT	BALANCE DEBIT	BALANCE CREDIT

[2, 4, 5]

GENERAL LEDGER

ACCOUNT Supplies Expense—Store ACCOUNT NO. 6180

DATE		ITEM	POST. REF.	DEBIT	CREDIT	BALANCE DEBIT	BALANCE CREDIT

ACCOUNT Utilities Expense ACCOUNT NO. 6190

DATE		ITEM	POST. REF.	DEBIT	CREDIT	BALANCE DEBIT	BALANCE CREDIT
19-- Dec.	31	Balance	✓			2 880 00	

[5]

ACCOUNT TITLE	DEBIT	CREDIT

Begin this problem on pages 286 and 287.

[2, 3]

			% OF NET SALES

[3, 4]

CHALLENGE PROBLEM 20-C, p. 483
[1–3, 5, 6, 8]

Plaza Book

Work

For Year Ended

ACCOUNT TITLE	1 TRIAL BALANCE DEBIT	2 TRIAL BALANCE CREDIT	3 ADJUSTMENTS DEBIT	4 ADJUSTMENTS CREDIT
Cash	21 340 00			
Accounts Receivable	8 955 00			
Merchandise Inventory	218 320 00			
Supplies—Office	5 180 00			
Supplies—Store	4 275 00			
Prepaid Insurance	3 960 00			
Accounts Payable		8 820 00		
Sales Tax Payable		1 270 00		
Karla Sykes, Capital		88 305 00		
Karla Sykes, Drawing	13 920 00			
Keith Sykes, Capital		85 135 00		
Keith Sykes, Drawing	13 670 00			
Income Summary				
Sales		255 420 00		
Purchases	127 250 00			
Advertising Expense	5 310 00			
Insurance Expense				
Miscellaneous Expense	2 370 00			
Rent Expense	14 400 00			
Supplies Expense—Office				
Supplies Expense—Store				
	438 950 00	438 950 00		

Name ______________________ Date ________ Class ______

CHALLENGE PROBLEM 20-C, continued
[1–3, 5, 6, 8]

Center

Sheet

December 31, 19--

	5	6	7	8	9	10	
	ADJUSTED TRIAL BALANCE		INCOME STATEMENT		BALANCE SHEET		
	DEBIT	CREDIT	DEBIT	CREDIT	DEBIT	CREDIT	
1							1
2							2
3							3
4							4
5							5
6							6
7							7
8							8
9							9
10							10
11							11
12							12
13							13
14							14
15							15
16							16
17							17
18							18
19							19
20							20
21							21
22							22
23							23
24							24
25							25
26							26
27							27
28							28
29							29
30							30
31							31
32							32

[4, 5]

[5]

[6–9]

GENERAL JOURNAL

PAGE 25

DATE		ACCOUNT TITLE	DOC. NO.	POST. REF.	DEBIT	CREDIT

Name ______________________ Date ________ Class ______

CHALLENGE PROBLEM 20-C, continued
[4, 7, 9, 10]

GENERAL LEDGER

ACCOUNT Cash — ACCOUNT NO. 1110

DATE		ITEM	POST. REF.	DEBIT	CREDIT	BALANCE DEBIT	BALANCE CREDIT
19-- Dec.	31	Balance	✓			21 340 00	

ACCOUNT Accounts Receivable — ACCOUNT NO. 1120

DATE		ITEM	POST. REF.	DEBIT	CREDIT	BALANCE DEBIT	BALANCE CREDIT
19-- Dec.	31	Balance	✓			8 955 00	

ACCOUNT Merchandise Inventory — ACCOUNT NO. 1130

DATE		ITEM	POST. REF.	DEBIT	CREDIT	BALANCE DEBIT	BALANCE CREDIT
19-- Jan.	1	Balance	✓			218 320 00	

ACCOUNT Supplies—Office — ACCOUNT NO. 1140

DATE		ITEM	POST. REF.	DEBIT	CREDIT	BALANCE DEBIT	BALANCE CREDIT
19-- Dec.	31	Balance	✓			5 180 00	

ACCOUNT Supplies—Store — ACCOUNT NO. 1150

DATE		ITEM	POST. REF.	DEBIT	CREDIT	BALANCE DEBIT	BALANCE CREDIT
19-- Dec.	31	Balance	✓			4 275 00	

ACCOUNT Prepaid Insurance — ACCOUNT NO. 1160

DATE		ITEM	POST. REF.	DEBIT	CREDIT	BALANCE DEBIT	BALANCE CREDIT
19-- Dec.	31	Balance	✓			3 960 00	

ACCOUNT Accounts Payable — ACCOUNT NO. 2110

DATE		ITEM	POST. REF.	DEBIT	CREDIT	BALANCE DEBIT	BALANCE CREDIT
19-- Dec.	31	Balance	✓				8 820 00

GENERAL LEDGER

ACCOUNT Sales Tax Payable — ACCOUNT NO. 2120

DATE		ITEM	POST. REF.	DEBIT	CREDIT	BALANCE DEBIT	BALANCE CREDIT
19-- Dec.	31	Balance	✓				1 270 00

ACCOUNT Karla Sykes, Capital — ACCOUNT NO. 3110

DATE		ITEM	POST. REF.	DEBIT	CREDIT	BALANCE DEBIT	BALANCE CREDIT
19-- Dec.	31	Balance	✓				88 305 00

ACCOUNT Karla Sykes, Drawing — ACCOUNT NO. 3120

DATE		ITEM	POST. REF.	DEBIT	CREDIT	BALANCE DEBIT	BALANCE CREDIT
19-- Dec.	31	Balance	✓			13 920 00	

ACCOUNT Keith Sykes, Capital — ACCOUNT NO. 3130

DATE		ITEM	POST. REF.	DEBIT	CREDIT	BALANCE DEBIT	BALANCE CREDIT
19-- Dec.	31	Balance	✓				85 135 00

ACCOUNT Keith Sykes, Drawing — ACCOUNT NO. 3140

DATE		ITEM	POST. REF.	DEBIT	CREDIT	BALANCE DEBIT	BALANCE CREDIT
19-- Dec.	31	Balance	✓			13 670 00	

ACCOUNT Income Summary — ACCOUNT NO. 3150

DATE		ITEM	POST. REF.	DEBIT	CREDIT	BALANCE DEBIT	BALANCE CREDIT

Name ______________________ Date ________ Class ______

CHALLENGE PROBLEM 20-C, continued
[4, 7, 9, 10]

GENERAL LEDGER

ACCOUNT Sales — ACCOUNT NO. 4110

DATE		ITEM	POST. REF.	DEBIT	CREDIT	BALANCE DEBIT	BALANCE CREDIT
19-- Dec.	31	Balance	✓				255 4 2 0 00

ACCOUNT Purchases — ACCOUNT NO. 5110

DATE		ITEM	POST. REF.	DEBIT	CREDIT	BALANCE DEBIT	BALANCE CREDIT
19-- Dec.	31	Balance	✓			127 2 5 0 00	

ACCOUNT Advertising Expense — ACCOUNT NO. 6110

DATE		ITEM	POST. REF.	DEBIT	CREDIT	BALANCE DEBIT	BALANCE CREDIT
19-- Dec.	31	Balance	✓			5 3 1 0 00	

ACCOUNT Insurance Expense — ACCOUNT NO. 6120

DATE		ITEM	POST. REF.	DEBIT	CREDIT	BALANCE DEBIT	BALANCE CREDIT

ACCOUNT Miscellaneous Expense — ACCOUNT NO. 6130

DATE		ITEM	POST. REF.	DEBIT	CREDIT	BALANCE DEBIT	BALANCE CREDIT
19-- Dec.	31	Balance	✓			2 3 7 0 00	

ACCOUNT Rent Expense — ACCOUNT NO. 6140

DATE		ITEM	POST. REF.	DEBIT	CREDIT	BALANCE DEBIT	BALANCE CREDIT
19-- Dec.	31	Balance	✓			14 4 0 0 00	

ACCOUNT Supplies Expense—Office — ACCOUNT NO. 6150

DATE		ITEM	POST. REF.	DEBIT	CREDIT	BALANCE DEBIT	BALANCE CREDIT

[4, 7, 9, 10]

GENERAL LEDGER

ACCOUNT Supplies Expense—Store ACCOUNT NO. 6160

DATE		ITEM	POST. REF.	DEBIT	CREDIT	BALANCE	
						DEBIT	CREDIT

[10]

ACCOUNT TITLE	DEBIT	CREDIT

Name ______________________ Date ________ Class ______

REINFORCEMENT ACTIVITY 2
PART B–p. 484

AN ACCOUNTING CYCLE FOR A PARTNERSHIP: END-OF-FISCAL-PERIOD WORK [12–18]

The ledgers used in Part A are needed to complete Part B.

		1	2	3	4	5	6	7	8	
	ACCOUNT TITLE	TRIAL BALANCE		ADJUSTMENTS		INCOME STATEMENT		BALANCE SHEET		
		DEBIT	CREDIT	DEBIT	CREDIT	DEBIT	CREDIT	DEBIT	CREDIT	
1										1
2										2
3										3
4										4
5										5
6										6
7										7
8										8
9										9
10										10
11										11
12										12
13										13
14										14
15										15
16										16
17										17
18										18
19										19
20										20
21										21
22										22
23										23
24										24
25										25
26										26
27										27

[12–18]

	ACCOUNT TITLE	1 TRIAL BALANCE DEBIT	2 TRIAL BALANCE CREDIT	3 ADJUSTMENTS DEBIT	4 ADJUSTMENTS CREDIT	5 INCOME STATEMENT DEBIT	6 INCOME STATEMENT CREDIT	7 BALANCE SHEET DEBIT	8 BALANCE SHEET CREDIT	
1										1
2										2
3										3
4										4
5										5
6										6
7										7
8										8
9										9
10										10
11										11
12										12
13										13
14										14
15										15
16										16
17										17
18										18
19										19
20										20
21										21
22										22
23										23
24										24
25										25
26										26
27										27

[14, 15]

% OF NET SALES

[15, 16]

[16, 17]

REINFORCEMENT ACTIVITY 2
PART B–continued
[18, 19]

GENERAL JOURNAL

PAGE 13

DATE		ACCOUNT TITLE	DOC. NO.	POST. REF.	DEBIT	CREDIT

Name ______________________ Date ________ Class ______

REINFORCEMENT ACTIVITY 2
PART B–continued
[20]

ACCOUNT TITLE	DEBIT	CREDIT

Extra form

ACCOUNT TITLE	DEBIT	CREDIT

Name ______________________ Date ________ Class ________

COMPUTER APPLICATION 4, p. 491

[3]

AUTOMATED ACCOUNTING CYCLE FOR A PARTNERSHIP: END-OF-FISCAL-PERIOD WORK

RUN DATE ____/____/____ (MM DD YY)

BATCH NO. ______

GENERAL LEDGER
Input Form

Problem No. ________

FORM GL-2

	1 DAY	2 DOC. NO.	3 ACCOUNT NUMBER	4 DEBIT AMOUNT	5 CREDIT AMOUNT	
1						1
2						2
3						3
4						4
5						5
6						6
7						7
8						8
9						9
10						10
11						11
12						12
13						13
14						14
15						15
16						16
17						17
18						18
19						19
20						20
21						21
22						22
23						23
24						24
25						25
			BATCH TOTALS			

RUN DATE ____/____/____
MM DD YY

BATCH NO. [ ]

GENERAL LEDGER
Input Form

Problem No. ________

FORM GL-2

	1	2	3	4	5	
	DAY	DOC. NO.	ACCOUNT NUMBER	DEBIT AMOUNT	CREDIT AMOUNT	
1						1
2						2
3						3
4						4
5						5
6						6
7						7
8						8
9						9
10						10
11						11
12						12
13						13
14						14
15						15
16						16
17						17
18						18
19						19
20						20
21						21
22						22
23						23
24						24
25						25
			BATCH TOTALS			

Perfect Score..... 51 Name ____________________

Deduct......... ___ Date ______________ Class ______________

Your Score..... ___ Checked by ____________________

STUDY GUIDE 21

UNIT A—Identifying Accounting Terms

DIRECTIONS: Select the one term in Column I that best fits each definition in Column II. Print the letter identifying your choice in the Answers column.

Column I

A. capital stock
B. cash discount
C. cash over
D. cash short
E. corporation
F. credit memorandum
G. debit memorandum
H. list price
I. purchases allowance
J. purchases discount
K. purchases return
L. sales allowance
M. sales discount
N. sales return
O. share of stock
P. trade discount

Column II	Answers	For Scoring
0. A business' printed or catalog price	H	**0.** ✓
1. An organization with the legal rights of a person and which may be owned by many persons		**1.**
2. A cash discount on purchases taken by a customer		**2.**
3. A cash discount on sales		**3.**
4. Total shares of ownership in a corporation		**4.**
5. A reduction in the list price granted to customers		**5.**
6. Each unit of ownership in a corporation		**6.**
7. A deduction that a vendor allows on the invoice amount to encourage prompt payment		**7.**
8. A petty cash on hand amount that is more than a recorded amount		**8.**
9. Credit allowed for the purchase price of returned merchandise, resulting in a decrease in the customer's accounts payable		**9.**
10. A form prepared by the vendor showing the amount deducted for sales returns and allowances		**10.**
11. A petty cash on hand amount that is less than a recorded amount		**11.**
12. Credit allowed to a customer for the sales price of returned merchandise, resulting in a decrease in the vendor's accounts receivable		**12.**
13. Credit allowed for part of the purchase price of merchandise that is not returned, resulting in a decrease in the customer's accounts payable		**13.**
14. Credit allowed a customer for part of the sales price of merchandise that is not returned, resulting in a decrease in the vendor's accounts receivable		**14.**
15. A form prepared by the customer showing the price deduction taken by the customer for returns and allowances		**15.**

UNIT B—Analyzing Discounts, Returns and Allowances, and Petty Cash

DIRECTIONS: Place a check mark in the proper Answers column to show whether each of the following statements is true or false.

	Answers		For Scoring
	True	False	
0. Purchases discounts are subtracted from the purchases journal total		✓	**0.** ✓
1. Each amount in the amount column of a purchases journal is posted individually as a credit to a vendor account in the accounts payable ledger			**1.**
2. Trade discounts are recorded in the purchases discount account			**2.**
3. The terms of sale 1/10, n/30 mean that the customer may deduct 1% of the invoice amount if payment is made within 30 days of the invoice date			**3.**
4. The terms of sale 2/15, n/30 mean that 2% of the invoice amount may be deducted if paid within 15 days of the invoice date or the total invoice amount must be paid within 30 days			**4.**
5. The amount recorded in the Debit column of a general journal for a purchases return must be posted to two different accounts			**5.**
6. A petty cash fund is always replenished at the end of a fiscal period			**6.**

UNIT B—Analyzing Discounts, Returns and Allowances, and Petty Cash *(continued)*

	Answers True	Answers False	For Scoring
7. The amount to replenish a petty cash fund will always equal the receipts total of petty cash expenditures			7.
8. Purchases on account are recorded in a purchases journal at list price...			8.
9. The practice of reporting financial information for a specific period of time is an application of the going concern concept			9.
10. Sales returns and allowances always reduce revenue			10.
11. Sales discounts are recorded as a debit to Sales			11.
12. A return of merchandise sold is recorded in a sales journal			12.
13. Sales Tax Payable is a contra account to the sales account			13.
14. Each amount in the Accounts Receivable Credit column of a cash receipts journal is posted individually to the account of the customer named in the Account Title column			14.
15. Each amount in the General Credit column of a cash receipts journal is posted separately to the accounts receivable ledger account named in the Account Title column			15.
16. The sales returns and allowances account has a normal debit balance...			16.
17. The sales discount account has a normal credit balance			17.
18. The account Sales Returns and Allowances is a contra account to Sales			18.
19. Sales discount is a percentage of the sales invoice amount			19.
20. Posting an amount to the wrong customer account results in an incorrect balance in the general ledger's accounts receivable account			20.
21. The best order to post special journal is (1) sales, (2) purchases, (3) general, (4) cash receipts, and (5) cash payments			21.

UNIT C—Analyzing Transactions Affecting Discounts, Returns and Allowances, and Petty Cash

DIRECTIONS: In Answers Column 1, print the abbreviation for the journal in which each transaction is to be recorded. In Columns 2 and 3, print the letters identifying the accounts to be debited and credited for each transaction.
S—sales journal G—general journal CP—cash payments journal

Account Title

A. Accounts Payable
B. Accounts Receivable
C. Mary Banks
D. Chris Gain
E. Cash
F. Cash Short and Over
G. Miscellaneous Expense
H. Purchases Discount
I. Purchases Returns and Allowances
J. Sales
K. Sales Discount
L. Sales Returns and Allowances
M. Sales Tax Payable
N. Sun Company
O. Supplies

Transaction	Answers: Journal	Answers: Debit	Answers: Credit	For Scoring: Journal	For Scoring: Debit	For Scoring: Credit
0–0–0. Sold merchandise on account to Mary Banks plus sales tax	S	B, C	L, O	0. ✓	0. ✓	0. ✓
1–2–3. Granted credit to Chris Gain for merchandise returned plus sales tax....				1.	2.	3.
4–5–6. Received cash on account from Mary Banks for sales with sales tax less sales discount				4.	5.	6.
7–8–9. Paid cash to replenish the petty cash fund: miscellaneous, supplies. Cash on hand is less than should be on hand				7.	8.	9.
10–11–12. Paid cash on account to Sun Co.; less a purchases discount				10.	11.	12.
13–14–15. Returned merchandise to Sun Company				13.	14.	15.

Analyzing the journalizing of purchases and cash payments transactions

The solution to Drill 21-D1 is needed to complete Drill 21-D2.

Trans. No.	(A) Account(s) Debited	(B) Account(s) Credited	(C) Journal in Which Recorded	(D) Name of Amount Column(s) Used in Journal	(E)
				For Amount Debited	For Amount Credited
1.	Accounts Pay. Hubburd Co.	Cash	Cash Payments	Accounts Pay. Debit	Cash Credit
2.					
3.					
4.					
5.					
6.					
7.					
8.					
9.					
10.					
11.					

Analyzing the posting of purchases and cash payments transactions

DRILL 21-D2, p. 533
[1, 2]

The solution to Drill 21-D1 is needed to complete Drill 21-D2.

Trans. No.	(A) Accounts Affected	(B) Amounts Posted Individually to: General Ledger	(C) Amounts Posted Individually to: Accounts Payable Ledger	(D) Amounts Not Posted Individually to Any Ledger
1.	Accounts Payable			✓
	Hubburd Co.		✓	
	Cash			✓
2.				
3.				
4.				
5.				
6.				
7.				
8.				
9.				
10.				
11.				

Figuring petty cash short and petty cash over

Company	Petty Cash Record				Amount of Cash in Cash Box	Amount of Cash over (+) or Cash short (−)
	Beginning Balance	Distribution of Payments				
		Supplies	Advertising Expense	Miscellaneous Expense		
A	$300.00	$46.25	$76.32	$91.87	$ 85.56	
B	250.00	24.76	82.35	18.21	120.68	
C	150.00	12.43	51.45	14.15	78.97	
D	200.00	53.98	25.34	34.25	84.43	

Analyzing replenishing a petty cash fund

DRILL 21-D4, p. 533

May 31 entry

July 31 entry

June 30 entry

August 31 entry

Analyzing the journalizing of sales and cash receipts transactions *DRILL 21-D5, p. 534*

The solution to Drill 21-D5 is needed to complete Drill 21-D6.

Trans. No.	(A) Account(s) Debited	(B) Account(s) Credited	(C) Journal in Which Recorded	(D) Name of Amount Column(s) Used in Journal	(E)
				For Amount Debited	For Amount Credited
1.	Accounts Rec. James Harding	Sales Sales Tax Payable	Sales	Accounts Rec. Debit	Sales Credit Sales Tax Pay. Credit
2.					
3.					
4.					
5.					
6.					
7.					
8.					

Analyzing the posting of sales and cash receipts transactions

The solution to Drill 21-D5 is needed to complete Drill 21-D6.

Trans. No.	(A) Accounts Affected	(B) Amounts Posted Individually to General Ledger	(C) Amounts Posted Individually to Accounts Receivable Ledger	(D) Amounts Not Posted Individually to Any Ledger
1.	Accounts Receivable			✓
	James Harding		✓	
	Sales			✓
	Sales Tax Payable			✓
2.				
3.				
4.				
5.				
6.				
7.				
8.				

PURCHASES JOURNAL

PAGE

DATE		ACCOUNT CREDITED	PURCH. NO.	POST. REF.	PURCHASES DR. ACCTS. PAY. CR.

Name ______________________ Date ________ Class ______

PROBLEM 21-1, p. 535
[1, 2]

Journalizing and posting purchase and cash payment transactions

PURCHASES JOURNAL

PAGE 4

	DATE		ACCOUNT CREDITED	PURCH. NO.	POST. REF.	PURCHASES DR. ACCTS. PAY. CR.	
1							1
2							2
3							3
4							4
5							5
6							6
7							7
8							8
9							9
10							10
11							11
12							12
13							13
14							14
15							15

[1]

GENERAL JOURNAL

PAGE 4

	DATE		ACCOUNT TITLE	DOC. NO.	POST. REF.	DEBIT	CREDIT	
1								1
2								2
3								3
4								4
5								5
6								6
7								7
8								8
9								9
10								10
11								11
12								12

[1, 3]

CASH PAYMENTS JOURNAL

PAGE 4

DATE		ACCOUNT TITLE	CK. NO.	POST. REF.	1 GENERAL DEBIT	2 GENERAL CREDIT	3 ACCOUNTS PAYABLE DEBIT	4 PURCHASES DISCOUNT CREDIT	5 CASH CREDIT

Name ______________________ Date ________ Class ______

PROBLEM 21-1, continued
[1–3]

GENERAL LEDGER

ACCOUNT Cash ACCOUNT NO. 1105

DATE		ITEM	POST. REF.	DEBIT	CREDIT	BALANCE DEBIT	BALANCE CREDIT
19-- April	1	Balance	✓			41 4 1 8 00	

ACCOUNT Petty Cash ACCOUNT NO. 1110

DATE		ITEM	POST. REF.	DEBIT	CREDIT	BALANCE DEBIT	BALANCE CREDIT
19-- April	1	Balance	✓			2 0 0 00	

ACCOUNT Supplies ACCOUNT NO. 1140

DATE		ITEM	POST. REF.	DEBIT	CREDIT	BALANCE DEBIT	BALANCE CREDIT
19-- April	1	Balance	✓			1 5 0 9 00	

ACCOUNT Accounts Payable ACCOUNT NO. 2115

DATE		ITEM	POST. REF.	DEBIT	CREDIT	BALANCE DEBIT	BALANCE CREDIT
19-- April	1	Balance	✓				7 5 3 2 00

ACCOUNT Purchases ACCOUNT NO. 5105

DATE		ITEM	POST. REF.	DEBIT	CREDIT	BALANCE DEBIT	BALANCE CREDIT

[1–3]

GENERAL LEDGER

ACCOUNT Purchases Discount — ACCOUNT NO. 5110

DATE		ITEM	POST. REF.	DEBIT	CREDIT	BALANCE DEBIT	BALANCE CREDIT

ACCOUNT Purchases Returns and Allowances — ACCOUNT NO. 5115

DATE		ITEM	POST. REF.	DEBIT	CREDIT	BALANCE DEBIT	BALANCE CREDIT

ACCOUNT Advertising Expense — ACCOUNT NO. 6105

DATE		ITEM	POST. REF.	DEBIT	CREDIT	BALANCE DEBIT	BALANCE CREDIT

ACCOUNT Miscellaneous Expense — ACCOUNT NO. 6130

DATE		ITEM	POST. REF.	DEBIT	CREDIT	BALANCE DEBIT	BALANCE CREDIT

ACCOUNT Rent Expense — ACCOUNT NO. 6140

DATE		ITEM	POST. REF.	DEBIT	CREDIT	BALANCE DEBIT	BALANCE CREDIT

ACCOUNT Cash Short and Over — ACCOUNT NO. 8105

DATE		ITEM	POST. REF.	DEBIT	CREDIT	BALANCE DEBIT	BALANCE CREDIT

Name ____________ Date ________ Class ______

PROBLEM 21-1, continued
[1, 4]

ACCOUNTS PAYABLE LEDGER

VENDOR Kelmans Supply **VENDOR NO.** 210

DATE		ITEM	POST. REF.	DEBIT	CREDIT	CREDIT BALANCE
19-- April	1	Balance	✓			1 678 00

VENDOR Office Emporium **VENDOR NO.** 220

DATE		ITEM	POST. REF.	DEBIT	CREDIT	CREDIT BALANCE

VENDOR Potters Equipment **VENDOR NO.** 230

DATE		ITEM	POST. REF.	DEBIT	CREDIT	CREDIT BALANCE
19-- April	1	Balance	✓			5 250 00

VENDOR Threads, Inc. **VENDOR NO.** 240

DATE		ITEM	POST. REF.	DEBIT	CREDIT	CREDIT BALANCE
19-- April	1	Balance	✓			604 00

VENDOR York Company **VENDOR NO.** 250

DATE		ITEM	POST. REF.	DEBIT	CREDIT	CREDIT BALANCE

PROBLEM 21-1, concluded

[4]

Extra form

Name ______________________________ Date ________ Class _______

PROBLEM 21-2, p. 537
[1, 2]

Journalizing and posting sales and cash receipts transactions

SALES JOURNAL

PAGE 6

DATE		ACCOUNT DEBITED	SALE NO.	POST. REF.	1 ACCOUNTS RECEIVABLE DEBIT	2 SALES CREDIT	3 SALES TAX PAYABLE CREDIT

[1]

GENERAL JOURNAL

PAGE 6

DATE		ACCOUNT TITLE	DOC. NO.	POST. REF.	DEBIT	CREDIT

[1, 3–5]

CASH RECEIPTS JOURNAL

PAGE 6

	DATE	ACCOUNT TITLE	Doc. No.	Post. Ref.	1 GENERAL DEBIT	2 GENERAL CREDIT	3 ACCOUNTS RECEIVABLE CREDIT	4 SALES CREDIT	5 SALES TAX PAYABLE DEBIT	6 SALES TAX PAYABLE CREDIT	7 SALES DISCOUNT DEBIT	8 CASH DEBIT	
1													1
2													2
3													3
4													4
5													5
6													6
7													7
8													8
9													9
10													10
11													11
12													12
13													13
14													14
15													15
16													16
17													17
18													18
19													19
20													20
21													21
22													22
23													23
24													24
25													25

Name ______________________ Date ________ Class ______

PROBLEM 21-2, continued
[1, 2, 5]

GENERAL LEDGER

ACCOUNT Cash — ACCOUNT NO. 1105

DATE		ITEM	POST. REF.	DEBIT	CREDIT	BALANCE DEBIT	BALANCE CREDIT
19-- June	1	Balance	✓			9 2 1 1 00	

ACCOUNT Accounts Receivable — ACCOUNT NO. 1125

DATE		ITEM	POST. REF.	DEBIT	CREDIT	BALANCE DEBIT	BALANCE CREDIT
19-- June	1	Balance	✓			3 3 6 1 48	

ACCOUNT Sales Tax Payable — ACCOUNT NO. 2135

DATE		ITEM	POST. REF.	DEBIT	CREDIT	BALANCE DEBIT	BALANCE CREDIT

ACCOUNT Sales — ACCOUNT NO. 4105

DATE		ITEM	POST. REF.	DEBIT	CREDIT	BALANCE DEBIT	BALANCE CREDIT

ACCOUNT Sales Discount — ACCOUNT NO. 4110

DATE		ITEM	POST. REF.	DEBIT	CREDIT	BALANCE DEBIT	BALANCE CREDIT

ACCOUNT Sales Returns and Allowances — ACCOUNT NO. 4115

DATE		ITEM	POST. REF.	DEBIT	CREDIT	BALANCE DEBIT	BALANCE CREDIT

[1, 6]

ACCOUNTS RECEIVABLE LEDGER

CUSTOMER Beverly's Gift Shop **CUSTOMER NO.** 110

DATE		ITEM	POST. REF.	DEBIT	CREDIT	DEBIT BALANCE
19-- June	1	Balance	✓			303 25

CUSTOMER Frank Finnely **CUSTOMER NO.** 120

DATE		ITEM	POST. REF.	DEBIT	CREDIT	DEBIT BALANCE
19-- June	1	Balance	✓			691 48

CUSTOMER Geno's **CUSTOMER NO.** 130

DATE		ITEM	POST. REF.	DEBIT	CREDIT	DEBIT BALANCE
19-- June	1	Balance	✓			346 00

CUSTOMER Susan Malta **CUSTOMER NO.** 140

DATE		ITEM	POST. REF.	DEBIT	CREDIT	DEBIT BALANCE
19-- June	1	Balance	✓			475 75

CUSTOMER Nan and Jenkins Decorators **CUSTOMER NO.** 150

DATE		ITEM	POST. REF.	DEBIT	CREDIT	DEBIT BALANCE

[1, 6]

ACCOUNTS RECEIVABLE LEDGER

CUSTOMER The Import Shop CUSTOMER NO. 160

DATE		ITEM	POST. REF.	DEBIT	CREDIT	DEBIT BALANCE
19-- June	1	Balance	✓			924 00

CUSTOMER Hana Victor CUSTOMER NO. 170

DATE		ITEM	POST. REF.	DEBIT	CREDIT	DEBIT BALANCE
19-- June	1	Balance	✓			621 00

[6]

Journalizing and posting sales, purchases, cash receipts, and cash payments transactions

MASTERY PROBLEM 21-M, p. 539
[1, 2]

SALES JOURNAL

PAGE 8

DATE		ACCOUNT DEBITED	SALE NO.	POST. REF.	1 ACCOUNTS RECEIVABLE DEBIT	2 SALES CREDIT	3 SALES TAX PAYABLE CREDIT

Name ______________________ Date ________ Class ________

MASTERY PROBLEM 21-M, continued
[1, 3]

PURCHASES JOURNAL

PAGE 8

DATE		ACCOUNT CREDITED	PURCH. NO.	POST. REF.	PURCHASES DR. ACCTS. PAY. CR.

[1]

GENERAL JOURNAL

PAGE 8

	DATE		ACCOUNT TITLE	DOC. NO.	POST. REF.	DEBIT	CREDIT	
1								1
2								2
3								3
4								4
5								5
6								6
7								7
8								8
9								9
10								10
11								11
12								12
13								13
14								14
15								15
16								16
17								17
18								18
19								19
20								20
21								21
22								22
23								23
24								24
25								25
26								26
27								27
28								28
29								29
30								30
31								31
32								32

CASH RECEIPTS JOURNAL

PAGE 8

	DATE	ACCOUNT TITLE	DOC. NO.	POST. REF.	1 GENERAL DEBIT	2 GENERAL CREDIT	3 ACCOUNTS RECEIVABLE CREDIT	4 SALES CREDIT	5 SALES TAX PAYABLE DEBIT	6 SALES TAX PAYABLE CREDIT	7 SALES DISCOUNT DEBIT	8 CASH DEBIT	
1													1
2													2
3													3
4													4
5													5
6													6
7													7
8													8
9													9
10													10
11													11
12													12
13													13
14													14
15													15
16													16
17													17
18													18
19													19
20													20
21													21
22													22
23													23
24													24
25													25

[1, 4, 5, 7]

CASH PAYMENTS JOURNAL

PAGE 8

	DATE	ACCOUNT TITLE	CK. NO.	POST. REF.	1 GENERAL DEBIT	2 GENERAL CREDIT	3 ACCOUNTS PAYABLE DEBIT	4 PURCHASES DISCOUNT CREDIT	5 CASH CREDIT	
1										1
2										2
3										3
4										4
5										5
6										6
7										7
8										8
9										9
10										10
11										11
12										12
13										13
14										14
15										15
16										16
17										17
18										18
19										19
20										20
21										21
22										22
23										23
24										24
25										25

GENERAL LEDGER

ACCOUNT Cash — ACCOUNT NO. 1105

DATE		ITEM	POST. REF.	DEBIT	CREDIT	BALANCE DEBIT	BALANCE CREDIT
19-- Aug.	1	Balance	✓			14 789 00	

ACCOUNT Petty Cash — ACCOUNT NO. 1110

DATE		ITEM	POST. REF.	DEBIT	CREDIT	BALANCE DEBIT	BALANCE CREDIT
19-- Aug.	1	Balance	✓			250 00	

ACCOUNT Accounts Receivable — ACCOUNT NO. 1125

DATE		ITEM	POST. REF.	DEBIT	CREDIT	BALANCE DEBIT	BALANCE CREDIT
19-- Aug.	1	Balance	✓			1 631 50	

ACCOUNT Supplies — ACCOUNT NO. 1140

DATE		ITEM	POST. REF.	DEBIT	CREDIT	BALANCE DEBIT	BALANCE CREDIT
19-- Aug.	1	Balance	✓			315 00	

GENERAL LEDGER

ACCOUNT Accounts Payable — ACCOUNT NO. 2115

DATE		ITEM	POST. REF.	DEBIT	CREDIT	BALANCE DEBIT	BALANCE CREDIT
19-- Aug.	1	Balance	✓				1 073 00

ACCOUNT Sales Tax Payable — ACCOUNT NO. 2135

DATE		ITEM	POST. REF.	DEBIT	CREDIT	BALANCE DEBIT	BALANCE CREDIT

ACCOUNT Sales — ACCOUNT NO. 4105

DATE		ITEM	POST. REF.	DEBIT	CREDIT	BALANCE DEBIT	BALANCE CREDIT

ACCOUNT Sales Discount — ACCOUNT NO. 4110

DATE		ITEM	POST. REF.	DEBIT	CREDIT	BALANCE DEBIT	BALANCE CREDIT

ACCOUNT Sales Returns and Allowances — ACCOUNT NO. 4115

DATE		ITEM	POST. REF.	DEBIT	CREDIT	BALANCE DEBIT	BALANCE CREDIT

GENERAL LEDGER

ACCOUNT Purchases ACCOUNT NO. 5105

DATE		ITEM	POST. REF.	DEBIT	CREDIT	BALANCE DEBIT	BALANCE CREDIT

ACCOUNT Purchases Discount ACCOUNT NO. 5110

DATE		ITEM	POST. REF.	DEBIT	CREDIT	BALANCE DEBIT	BALANCE CREDIT

ACCOUNT Purchases Returns and Allowances ACCOUNT NO. 5115

DATE		ITEM	POST. REF.	DEBIT	CREDIT	BALANCE DEBIT	BALANCE CREDIT

ACCOUNT Advertising Expense ACCOUNT NO. 6105

DATE		ITEM	POST. REF.	DEBIT	CREDIT	BALANCE DEBIT	BALANCE CREDIT

ACCOUNT Miscellaneous Expense ACCOUNT NO. 6130

DATE		ITEM	POST. REF.	DEBIT	CREDIT	BALANCE DEBIT	BALANCE CREDIT

ACCOUNT Cash Short and Over ACCOUNT NO. 8105

DATE		ITEM	POST. REF.	DEBIT	CREDIT	BALANCE DEBIT	BALANCE CREDIT

[1, 8]

ACCOUNTS RECEIVABLE LEDGER

CUSTOMER Andrew Anderson CUSTOMER NO. 110

DATE		ITEM	POST. REF.	DEBIT	CREDIT	DEBIT BALANCE
19-- Aug.	1	Balance	✓			229 50

CUSTOMER Jessica Howe CUSTOMER NO. 120

DATE		ITEM	POST. REF.	DEBIT	CREDIT	DEBIT BALANCE
19-- Aug.	1	Balance	✓			376 00

CUSTOMER Alford Lein CUSTOMER NO. 130

DATE		ITEM	POST. REF.	DEBIT	CREDIT	DEBIT BALANCE
19-- Aug.	1	Balance	✓			216 00

CUSTOMER Mandon, Inc. CUSTOMER NO. 140

DATE		ITEM	POST. REF.	DEBIT	CREDIT	DEBIT BALANCE
19-- Aug.	1	Balance	✓			378 00

CUSTOMER Platter Company CUSTOMER NO. 150

DATE		ITEM	POST. REF.	DEBIT	CREDIT	DEBIT BALANCE
19-- Aug.	1	Balance	✓			432 00

Name ______________________ Date ________ Class ________

MASTERY PROBLEM 21-M, continued

[1, 8]

ACCOUNTS PAYABLE LEDGER

VENDOR Barker Pipe Co. VENDOR NO. 210

DATE		ITEM	POST. REF.	DEBIT	CREDIT	CREDIT BALANCE
19-- Aug.	1	Balance	✓			3 6 5 00

VENDOR Fullers Tape Company VENDOR NO. 220

DATE		ITEM	POST. REF.	DEBIT	CREDIT	CREDIT BALANCE
19-- Aug.	1	Balance	✓			7 0 8 00

VENDOR TenCorp Tubing VENDOR NO. 230

DATE		ITEM	POST. REF.	DEBIT	CREDIT	CREDIT BALANCE

VENDOR VENDOR NO.

DATE		ITEM	POST. REF.	DEBIT	CREDIT	CREDIT BALANCE

[8]

Extra Form

MASTERY PROBLEM 21-M, concluded

[8]

Extra Form

Journalizing and posting sales, purchases, cash receipts, and cash payments transactions

CHALLENGE PROBLEM 21-C, p. 540
[1, 2]

SALES JOURNAL

PAGE 4

DATE		ACCOUNT DEBITED	SALE NO.	POST. REF.	1 ACCOUNTS RECEIVABLE DEBIT	2 SALES CREDIT	3 SALES TAX PAYABLE CREDIT

Name ______________________ Date ________ Class ______

CHALLENGE PROBLEM 21-C, continued

[1, 3]

PURCHASES JOURNAL

PAGE 4

DATE		ACCOUNT CREDITED	PURCH. NO.	POST. REF.	PURCHASES DR. ACCTS. PAY. CR.

[1]

GENERAL JOURNAL

PAGE 4

DATE		ACCOUNT TITLE	DOC. NO.	POST. REF.	DEBIT	CREDIT

[1, 4–6]

CASH RECEIPTS JOURNAL

PAGE 4

	DATE	ACCOUNT TITLE	Doc. No.	Post. Ref.	1 GENERAL DEBIT	2 GENERAL CREDIT	3 ACCOUNTS RECEIVABLE CREDIT	4 SALES CREDIT	5 SALES TAX PAYABLE DEBIT	6 SALES TAX PAYABLE CREDIT	7 SALES DISCOUNT DEBIT	8 CASH DEBIT	
1													1
2													2
3													3
4													4
5													5
6													6
7													7
8													8
9													9
10													10
11													11
12													12
13													13
14													14
15													15
16													16
17													17
18													18
19													19
20													20
21													21
22													22
23													23
24													24
25													25

[1, 4, 5, 7]

CASH PAYMENTS JOURNAL

PAGE 4

	DATE	ACCOUNT TITLE	CK. NO.	POST. REF.	1 GENERAL DEBIT	2 GENERAL CREDIT	3 ACCOUNTS PAYABLE DEBIT	4 PURCHASES DISCOUNT CREDIT	5 CASH CREDIT	
1										1
2										2
3										3
4										4
5										5
6										6
7										7
8										8
9										9
10										10
11										11
12										12
13										13
14										14
15										15
16										16
17										17
18										18
19										19
20										20
21										21
22										22
23										23
24										24

GENERAL LEDGER

ACCOUNT Cash — ACCOUNT NO. 1105

DATE		ITEM	POST. REF.	DEBIT	CREDIT	BALANCE DEBIT	BALANCE CREDIT
19-- Apr.	1	Balance	✓			7 6 9 0 00	

ACCOUNT Petty Cash — ACCOUNT NO. 1110

DATE		ITEM	POST. REF.	DEBIT	CREDIT	BALANCE DEBIT	BALANCE CREDIT
19-- Apr.	1	Balance	✓			3 0 0 00	

ACCOUNT Accounts Receivable — ACCOUNT NO. 1125

DATE		ITEM	POST. REF.	DEBIT	CREDIT	BALANCE DEBIT	BALANCE CREDIT
19-- Apr.	1	Balance	✓			1 4 7 9 60	

ACCOUNT Supplies — ACCOUNT NO. 1140

DATE		ITEM	POST. REF.	DEBIT	CREDIT	BALANCE DEBIT	BALANCE CREDIT
19-- Apr.	1	Balance	✓			2 4 0 00	

ACCOUNT Accounts Payable — ACCOUNT NO. 2115

DATE		ITEM	POST. REF.	DEBIT	CREDIT	BALANCE DEBIT	BALANCE CREDIT
19-- Apr.	1	Balance	✓				6 7 3 4 00

GENERAL LEDGER

ACCOUNT Sales Tax Payable — ACCOUNT NO. 2135

DATE		ITEM	POST. REF.	DEBIT	CREDIT	BALANCE DEBIT	BALANCE CREDIT

ACCOUNT Sales — ACCOUNT NO. 4105

DATE		ITEM	POST. REF.	DEBIT	CREDIT	BALANCE DEBIT	BALANCE CREDIT

ACCOUNT Sales Discount — ACCOUNT NO. 4110

DATE		ITEM	POST. REF.	DEBIT	CREDIT	BALANCE DEBIT	BALANCE CREDIT

ACCOUNT Sales Returns and Allowances — ACCOUNT NO. 4115

DATE		ITEM	POST. REF.	DEBIT	CREDIT	BALANCE DEBIT	BALANCE CREDIT

ACCOUNT Purchases — ACCOUNT NO. 5105

DATE		ITEM	POST. REF.	DEBIT	CREDIT	BALANCE DEBIT	BALANCE CREDIT

ACCOUNT Purchases Discount — ACCOUNT NO. 5110

DATE		ITEM	POST. REF.	DEBIT	CREDIT	BALANCE DEBIT	BALANCE CREDIT

[1–3, 6, 7]

GENERAL LEDGER

ACCOUNT Purchases Returns and Allowances — ACCOUNT NO. 5115

DATE	ITEM	POST. REF.	DEBIT	CREDIT	BALANCE DEBIT	BALANCE CREDIT

ACCOUNT Advertising Expense — ACCOUNT NO. 6105

DATE	ITEM	POST. REF.	DEBIT	CREDIT	BALANCE DEBIT	BALANCE CREDIT

ACCOUNT Miscellaneous Expense — ACCOUNT NO. 6130

DATE	ITEM	POST. REF.	DEBIT	CREDIT	BALANCE DEBIT	BALANCE CREDIT

ACCOUNT Rent Expense — ACCOUNT NO. 6140

DATE	ITEM	POST. REF.	DEBIT	CREDIT	BALANCE DEBIT	BALANCE CREDIT

ACCOUNT Cash Short and Over — ACCOUNT NO. 8105

DATE	ITEM	POST. REF.	DEBIT	CREDIT	BALANCE DEBIT	BALANCE CREDIT

ACCOUNT — ACCOUNT NO.

DATE	ITEM	POST. REF.	DEBIT	CREDIT	BALANCE DEBIT	BALANCE CREDIT

[1, 8]

ACCOUNTS RECEIVABLE LEDGER

CUSTOMER Barbra Almon — CUSTOMER NO. 110

DATE		ITEM	POST. REF.	DEBIT	CREDIT	DEBIT BALANCE
19-- Apr.	1	Balance	✓			330 48

CUSTOMER Bland Company — CUSTOMER NO. 120

DATE		ITEM	POST. REF.	DEBIT	CREDIT	DEBIT BALANCE

CUSTOMER James Hart — CUSTOMER NO. 130

DATE		ITEM	POST. REF.	DEBIT	CREDIT	DEBIT BALANCE
19-- Apr.	1	Balance	✓			167 40

CUSTOMER Jefferson Co. — CUSTOMER NO. 140

DATE		ITEM	POST. REF.	DEBIT	CREDIT	DEBIT BALANCE
19-- Apr.	1	Balance	✓			556 20

CUSTOMER Linda Ponder — CUSTOMER NO. 150

DATE		ITEM	POST. REF.	DEBIT	CREDIT	DEBIT BALANCE
19-- Apr.	1	Balance	✓			425 52

Name ______________________ Date ________ Class ________ *CHALLENGE PROBLEM 21-C, continued*

[1, 8]

ACCOUNTS PAYABLE LEDGER

VENDOR Dunn Supplies VENDOR NO. 210

DATE		ITEM	POST. REF.	DEBIT	CREDIT	CREDIT BALANCE
19-- Apr.	1	Balance	✓			1 4 1 3 00

VENDOR Gibson Electric Co. VENDOR NO. 220

DATE		ITEM	POST. REF.	DEBIT	CREDIT	CREDIT BALANCE
19-- Apr.	1	Balance	✓			1 9 4 5 00

VENDOR Roland and Barnes VENDOR NO. 230

DATE		ITEM	POST. REF.	DEBIT	CREDIT	CREDIT BALANCE
19-- Apr.	1	Balance	✓			3 6 6 00

VENDOR Webb Co. VENDOR NO. 240

DATE		ITEM	POST. REF.	DEBIT	CREDIT	CREDIT BALANCE
19-- Apr.	1	Balance	✓			3 0 1 0 00

[8]

[8]

Name ______________________ Date ________ Class ______

REINFORCEMENT ACTIVITY 3
PART A, p. 543
[1, 4, 5]

AN ACCOUNTING CYCLE FOR A CORPORATION:
JOURNALIZING AND POSTING TRANSACTIONS

SALES JOURNAL

PAGE 12

DATE		ACCOUNT DEBITED	SALE NO.	POST. REF.	1 ACCOUNTS RECEIVABLE DEBIT	2 SALES CREDIT	3 SALES TAX PAYABLE CREDIT

PURCHASES JOURNAL

PAGE 12

DATE		ACCOUNT CREDITED	PURCH. NO.	POST. REF.	PURCHASES DR. ACCTS. PAY. CR.

Name ______________________ Date ________ Class ______

REINFORCEMENT ACTIVITY 3
PART A, continued
[1, 4]

GENERAL JOURNAL

PAGE 12

DATE		ACCOUNT TITLE	DOC. NO.	POST. REF.	DEBIT	CREDIT

[1, 4, 7–9]

CASH RECEIPTS JOURNAL

PAGE 12

	DATE	ACCOUNT TITLE	DOC. NO.	POST. REF.	1 GENERAL DEBIT	2 GENERAL CREDIT	3 ACCOUNTS RECEIVABLE CREDIT	4 SALES CREDIT	5 SALES TAX PAYABLE DEBIT	6 SALES TAX PAYABLE CREDIT	7 SALES DISCOUNT DEBIT	8 CASH DEBIT	
1													1
2													2
3													3
4													4
5													5
6													6
7													7
8													8
9													9
10													10
11													11
12													12
13													13
14													14
15													15
16													16
17													17
18													18
19													19
20													20
21													21
22													22
23													23
24													24
25													25

[1–3]

CASH PAYMENTS JOURNAL

PAGE 23

	DATE	ACCOUNT TITLE	CK. NO.	POST. REF.	GENERAL DEBIT (1)	GENERAL CREDIT (2)	ACCOUNTS PAYABLE DEBIT (3)	PURCHASES DISCOUNT CREDIT (4)	CASH CREDIT (5)	
1										1
2										2
3										3
4										4
5										5
6										6
7										7
8										8
9										9
10										10
11										11
12										12
13										13
14										14
15										15
16										16
17										17
18										18
19										19
20										20
21										21
22										22
23										23
24										24
25										25

[4, 7, 8, 10]

CASH PAYMENTS JOURNAL

PAGE 24

	DATE	ACCOUNT TITLE	CK. NO.	POST. REF.	1 GENERAL DEBIT	2 GENERAL CREDIT	3 ACCOUNTS PAYABLE DEBIT	4 PURCHASES DISCOUNT CREDIT	5 CASH CREDIT	
1										1
2										2
3										3
4										4
5										5
6										6
7										7
8										8
9										9
10										10
11										11
12										12
13										13
14										14
15										15
16										16
17										17
18										18
19										19
20										20
21										21
22										22
23										23
24										24
25										25

Name ______________________ Date ________ Class ______

REINFORCEMENT ACTIVITY 3
PART A, *continued*
[1, 4–6, 9, 10, 12, 18–21]

The general ledger used in Reinforcement Activity 3, Part A, is needed to complete Part B.

GENERAL LEDGER

ACCOUNT Cash — ACCOUNT NO. 1105

DATE		ITEM	POST. REF.	DEBIT	CREDIT	BALANCE DEBIT	BALANCE CREDIT
19-- Dec.	1	Balance	✓			33 8 5 6 80	

ACCOUNT Petty Cash — ACCOUNT NO. 1110

DATE		ITEM	POST. REF.	DEBIT	CREDIT	BALANCE DEBIT	BALANCE CREDIT
19-- Dec.	1	Balance	✓			2 0 0 00	

ACCOUNT Notes Receivable — ACCOUNT NO. 1115

DATE		ITEM	POST. REF.	DEBIT	CREDIT	BALANCE DEBIT	BALANCE CREDIT
19-- Dec.	1	Balance	✓			4 2 0 0 00	

ACCOUNT Interest Receivable — ACCOUNT NO. 1120

DATE		ITEM	POST. REF.	DEBIT	CREDIT	BALANCE DEBIT	BALANCE CREDIT

ACCOUNT Accounts Receivable — ACCOUNT NO. 1125

DATE		ITEM	POST. REF.	DEBIT	CREDIT	BALANCE DEBIT	BALANCE CREDIT
19-- Dec.	1	Balance	✓			19 8 6 6 60	

ACCOUNT Allowance for Uncollectible Accounts — ACCOUNT NO. 1130

DATE		ITEM	POST. REF.	DEBIT	CREDIT	BALANCE DEBIT	BALANCE CREDIT
19-- Dec.	1	Balance	✓				3 3 70

GENERAL LEDGER

ACCOUNT Merchandise Inventory — ACCOUNT NO. 1135

DATE		ITEM	POST. REF.	DEBIT	CREDIT	BALANCE DEBIT	BALANCE CREDIT
19-- Dec.	1	Balance	✓			59 5 9 6 00	

ACCOUNT Supplies — ACCOUNT NO. 1140

DATE		ITEM	POST. REF.	DEBIT	CREDIT	BALANCE DEBIT	BALANCE CREDIT
19-- Dec.	1	Balance	✓			1 8 7 1 60	

ACCOUNT Prepaid Insurance — ACCOUNT NO. 1145

DATE		ITEM	POST. REF.	DEBIT	CREDIT	BALANCE DEBIT	BALANCE CREDIT
19-- Dec.	1	Balance	✓			6 6 2 0 00	

ACCOUNT Office Equipment — ACCOUNT NO. 1205

DATE		ITEM	POST. REF.	DEBIT	CREDIT	BALANCE DEBIT	BALANCE CREDIT
19-- Dec.	1	Balance	✓			17 7 3 0 00	

ACCOUNT Accumulated Depreciation—Office Equipment — ACCOUNT NO. 1210

DATE		ITEM	POST. REF.	DEBIT	CREDIT	BALANCE DEBIT	BALANCE CREDIT
19-- Dec.	1	Balance	✓				5 9 1 0 00

ACCOUNT Store Equipment — ACCOUNT NO. 1215

DATE		ITEM	POST. REF.	DEBIT	CREDIT	BALANCE DEBIT	BALANCE CREDIT
19-- Dec.	1	Balance	✓			44 9 1 0 00	

Name ______________________ Date ________ Class ______

REINFORCEMENT ACTIVITY 3
PART A, *continued*
[1, 4–6, 9, 10, 12, 18–21]

GENERAL LEDGER

ACCOUNT Accumulated Depreciation—Store Equipment ACCOUNT NO. 1220

DATE		ITEM	POST. REF.	DEBIT	CREDIT	BALANCE DEBIT	BALANCE CREDIT
19-- Dec.	1	Balance	✓				14 2 2 0 00

ACCOUNT Notes Payable ACCOUNT NO. 2105

DATE		ITEM	POST. REF.	DEBIT	CREDIT	BALANCE DEBIT	BALANCE CREDIT
19-- Dec.	1	Balance	✓				30 0 0 0 00

ACCOUNT Interest Payable ACCOUNT NO. 2110

DATE		ITEM	POST. REF.	DEBIT	CREDIT	BALANCE DEBIT	BALANCE CREDIT

ACCOUNT Accounts Payable ACCOUNT NO. 2115

DATE		ITEM	POST. REF.	DEBIT	CREDIT	BALANCE DEBIT	BALANCE CREDIT
19-- Dec.	1	Balance	✓				17 7 6 0 00

ACCOUNT Employee Income Tax Payable ACCOUNT NO. 2120

DATE		ITEM	POST. REF.	DEBIT	CREDIT	BALANCE DEBIT	BALANCE CREDIT
19-- Dec.	1	Balance	✓				1 0 7 5 00

ACCOUNT Federal Income Tax Payable ACCOUNT NO. 2125

DATE		ITEM	POST. REF.	DEBIT	CREDIT	BALANCE DEBIT	BALANCE CREDIT

GENERAL LEDGER

ACCOUNT FICA Tax Payable — ACCOUNT NO. 2130

DATE		ITEM	POST. REF.	DEBIT	CREDIT	BALANCE DEBIT	BALANCE CREDIT
19-- Dec.	1	Balance	✓				1 3 6 0 00

ACCOUNT Sales Tax Payable — ACCOUNT NO. 2135

DATE		ITEM	POST. REF.	DEBIT	CREDIT	BALANCE DEBIT	BALANCE CREDIT
19-- Dec.	1	Balance	✓				4 9 7 7 00

ACCOUNT Unemployment Tax Payable—Federal — ACCOUNT NO. 2140

DATE		ITEM	POST. REF.	DEBIT	CREDIT	BALANCE DEBIT	BALANCE CREDIT
19-- Dec.	1	Balance	✓				1 2 00

ACCOUNT Unemployment Tax Payable—State — ACCOUNT NO. 2145

DATE		ITEM	POST. REF.	DEBIT	CREDIT	BALANCE DEBIT	BALANCE CREDIT
19-- Dec.	1	Balance	✓				8 1 00

ACCOUNT Health Insurance Premiums Payable — ACCOUNT NO. 2150

DATE		ITEM	POST. REF.	DEBIT	CREDIT	BALANCE DEBIT	BALANCE CREDIT
19-- Dec.	1	Balance	✓				6 2 5 00

GENERAL LEDGER

ACCOUNT Dividends Payable — ACCOUNT NO. 2155

DATE		ITEM	POST. REF.	DEBIT	CREDIT	BALANCE DEBIT	BALANCE CREDIT

ACCOUNT Capital Stock — ACCOUNT NO. 3105

DATE		ITEM	POST. REF.	DEBIT	CREDIT	BALANCE DEBIT	BALANCE CREDIT
19-- Dec.	1	Balance	✓				40 0 0 0 00

ACCOUNT Retained Earnings — ACCOUNT NO. 3110

DATE		ITEM	POST. REF.	DEBIT	CREDIT	BALANCE DEBIT	BALANCE CREDIT
19-- Dec.	1	Balance	✓				34 8 9 4 40

ACCOUNT Dividends — ACCOUNT NO. 3115

DATE		ITEM	POST. REF.	DEBIT	CREDIT	BALANCE DEBIT	BALANCE CREDIT
19-- Dec.	1	Balance	✓			30 0 0 0 00	

ACCOUNT Income Summary — ACCOUNT NO. 3120

DATE		ITEM	POST. REF.	DEBIT	CREDIT	BALANCE DEBIT	BALANCE CREDIT

ACCOUNT Sales — ACCOUNT NO. 4105

DATE		ITEM	POST. REF.	DEBIT	CREDIT	BALANCE DEBIT	BALANCE CREDIT
19-- Dec.	1	Balance	✓				684 3 4 5 00

GENERAL LEDGER

ACCOUNT Sales Discount — ACCOUNT NO. 4110

DATE		ITEM	POST. REF.	DEBIT	CREDIT	BALANCE DEBIT	BALANCE CREDIT
19-- Dec.	1	Balance	✓			1 710 80	

ACCOUNT Sales Returns and Allowances — ACCOUNT NO. 4115

DATE		ITEM	POST. REF.	DEBIT	CREDIT	BALANCE DEBIT	BALANCE CREDIT
19-- Dec.	1	Balance	✓			5 152 00	

ACCOUNT Purchases — ACCOUNT NO. 5105

DATE		ITEM	POST. REF.	DEBIT	CREDIT	BALANCE DEBIT	BALANCE CREDIT
19-- Dec.	1	Balance	✓			447 266 00	

ACCOUNT Purchases Discount — ACCOUNT NO. 5110

DATE		ITEM	POST. REF.	DEBIT	CREDIT	BALANCE DEBIT	BALANCE CREDIT
19-- Dec.	1	Balance	✓				3 354 50

ACCOUNT Purchases Returns and Allowances — ACCOUNT NO. 5115

DATE		ITEM	POST. REF.	DEBIT	CREDIT	BALANCE DEBIT	BALANCE CREDIT
19-- Dec.	1	Balance	✓				1 621 00

Name ______________________ Date ________ Class ______

REINFORCEMENT ACTIVITY 3
PART A, *continued*
[1, 4–6, 9, 10, 12, 18–21]

GENERAL LEDGER

ACCOUNT Advertising Expense — ACCOUNT NO. 6105

DATE		ITEM	POST. REF.	DEBIT	CREDIT	BALANCE DEBIT	BALANCE CREDIT
19-- Dec.	1	Balance	✓			8 5 1 2 00	

ACCOUNT Credit Card Fee Expense — ACCOUNT NO. 6110

DATE		ITEM	POST. REF.	DEBIT	CREDIT	BALANCE DEBIT	BALANCE CREDIT
19-- Dec.	1	Balance	✓			12 3 1 8 00	

ACCOUNT Depreciation Expense—Office Equipment — ACCOUNT NO. 6115

DATE		ITEM	POST. REF.	DEBIT	CREDIT	BALANCE DEBIT	BALANCE CREDIT

ACCOUNT Depreciation Expense—Store Equipment — ACCOUNT NO. 6120

DATE		ITEM	POST. REF.	DEBIT	CREDIT	BALANCE DEBIT	BALANCE CREDIT

ACCOUNT Insurance Expense — ACCOUNT NO. 6125

DATE		ITEM	POST. REF.	DEBIT	CREDIT	BALANCE DEBIT	BALANCE CREDIT

GENERAL LEDGER

ACCOUNT Miscellaneous Expense ACCOUNT NO. 6130

DATE		ITEM	POST. REF.	DEBIT	CREDIT	BALANCE DEBIT	BALANCE CREDIT
19-- Dec.	1	Balance	✓			5 2 1 8 80	

ACCOUNT Payroll Taxes Expense ACCOUNT NO. 6135

DATE		ITEM	POST. REF.	DEBIT	CREDIT	BALANCE DEBIT	BALANCE CREDIT
19-- Dec.	1	Balance	✓			9 6 5 0 00	

ACCOUNT Rent Expense ACCOUNT NO. 6140

DATE		ITEM	POST. REF.	DEBIT	CREDIT	BALANCE DEBIT	BALANCE CREDIT
19-- Dec.	1	Balance	✓			19 2 5 0 00	

ACCOUNT Salary Expense ACCOUNT NO. 6145

DATE		ITEM	POST. REF.	DEBIT	CREDIT	BALANCE DEBIT	BALANCE CREDIT
19-- Dec.	1	Balance	✓			93 5 0 0 00	

ACCOUNT Supplies Expense ACCOUNT NO. 6150

DATE		ITEM	POST. REF.	DEBIT	CREDIT	BALANCE DEBIT	BALANCE CREDIT

Name ______________________ Date ________ Class ________

REINFORCEMENT ACTIVITY 3
PART A, *continued*
[1, 4–6, 9, 10, 12, 18–21]

GENERAL LEDGER

ACCOUNT Uncollectible Accounts Expense — ACCOUNT NO. 6155

DATE		ITEM	POST. REF.	DEBIT	CREDIT	BALANCE DEBIT	BALANCE CREDIT

ACCOUNT Utilities Expense — ACCOUNT NO. 6160

DATE		ITEM	POST. REF.	DEBIT	CREDIT	BALANCE DEBIT	BALANCE CREDIT
19-- Dec.	1	Balance	✓			6 5 1 0 00	

ACCOUNT Gain on Plant Assets — ACCOUNT NO. 7105

DATE		ITEM	POST. REF.	DEBIT	CREDIT	BALANCE DEBIT	BALANCE CREDIT
19-- Dec.	1	Balance	✓				1 8 0 00

ACCOUNT Interest Income — ACCOUNT NO. 7110

DATE		ITEM	POST. REF.	DEBIT	CREDIT	BALANCE DEBIT	BALANCE CREDIT
19-- Dec.	1	Balance	✓				5 6 2 00

ACCOUNT Cash Short and Over — ACCOUNT NO. 8105

DATE		ITEM	POST. REF.	DEBIT	CREDIT	BALANCE DEBIT	BALANCE CREDIT
19-- Dec.	1	Balance	✓			1 2 00	

[1, 4–6, 9, 10, 12, 18–21]

GENERAL LEDGER

ACCOUNT Interest Expense — ACCOUNT NO. 8110

DATE		ITEM	POST. REF.	DEBIT	CREDIT	BALANCE DEBIT	BALANCE CREDIT
19-- Dec.	1	Balance	✓			2 1 0 0 00	

ACCOUNT Loss on Plant Assets — ACCOUNT NO. 8115

DATE		ITEM	POST. REF.	DEBIT	CREDIT	BALANCE DEBIT	BALANCE CREDIT
19-- Dec.	1	Balance	✓			4 6 0 00	

ACCOUNT Federal Income Tax Expense — ACCOUNT NO. 9105

DATE		ITEM	POST. REF.	DEBIT	CREDIT	BALANCE DEBIT	BALANCE CREDIT
19-- Dec.	1	Balance	✓			10 5 0 0 00	

ACCOUNTS RECEIVABLE LEDGER

[1, 4, 11]

CUSTOMER Gerald Bell — CUSTOMER NO. 110

DATE		ITEM	POST. REF.	DEBIT	CREDIT	DEBIT BALANCE
19-- Dec.	1	Balance	✓			3 1 7 5 20

CUSTOMER Linda Franz — CUSTOMER NO. 120

DATE		ITEM	POST. REF.	DEBIT	CREDIT	DEBIT BALANCE
19-- Dec.	1	Balance	✓			3 5 7 4 80

Name ______________ Date ________ Class ________

REINFORCEMENT ACTIVITY 3
PART A, *continued*
[1, 4, 11]

ACCOUNTS RECEIVABLE LEDGER

CUSTOMER Roy Heflin — CUSTOMER NO. 130

DATE		ITEM	POST. REF.	DEBIT	CREDIT	DEBIT BALANCE
19-- Dec.	1	Balance	✓			4 374 00

CUSTOMER Patricia Nielsen — CUSTOMER NO. 140

DATE		ITEM	POST. REF.	DEBIT	CREDIT	DEBIT BALANCE
19-- Dec.	1	Balance	✓			2 381 40

CUSTOMER Paul Rodriquez — CUSTOMER NO. 150

DATE		ITEM	POST. REF.	DEBIT	CREDIT	DEBIT BALANCE
19-- Dec.	1	Balance	✓			5 167 80

CUSTOMER Kay Walker — CUSTOMER NO. 160

DATE		ITEM	POST. REF.	DEBIT	CREDIT	DEBIT BALANCE
19-- Dec.	1	Balance	✓			1 193 40

ACCOUNTS PAYABLE LEDGER

VENDOR Beta Hardware Supplies — VENDOR NO. 210

DATE		ITEM	POST. REF.	DEBIT	CREDIT	CREDIT BALANCE
19-- Dec.	1	Balance	✓			4 261 60

[1, 4, 11]

ACCOUNTS PAYABLE LEDGER

VENDOR Decorator Systems — VENDOR NO. 220

DATE		ITEM	POST. REF.	DEBIT	CREDIT	CREDIT BALANCE
19-- Dec.	1	Balance	✓			3 5 5 2 50

VENDOR Granger Company — VENDOR NO. 230

DATE		ITEM	POST. REF.	DEBIT	CREDIT	CREDIT BALANCE
19-- Dec.	1	Balance	✓			4 0 8 4 70

VENDOR HiValue Electrical Co. — VENDOR NO. 240

DATE		ITEM	POST. REF.	DEBIT	CREDIT	CREDIT BALANCE

VENDOR Sunbelt Corp. — VENDOR NO. 250

DATE		ITEM	POST. REF.	DEBIT	CREDIT	CREDIT BALANCE
19-- Dec.	1	Balance	✓			3 1 9 6 80

VENDOR Western Tools — VENDOR NO. 260

DATE		ITEM	POST. REF.	DEBIT	CREDIT	CREDIT BALANCE
19-- Dec.	1	Balance	✓			2 6 6 4 40

[11]

[11]

SALES JOURNAL

PAGE

	DATE	ACCOUNT DEBITED	SALE NO.	POST. REF.	1 ACCOUNTS RECEIVABLE DEBIT	2 SALES CREDIT	3 SALES TAX PAYABLE CREDIT	
1								1
2								2
3								3
4								4
5								5
6								6
7								7
8								8
9								9
10								10
11								11
12								12
13								13
14								14

Extra form

PURCHASES JOURNAL

PAGE

	DATE	ACCOUNT CREDITED	PURCH. NO.	POST. REF.	PURCHASES DR. ACCTS. PAY. CR.	
1						1
2						2
3						3
4						4
5						5
6						6
7						7
8						8
9						9
10						10
11						11
12						12
13						13
14						14

Name ______________________ Date __________ Class ________

COMPUTER APPLICATION 5, p. 548
[1]

AUTOMATED ACCOUNTING CYCLE FOR A CORPORATION: JOURNALIZING AND POSTING TRANSACTIONS

RUN DATE ____/____/____
MM DD YY

BATCH NO. [ ]

GENERAL LEDGER
Input Form

Problem No. ________

FORM GL-2

	1	2	3	4	5	
	DAY	DOC. NO.	ACCOUNT NUMBER	DEBIT AMOUNT	CREDIT AMOUNT	
1						1
2						2
3						3
4						4
5						5
6						6
7						7
8						8
9						9
10						10
11						11
12						12
13						13
14						14
15						15
16						16
17						17
18						18
19						19
20						20
21						21
22						22
23						23
24						24
25						25
			BATCH TOTALS			

[1]

RUN DATE ____/____/____
MM DD YY

BATCH NO. [ ]

GENERAL LEDGER
Input Form

Problem No. ________

FORM GL-2

	1	2	3	4	5	
	DAY	DOC. NO.	ACCOUNT NUMBER	DEBIT AMOUNT	CREDIT AMOUNT	
1						1
2						2
3						3
4						4
5						5
6						6
7						7
8						8
9						9
10						10
11						11
12						12
13						13
14						14
15						15
16						16
17						17
18						18
19						19
20						20
21						21
22						22
23						23
24						24
25						25
			BATCH TOTALS			

[1]

RUN DATE ___/___/___
MM DD YY

BATCH NO. [ ]

ACCOUNTS PAYABLE
Input Form

Problem No. ________

FORM AP-3

	1	2	3			4	5	6			7	8	9			10	11	12	
		PURCHASES						DEBIT MEMOS					CASH PAYMENTS						
	PURCH. INVOICE NO.	VEND. NO.	DATE			GEN. LEDGER ACCT. NO.	INVOICE AMOUNT	DATE			MEMO. NO.	DEBIT MEMO. AMOUNT	DATE			DISC. %	DISP. CODE	MANUAL CHECK NO.	
			MO.	DAY	YR.			MO.	DAY	YR.			MO.	DAY	YR.				
1																			1
2																			2
3																			3
4																			4
5																			5
6																			6
7																			7
8																			8
9																			9
10																			10
11																			11
12																			12
13																			13
14																			14
15																			15
16																			16
17																			17
18																			18

BATCH TOTALS [ ] [ ]

DISPOSITION CODE:
A = ON ACCOUNT
M = MANUAL CHECK

[1]

RUN DATE ___/___/___
MM DD YY

BATCH NO. ☐

ACCOUNTS RECEIVABLE
Input Form

Problem No. ______

FORM AR-3

	1	2	3			4	5	6	7			8	9	10			11	12	13	
		SALES							CREDIT MEMOS					CASH RECEIPTS						
	SALES INVOICE NO.	CUST. NO.	DATE			GEN. LEDGER ACCT. NO.	INVOICE AMOUNT	SALES TAX %	DATE			MEMO. NO.	CREDIT MEMO. AMOUNT	DATE			DOC. NO.	DISC. %	CASH RECEIVED	
			MO.	DAY	YR.				MO.	DAY	YR.			MO.	DAY	YR.				
1																				1
2																				2
3																				3
4																				4
5																				5
6																				6
7																				7
8																				8
9																				9
10																				10
11																				11
12																				12
13																				13
14																				14
15																				15
16																				16
17																				17
18																				18
						BATCH TOTALS	☐						☐						☐	

Perfect Score..... 36 | Name ____________________

Deduct......... ___ | Date ____________ Class ____________

Your Score..... ___ | Checked by ____________________

STUDY GUIDE 22

UNIT A—Analyzing Uncollectible Accounts Expense and Allowance for Uncollectible Accounts

DIRECTIONS: Place a check mark in the proper Answers column to show whether each of the following statements is true or false.

Statement	True	False	For Scoring
0. A business generally sells on account to encourage sales	✓		**0.** ✓
1. Uncollectible accounts also are known as bad debts			**1.**
2. An uncollectible amount of accounts receivable decreases revenue			**2.**
3. Risk of loss occurs when a business sells on account			**3.**
4. Accurate financial reporting requires that expenses be recorded in the fiscal period in which cash is spent			**4.**
5. A business knows at the time sales are made which customer account will become uncollectible			**5.**
6. Estimating and recording uncollectible accounts expense at the end of a fiscal period prevents an overstatement of the value of accounts receivable on the balance sheet			**6.**
7. The Uncollectible Accounts Expense account is increased by a debit and decreased by a credit			**7.**
8. Allowance for Uncollectible Accounts is a contra account to its related account, Uncollectible Accounts Expense			**8.**
9. The account Allowance for Uncollectible Accounts is increased by a debit and decreased by a credit			**9.**
10. When the account Allowance for Uncollectible Accounts is used, the amount of uncollectible accounts expense shown on the income statement is an estimated amount			**10.**
11. Adjustments for uncollectible accounts expense are planned on a work sheet			**11.**
12. Allowance for Uncollectible Accounts is debited to write off a customer account			**12.**
13. Accounts Receivable is debited to write off a customer account			**13.**
14. When an adjusting entry for uncollectible accounts expense is recorded, Accounts Receivable is debited			**14.**
15. When an adjusting entry for uncollectible accounts expense is recorded, Allowance for Uncollectible Accounts is credited			**15.**
16. When an adjusting entry for uncollectible accounts expense is recorded, Uncollectible Account Expense is credited			**16.**
17. Information used for an uncollectible accounts expense entry is obtained from a work sheet's Adjustments columns			**17.**
18. After an adjusting entry for uncollectible accounts expense is posted, the uncollectible accounts expense account has a debit balance			**18.**
19. The percentage of total sales on account method of estimating uncollectible accounts expense assumes that a portion of every sale on account dollar will become uncollectible			**19.**
20. When an account is written off, Uncollectible Accounts Expense is debited and Allowance for Uncollectible Accounts is credited			**20.**
21. When a customer account is written off under the allowance method, book value of accounts receivable decreases			**21.**
22. When an account is written off, the account is transferred to Uncollectible Accounts Expense			**22.**
23. When a previously written off account is collected, Accounts Receivable is debited and credited for the amount collected			**23.**

UNIT B—Analyzing Uncollectible Accounts Receivable

DIRECTIONS: For each of the following items, select the choice that best completes the statement. Print the letter identifying your choice in the Answers column.

	Answers	For Scoring
0. Accounts receivable that cannot be collected are called **(A)** uncollectible accounts, **(B)** allowance for uncollectible accounts, **(C)** lost accounts, **(D)** book value of accounts receivable	A	**0.** ✔
1. Uncollectible Accounts Expense is a(an) **(A)** revenue account, **(B)** expense account, **(C)** asset account, **(D)** liability account		**1.**
2. Accounts Receivable is a(an) **(A)** revenue account, **(B)** expense account, **(C)** asset account, **(D)** liability account		**2.**
3. Allowance for Uncollectible Accounts is a(an) **(A)** asset account, **(B)** contra asset account, **(C)** liability account, **(D)** contra liability account		**3.**
4. Crediting the estimated value of uncollectible accounts to a contra account is known as **(A)** proving the uncollectible accounts expense account, **(B)** the allowance method of recording losses from uncollectible accounts, **(C)** the direct write off, **(D)** writing off an account		**4.**
5. At the end of a fiscal period, the account debited to show the estimated amount of uncollectible accounts is **(A)** Cash, **(B)** Accounts Receivable, **(C)** Allowance for Uncollectible Accounts, **(D)** Uncollectible Accounts Expense		**5.**
6. At the end of a fiscal period, the account credited to show the estimated amount of uncollectible accounts is **(A)** Cash, **(B)** Accounts Receivable, **(C)** Allowance for Uncollectible Accounts, **(D)** Uncollectible Accounts Expense		**6.**
7. When the account Allowance for Uncollectible Accounts is used, a customer past-due account is written off as uncollectible by **(A)** debiting Uncollectible Accounts Expense and crediting Accounts Receivable and the customer account, **(B)** debiting Allowance for Uncollectible Accounts and crediting Accounts Receivable and the customer account, **(C)** debiting Accounts Receivable and the customer account and crediting Allowance for Uncollectible Accounts, **(D)** none of these		**7.**
8. An Allowance for Uncollectible Accounts balance in the Trial Balance Credit column means **(A)** too many accounts have been written off, **(B)** an error has been made, **(C)** previous fiscal period estimates are not yet identified as uncollectible, **(D)** uncollectible accounts expense has been underestimated...		**8.**
9. The difference between the balance of Accounts Receivable and the estimated uncollectible accounts is known as **(A)** book value of accounts receivable, **(B)** uncollectible accounts expense, **(C)** allowance for uncollectible accounts, **(D)** a contra account		**9.**
10. When the allowance method of recording uncollectible accounts is used and a customer account is written off **(A)** revenues decrease, **(B)** expenses increase, **(C)** retained earnings decrease, **(D)** revenues and expenses do not change		**10.**
11. After an account has been written off, the book value of accounts receivable is **(A)** more than before the write-off, **(B)** less than before the write-off, **(C)** the same as before the write-off, **(D)** reported on the income statement		**11.**
12. When an account is collected that was previously written off as uncollectible **(A)** debit Cash and credit Accounts Receivable, **(B)** debit Accounts Receivable and credit Allowance for Uncollectible Accounts, then debit Cash and credit Accounts Receivable, **(C)** debit Allowance for Uncollectible Accounts and credit Accounts Receivable, then debit Cash and credit Accounts Receivable, **(D)** debit Accounts Receivable and credit Allowance for Uncollectible Accounts, then debit Cash and credit Uncollectible Accounts Expense		**12.**
13. When an account is collected that was previously written off as uncollectible, **(A)** revenue is increased, **(B)** expenses are decreased, **(C)** expenses are increased, **(D)** neither revenue nor expenses are affected		**13.**

Name ______________________ Date ________ Class ________ *DRILL 22-D1, p. 567*

Estimating uncollectible accounts expense

Store	Total Sales on Account	Estimated Uncollectible Accounts as Percentage of Sales on Account	Balance of Allowance for Uncollectible Accounts Before Adjustment	(A) Uncollectible Accounts Expense	(B) Balance of Allowance for Uncollectible Accounts After Adjustment
1	$48,700.00	0.6%	32.00 Credit		
2	73,900.00	0.5%	63.00 Credit		
3	95,200.00	1.0%	24.00 Debit		
4	61,400.00	0.7%	79.00 Credit		
5	54,800.00	0.4%	0		
6	89,600.00	0.8%	57.00 Debit		

Analyzing entries for uncollectible accounts *DRILL 22-D2, p. 567*

Transaction	General Ledger				Accounts Receivable Ledger Customer Account
	Cash	Accounts Receivable	Allowance for Uncollectible Accounts	Uncollectible Accounts Expense	
A. Adjusting entry for uncollectible accounts expense at end of fiscal period					
B. Wrote off an uncollectible account					
C. Collected account previously written off 1) Entry 1:					
2) Entry 2:					

Estimating and journalizing entries for uncollectible accounts expense

PROBLEM 22-1, p. 568

[1]

Caraway Company

Work Sheet

For Year Ended December 31, 19X1

	ACCOUNT TITLE	1 TRIAL BALANCE DEBIT	2 TRIAL BALANCE CREDIT	3 ADJUSTMENTS DEBIT	4 ADJUSTMENTS CREDIT	
6	Allowance for Uncoll. Accounts		171 00			6
45	Uncollectible Accounts Expense					45
46						46
47						47

Caraway Company

Work Sheet

For Year Ended December 31, 19X2

	ACCOUNT TITLE	1 TRIAL BALANCE DEBIT	2 TRIAL BALANCE CREDIT	3 ADJUSTMENTS DEBIT	4 ADJUSTMENTS CREDIT	
6	Allowance for Uncoll. Accounts		279 00			6
45	Uncollectible Accounts Expense					45
46						46
47						47

Caraway Company

Work Sheet

For Year Ended December 31, 19X3

	ACCOUNT TITLE	1 TRIAL BALANCE DEBIT	2 TRIAL BALANCE CREDIT	3 ADJUSTMENTS DEBIT	4 ADJUSTMENTS CREDIT	
6	Allowance for Uncoll. Accounts		392 80			6
45	Uncollectible Accounts Expense					45
46						46
47						47

[2]

GENERAL JOURNAL

PAGE 13

DATE		ACCOUNT TITLE	DOC. NO.	POST. REF.	DEBIT	CREDIT

GENERAL JOURNAL

PAGE 13

DATE		ACCOUNT TITLE	DOC. NO.	POST. REF.	DEBIT	CREDIT

GENERAL JOURNAL

PAGE 13

DATE		ACCOUNT TITLE	DOC. NO.	POST. REF.	DEBIT	CREDIT

[1, 2]

GENERAL JOURNAL

PAGE 6

DATE		ACCOUNT TITLE	DOC. NO.	POST. REF.	DEBIT	CREDIT

Name ______________ Date ________ Class ________

PROBLEM 22-2, concluded

[2]

ACCOUNTS RECEIVABLE LEDGER

CUSTOMER Davidson Corporation — CUSTOMER NO. 140

DATE		ITEM	POST. REF.	DEBIT	CREDIT	DEBIT BALANCE
19-- Jan.	6		S1	347 00		347 00

CUSTOMER Jordan Equipment Co. — CUSTOMER NO. 165

DATE		ITEM	POST. REF.	DEBIT	CREDIT	DEBIT BALANCE
19-- Jan.	13		S1	521 00		521 00

CUSTOMER Porter, Inc. — CUSTOMER NO. 180

DATE		ITEM	POST. REF.	DEBIT	CREDIT	DEBIT BALANCE
19-- Feb.	1		S2	179 00		179 00

CUSTOMER — CUSTOMER NO.

DATE		ITEM	POST. REF.	DEBIT	CREDIT	DEBIT BALANCE

PROBLEM 22-3, p. 568

Recording transactions for collection of written-off accounts receivable [1, 2]

GENERAL JOURNAL

PAGE 8

	DATE		ACCOUNT TITLE	DOC. NO.	POST. REF.	DEBIT	CREDIT	
1								1
2								2
3								3
4								4
5								5
6								6
7								7
8								8
9								9
10								10
11								11
12								12
13								13
14								14
15								15

[1, 3]

CASH RECEIPTS JOURNAL

PAGE 15

	DATE		ACCOUNT TITLE	Doc. No.	Post. Ref.	1 GENERAL DEBIT	2 GENERAL CREDIT	3 ACCOUNTS RECEIVABLE CREDIT	4 SALES CREDIT	5 SALES TAX PAYABLE DEBIT	6 SALES TAX PAYABLE CREDIT	7 SALES DISCOUNT DEBIT	8 CASH DEBIT	
1														1
2														2
3														3
4														4
5														5

[2]

ACCOUNTS RECEIVABLE LEDGER

CUSTOMER Andrews Corp. CUSTOMER NO. 110

DATE		ITEM	POST. REF.	DEBIT	CREDIT	DEBIT BALANCE
19-- Feb.	3		S2	384 00		384 00
July	15	Written off	G7		384 00	———

CUSTOMER Hargrove, Inc. CUSTOMER NO. 170

DATE		ITEM	POST. REF.	DEBIT	CREDIT	DEBIT BALANCE
19-- Mar.	2		S3	715 00		715 00
July	30	Written off	G7		715 00	———

CUSTOMER Tyler Co. CUSTOMER NO. 185

DATE		ITEM	POST. REF.	DEBIT	CREDIT	DEBIT BALANCE
19-- Feb.	25		S2	443 00		443 00
July	28	Written off	G7		443 00	———

CUSTOMER CUSTOMER NO.

DATE		ITEM	POST. REF.	DEBIT	CREDIT	DEBIT BALANCE

[1]

GENERAL JOURNAL

PAGE 10

DATE		ACCOUNT TITLE	DOC. NO.	POST. REF.	DEBIT	CREDIT

GENERAL JOURNAL

PAGE 11

DATE		ACCOUNT TITLE	DOC. NO.	POST. REF.	DEBIT	CREDIT

GENERAL JOURNAL

PAGE 12

DATE		ACCOUNT TITLE	DOC. NO.	POST. REF.	DEBIT	CREDIT

[1]

CASH RECEIPTS JOURNAL

PAGE 11

				1	2	3	4	5	6	7	8	
	DATE	ACCOUNT TITLE	DOC. NO.	POST. REF.	GENERAL DEBIT	GENERAL CREDIT	ACCOUNTS RECEIVABLE CREDIT	SALES CREDIT	SALES TAX PAYABLE DEBIT	SALES TAX PAYABLE CREDIT	SALES DISCOUNT DEBIT	CASH DEBIT	
1													1
2													2
3													3
4													4
5													5
6													6
7													7
8													8
9													9

[1]

CASH RECEIPTS JOURNAL

PAGE 12

				1	2	3	4	5	6	7	8	
	DATE	ACCOUNT TITLE	DOC. NO.	POST. REF.	GENERAL DEBIT	GENERAL CREDIT	ACCOUNTS RECEIVABLE CREDIT	SALES CREDIT	SALES TAX PAYABLE DEBIT	SALES TAX PAYABLE CREDIT	SALES DISCOUNT DEBIT	CASH DEBIT	
1													1
2													2
3													3
4													4
5													5
6													6
7													7
8													8
9													9

[1]

ACCOUNTS RECEIVABLE LEDGER

CUSTOMER Burrell Company — CUSTOMER NO. 125

DATE		ITEM	POST. REF.	DEBIT	CREDIT	DEBIT BALANCE
19-- Mar.	28		S3	714 15		714 15

CUSTOMER Fiber-Tech — CUSTOMER NO. 135

DATE		ITEM	POST. REF.	DEBIT	CREDIT	DEBIT BALANCE
19-- Mar.	15		S3	829 35		829 35

CUSTOMER Gentry Corporation — CUSTOMER NO. 140

DATE		ITEM	POST. REF.	DEBIT	CREDIT	DEBIT BALANCE
19-- Jan.	16		S1	482 50		482 50

CUSTOMER Kingston Corporation — CUSTOMER NO. 150

DATE		ITEM	POST. REF.	DEBIT	CREDIT	DEBIT BALANCE
19-- Feb.	4		S2	247 60		247 60

[2]

GENERAL JOURNAL

PAGE 13

	DATE		ACCOUNT TITLE	DOC. NO.	POST. REF.	DEBIT	CREDIT	
1								1
2								2
3								3
4								4
5								5
6								6

Name ______________________ Date ________ Class ______

PROBLEM 22-C, p. 569
[1]

Recording entries for uncollectible accounts

GENERAL JOURNAL

PAGE 1

	DATE		ACCOUNT TITLE	DOC. NO.	POST. REF.	DEBIT	CREDIT	
1								1
2								2
3								3
4								4
5								5
6								6
7								7
8								8
9								9
10								10
11								11
12								12
13								13
14								14
15								15
16								16
17								17
18								18
19								19
20								20
21								21
22								22
23								23
24								24
25								25
26								26
27								27
28								28
29								29
30								30
31								31
32								32

[1]

CASH RECEIPTS JOURNAL

PAGE 1

	DATE	ACCOUNT TITLE	DOC. NO.	POST. REF.	1 GENERAL DEBIT	2 GENERAL CREDIT	3 ACCOUNTS RECEIVABLE CREDIT	4 SALES CREDIT	5 SALES TAX PAYABLE DEBIT	6 SALES TAX PAYABLE CREDIT	7 SALES DISCOUNT DEBIT	8 CASH DEBIT	
1													1
2													2
3													3
4													4
5													5
6													6
7													7
8													8
9													9
10													10
11													11
12													12
13													13
14													14
15													15
16													16
17													17
18													18
19													19
20													20
21													21
22													22
23													23
24													24
25													25

[1]

GENERAL LEDGER

ACCOUNT Allowance for Uncollectible Accounts ACCOUNT NO. 1130

DATE		ITEM	POST. REF.	DEBIT	CREDIT	BALANCE DEBIT	BALANCE CREDIT
19-- Jan.	1	Balance	✓				1 5 7 3 25

ACCOUNT Uncollectible Accounts Expense ACCOUNT NO. 6165

DATE		ITEM	POST. REF.	DEBIT	CREDIT	BALANCE DEBIT	BALANCE CREDIT

[2]

Perfect Score..... 39	Name ______	
Deduct......... ___	Date ______	Class ______
Your Score..... ___	Checked by ______	

STUDY GUIDE 23

UNIT A—Identifying Accounting Terms

DIRECTIONS: Select the term in Column I that best fits each definition in Column II. Print the letter identifying your choice in the Answers column.

Column I

A. accumulated depreciation
B. book value of a plant asset
C. current assets
D. depreciation expense
E. gain on plant assets
F. loss on plant assets
G. plant asset record
H. plant assets
I. straight-line method of depreciation

Column II	Answers	For Scoring
0. An accounting form on which a business records information about each plant asset....................	G	**0.** ✓
1. Revenue that results when a plant asset is sold for more than book value		**1.**
2. The portion of a plant asset's cost that is transferred to an expense account in each fiscal period during a plant asset's useful life....................		**2.**
3. The original cost of a plant asset minus accumulated depreciation....................		**3.**
4. Assets which will be used for a number of years in the operation of a business....................		**4.**
5. Charging an equal amount of depreciation expense for a plant asset in each year of useful life		**5.**
6. The total amount of depreciation expense that has been recorded since the purchase of a plant asset....		**6.**
7. Cash and other assets expected to be exchanged for cash or consumed within a year		**7.**
8. Loss that results when a plant asset is sold for less than book value		**8.**

UNIT B—Analyzing Plant Asset Transactions

DIRECTIONS: Analyze each of the following transactions into debit and credit parts. Print the letters identifying your choices in the proper Answers column.

Account Title

A. Accumulated Depreciation—Office Equipment
B. Accumulated Depreciation—Store Equipment
C. Cash
D. Depreciation Expense—Office Equipment
E. Depreciation Expense—Store Equipment
F. Gain on Plant Assets
G. Loss on Plant Assets
H. Office Equipment
I. Store Equipment

Transaction	Answers Debit	Answers Credit	For Scoring Debit	For Scoring Credit
0–0. Paid cash for new typewriter....................	H	C	**0.** ✓	**0.** ✓
1–2. Recorded annual store equipment depreciation			**1.**	**2.**
3–4. Sold store display case for book value....................			**3.**	**4.**
5–6. Paid cash for new cash register for store....................			**5.**	**6.**
7–8. Sold office computer for less than book value			**7.**	**8.**
9–10. Paid cash for new store equipment....................			**9.**	**10.**
11–12. Sold office typewriter for more than book value			**11.**	**12.**
13–14. Recorded annual office equipment depreciation....................			**13.**	**14.**
15–16. Sold store equipment for less than book value....................			**15.**	**16.**

UNIT C—Analyzing Plant Assets and Depreciation

DIRECTIONS: For each of the following items, select the choice that best completes the statement. Print the letter identifying your choice in the Answers column.

	Answers	For Scoring
0. A business buys plant assets **(A)** to use as an investment **(B)** to sell for a profit **(C)** to use in earning revenue **(D)** for employees' personal use	C	**0.** ✓
1. A factor affecting the amount of plant asset depreciation expense for a fiscal period is **(A)** the contra account **(B)** cash **(C)** estimated salvage value **(D)** accumulated depreciation		**1.**
2. Recording depreciation expense is an application of the concept **(A)** Going Concern **(B)** Matching Expenses with Revenue **(C)** Objective Evidence **(D)** Historical Cost		**2.**
3. The amount by which a plant asset depreciates is classified as a(an) **(A)** asset **(B)** expense **(C)** liability **(D)** revenue................................		**3.**
4. Accumulated Depreciation—Equipment is classified as a(an) **(A)** contra asset account **(B)** liability account **(C)** contra expense account, **(D)** asset account		**4.**
5. Depreciation expense for a plant asset is recorded **(A)** when the asset is bought **(B)** after the asset is sold **(C)** when the asset is repaired **(D)** at the end of each fiscal period during the asset's estimated useful life.......		**5.**
6. Gain on disposal of a plant asset is figured as **(A)** value of asset received less book value of asset sold **(B)** value of asset received plus book value of asset sold **(C)** book value of asset sold less value of asset received **(D)** original cost of asset less accumulated depreciation		**6.**
7. The amount appearing in a work sheet's Adjustments Credit column for Accumulated Depreciation—Equipment is extended to the **(A)** Income Statement Credit column **(B)** Income Statement Debit column **(C)** Balance Sheet Credit column **(D)** Balance Sheet Debit column		**7.**
8. The amount appearing in a work sheet's Adjustments Debit column for Depreciation Expense—Equipment is included in the amount extended to the **(A)** Balance Sheet Credit column **(B)** Balance Sheet Debit column **(C)** Income Statement Credit column **(D)** Income Statement Debit column...		**8.**
9. When a plant asset is sold for less than the asset's book value **(A)** cash received plus accumulated depreciation plus gain on disposal equals original cost **(B)** cash received plus accumulated depreciation equals original cost plus gain on disposal **(C)** cash received plus accumulated depreciation plus loss on disposal equals original cost **(D)** cash received plus accumulated depreciation equals original cost plus loss on disposal		**9.**
10. When a plant asset is sold for the asset's book value, **(A)** cash received plus accumulated depreciation equals original cost **(B)** cash received plus salvage value equals original cost **(C)** cash received plus accumulated depreciation plus salvage value equals original cost..		**10.**
11. The annual depreciation for a plant asset with original cost of $1,000.00, estimated salvage value of $100.00, and estimated useful life of 10 years, using the straight-line method, is **(A)** $100.00 **(B)** $1,000.00 **(C)** $90.00 **(D)** $200.00 ..		**11.**
12. Loss on disposal of a plant asset is figured as **(A)** value of asset received less book value of asset sold **(B)** value of asset received plus book value of asset sold **(C)** book value of asset sold less value of asset received **(D)** original cost of assets less accumulated depreciation		**12.**
13. The accumulated depreciation account should show **(A)** total depreciation for plant assets since the business was formed **(B)** only total depreciation expense for plant assets for the current year **(C)** total depreciation for plant assets still in use **(D)** next year's estimated depreciation for plant assets		**13.**
14. When a plant asset is sold for more than the asset's book value **(A)** cash received plus accumulated depreciation plus gain on disposal equals original cost plus gain on disposal **(B)** cash received plus accumulated depreciation equals original cost plus gain on disposal **(C)** cash received plus accumulated depreciation plus loss on disposal equals original cost **(D)** cash received plus accumulated depreciation equals original cost plus loss on disposal................		**14.**
15. Recording a plant asset at its original cost is an application of the concept **(A)** Going Concern **(B)** Matching Expenses with Revenue **(C)** Objective Evidence **(D)** Historical Cost...		**15.**

Calculating depreciation expense

Plant Asset	Original Cost	Estimated Salvage Value	Estimated Useful Life	Amount of Annual Depreciation
1	$ 730.00	$ 50.00	4 years	
2	5,200.00	1,400.00	5 years	
3	2,170.00	250.00	3 years	
4	1,610.00	170.00	6 years	
5	8,950.00	2,350.00	8 years	
6	17,480.00	950.00	10 years	
7	12,600.00	3,150.00	9 years	
8	57,200.00	5,500.00	25 years	
9	9,220.00	480.00	4 years	
10	26,500.00	5,950.00	15 years	

Calculating book value of plant assets DRILL 23-D2, p. 593

Plant Asset	Date Bought	Original Cost	Estimated Salvage Value	Estimated Useful Life	(A) Total Accumulated Depreciation as of 12/31/X6	(B) Ending Book Value 12/31/X6
1	Jan. 1, 19X1	$ 1,050.00	$ 150.00	6 years		
2	July 1, 19X1	4,700.00	400.00	10 years		
3	Apr. 1, 19X2	25,500.00	1,500.00	15 years		
4	Sept. 1, 19X2	12,800.00	1,250.00	7 years		
5	Mar. 1, 19X3	10,700.00	1,100.00	8 years		
6	Aug. 1, 19X4	6,200.00	500.00	5 years		
7	Dec. 31, 19X4	930.00	110.00	4 years		
8	Oct. 1, 19X5	2,700.00	300.00	3 years		
9	May 1, 19X6	15,600.00	3,600.00	8 years		
10	Nov. 1, 19X6	7,800.00	240.00	9 years		

PROBLEMS 23-1 and 23-2, p. 593

Journalizing the buying of plant assets

CASH PAYMENTS JOURNAL

PAGE 12

	DATE		ACCOUNT TITLE	CK. NO.	POST. REF.	1 GENERAL DEBIT	2 GENERAL CREDIT	3 ACCOUNTS PAYABLE DEBIT	4 PURCHASES DISCOUNT CREDIT	5 CASH CREDIT	
1											1
2											2
3											3
4											4
5											5
6											6
7											7
8											8
9											9

Calculating depreciation expense

PROBLEM 23-2, p. 594

Plant Asset	Date Bought	Original Cost	Estimated Salvage Value	Estimated Useful Life	Depreciation Expense 19X3
1	July 1, 19X1	$ 5,600.00	$ 800.00	12 years	
2	Nov. 1, 19X1	5,000.00	380.00	7 years	
3	May 1, 19X2	21,600.00	2,250.00	15 years	
4	Feb. 1, 19X3	10,750.00	1,750.00	9 years	
5	Apr. 1, 19X3	3,820.00	220.00	6 years	
6	Aug. 1, 19X3	1,440.00	200.00	2 years	

Name ______________________ Date ________ Class ______ *PROBLEM 23-3, p. 594*

Preparing a plant asset record

PLANT ASSET RECORD General Ledger Account No. ____________

Description ______________________ General Ledger Account ______________________

Date Bought ____________ Serial Number ____________ Original Cost ____________

Estimated Useful Life ____________ Estimated Salvage Value ____________ Annual Depreciation ____________

Disposed of: Discarded ________ Sold ________ Traded ________

Date ______________________ Disposal Amount ______________________

YEAR	ANNUAL DEPRECIATION EXPENSE	ACCUMULATED DEPRECIATION	ENDING BOOK VALUE

Continue record on back of card

Recording work sheet adjustments and journal entries for depreciation expense

PROBLEM 23-4, p. 594
[1–3]

	ACCOUNT TITLE	TRIAL BALANCE DEBIT (1)	TRIAL BALANCE CREDIT (2)	ADJUSTMENTS DEBIT (3)	ADJUSTMENTS CREDIT (4)	
8						8
9						9
10						10
11						11
37						37
38						38
39						39
40						40

[3]

GENERAL JOURNAL

PAGE 13

	DATE		ACCOUNT TITLE	DOC. NO.	POST. REF.	DEBIT	CREDIT	
1								1
2								2
3								3
4								4
5								5
6								6
7								7
8								8
9								9
10								10
11								11
12								12
13								13
14								14
15								15
16								16

Name ______________________ Date ________ Class ______ *PROBLEM 23-5, p. 595*

Journalizing the disposing of plant assets

GENERAL JOURNAL

PAGE 12

	DATE		ACCOUNT TITLE	DOC. NO.	POST. REF.	DEBIT	CREDIT	
1								1
2								2
3								3
4								4
5								5
6								6
7								7
8								8
9								9
10								10
11								11
12								12
13								13
14								14
15								15
16								16
17								17
18								18
19								19
20								20
21								21
22								22
23								23
24								24
25								25
26								26
27								27
28								28
29								29
30								30
31								31
32								32

CASH RECEIPTS JOURNAL

PAGE 12

	DATE	ACCOUNT TITLE	DOC. NO.	POST. REF.	1 GENERAL DEBIT	2 GENERAL CREDIT	3 ACCOUNTS RECEIVABLE CREDIT	4 SALES CREDIT	5 SALES TAX PAYABLE DEBIT	6 SALES TAX PAYABLE CREDIT	7 SALES DISCOUNT DEBIT	8 CASH DEBIT	
1													1
2													2
3													3
4													4
5													5
6													6
7													7
8													8
9													9
10													10
11													11
12													12
13													13
14													14
15													15
16													16
17													17
18													18
19													19
20													20
21													21
22													22
23													23
24													24
25													25

Name ______________________ Date ________ Class ________

MASTERY PROBLEM 23-M, p. 595

[1, 2]

Calculating depreciation expense and book value of plant assets; journalizing entries affecting plant assets

Plant Asset	Asset Account	Date Bought	Original Cost	Estimated Salavage Value	Estimated Useful Life	Depreciation Expense 19X4	Book Value 12/31/X4
1	Office Equipment	Apr. 1, 19X1	$ 7,300.00	$ 700.00	6 years		
2	Store Equipment	July 1, 19X1	6,900.00	600.00	9 years		
3	Store Equipment	Oct. 1, 19X1	5,700.00	900.00	3 years		
4	Store Equipment	Aug. 1, 19X2	2,600.00	500.00	5 years		
5	Store Equipment	Sept. 1, 19X2	3,100.00	700.00	4 years		
6	Office Equipment	Nov. 1, 19X3	10,800.00	1,800.00	10 years		
7	Office Equipment	May 1, 19X4	1,400.00	200.00	4 years		
8	Office Equipment	July 1, 19X4	22,500.00	1,500.00	14 years		

[3, 4]

GENERAL JOURNAL

PAGE 13

	DATE		ACCOUNT TITLE	DOC. NO.	POST. REF.	DEBIT	CREDIT	
1								1
2								2
3								3
4								4
5								5
6								6
7								7
8								8
9								9
10								10
11								11
12								12

[4]

CASH RECEIPTS JOURNAL

PAGE 4

	DATE	ACCOUNT TITLE	DOC. NO.	POST. REF.	1 GENERAL DEBIT	2 GENERAL CREDIT	3 ACCOUNTS RECEIVABLE CREDIT	4 SALES CREDIT	5 SALES TAX PAYABLE DEBIT	6 SALES TAX PAYABLE CREDIT	7 SALES DISCOUNT DEBIT	8 CASH DEBIT	
1													1
2													2
3													3
4													4
5													5
6													6
7													7
8													8
9													9
10													10
11													11
12													12
13													13
14													14
15													15
16													16
17													17
18													18
19													19
20													20
21													21
22													22
23													23
24													24
25													25

Name ______________________ Date __________ Class ________

CHALLENGE PROBLEM 23-C, p. 596

[1–3]

Calculating depreciation expense and book value of plant assets; journalizing entries affecting plant assets

Plant Asset	Asset Account	Date Bought	Original Cost	Estimated Salvage Value	Estimated Useful Life	Depreciation Expense 19X5	Accumulated Depreciation 12/31/X5	Ending Book Value 12/31/X5
1	Office Equipment	Jan. 1, 19X1	$1,750.00	$ 250.00	5 years			
2	Store Equipment	Jan. 1, 19X2	7,250.00	1,000.00	5 years			
3	Store Equipment	Apr. 1, 19X2	12,500.00	1,500.00	10 years			
4	Office Equipment	July 1, 19X2	3,500.00	300.00	4 years			
5	Office Equipment	April 1, 19X3	4,400.00	500.00	6 years			
6	Store Equipment	July 1, 19X3	1,400.00	200.00	3 years			
7	Store Equipment	July 1, 19X5	6,050.00	800.00	7 years			
8	Office Equipment	Oct. 1, 19X5	3,000.00	600.00	8 years			

[4, 5]

GENERAL JOURNAL

PAGE 13

DATE		ACCOUNT TITLE	DOC. NO.	POST. REF.	DEBIT	CREDIT

[5]

CASH RECEIPTS JOURNAL

PAGE 25

	DATE	ACCOUNT TITLE	Doc. No.	Post. Ref.	1 GENERAL DEBIT	2 GENERAL CREDIT	3 ACCOUNTS RECEIVABLE CREDIT	4 SALES CREDIT	5 SALES TAX PAYABLE DEBIT	6 SALES TAX PAYABLE CREDIT	7 SALES DISCOUNT DEBIT	8 CASH DEBIT	
1													1
2													2
3													3
4													4
5													5
6													6
7													7
8													8
9													9
10													10
11													11
12													12
13													13
14													14
15													15
16													16
17													17
18													18
19													19
20													20
21													21
22													22
23													23
24													24
25													25

Perfect Score..... 49 Name ____________________

Deduct......... ___ Date ____________ Class ____________

Your Score..... ___ Checked by ____________________

STUDY GUIDE 24

UNIT A—Identifying Accounting Terms

DIRECTIONS: Select the term in Column I that best fits each definition in Column II. Print the letter identifying your choice in the Answers column.

Column I

A. bank discount
B. creditor
C. current liabilities
D. date of a note
E. discounted note
F. dishonored note
G. interest
H. interest-bearing note
I. interest expense
J. interest income
K. interest rate of a note
L. maker of a note
M. maturity date of a note
N. maturity value
O. non-interest-bearing note
P. notes payable
Q. notes receivable
R. number of a note
S. payee of a note
T. principal of a note
U. proceeds
V. promissory note
W. time of a note

Column II	Answers	For Scoring
0. Promissory notes that a business issues to creditors ...	P	**0.** ✓
1. Interest collected in advance on a note		**1.**
2. The original amount of a note		**2.**
3. The amount that is due on the maturity date of a note		**3.**
4. An amount paid for the use of money for a period of time		**4.**
5. A person or organization to whom a liability is owed		**5.**
6. The interest accrued on money borrowed.............		**6.**
7. The date a note is due....................................		**7.**
8. A note that is not paid when due.........................		**8.**
9. The day a note is issued		**9.**
10. The interest earned on money loaned...................		**10.**
11. A note on which interest is paid in advance...........		**11.**
12. A promissory note that requires only the payment of the principal when the note is due		**12.**
13. The amount received for a note after the bank discount has been deducted...............................		**13.**
14. The person or business to whom the amount of a note is payable..		**14.**
15. The person or business who signs a note and thus promises to make payment...............................		**15.**
16. Promissory notes that a business accepts from customers		**16.**
17. The days, months, or years from the date of issue until a note is to be paid		**17.**
18. A written and signed promise to pay a sum of money at a specified time		**18.**
19. The percentage of the principal that is paid for use of the money		**19.**
20. The number assigned by the maker to identify a specific note...		**20.**
21. A promissory note that requires the payment of principal plus interest when the note is due		**21.**
22. Liabilities due within a short time, usually within a year		**22.**

UNIT B—Analyzing Notes Payable and Notes Receivable Transactions

DIRECTIONS: Analyze each of the following transactions into debit and credit parts. Print the letters identifying your choices in the proper Answers column.

Account Title

GENERAL LEDGER:

A. Accounts Payable
B. Accounts Receivable
C. Allowance for Uncoll. Accounts
D. Bad Debts Expense
E. Cash
F. Equipment
G. Interest Expense
H. Interest Income
I. Notes Payable
J. Notes Receivable

ACCTS. REC. LEDGER:

K. Alpha Ceramics
L. Anita Scott

ACCTS. PAYABLE LEDGER:

M. Citation Company

Transaction	Answers Debit	Answers Credit	For Scoring Debit	For Scoring Credit
0–0. Issued an interest–bearing note.......	E	I	**0.** ✓	**0.** ✓
1–2. Received an interest–bearing note from Alpha Ceramics for an extension of time on their account			**1.**	**2.**
3–4. Received a check from Alpha Ceramics in settlement of their note and interest..............................			**3.**	**4.**
5–6. Paid principal and interest on an interest–bearing note..................			**5.**	**6.**
7–8. Anita Scott dishonored her note receivable plus interest due today....			**7.**	**8.**
9–10. Issued an interest–bearing note to Citation Company for an extension of time on this account payable...................................			**9.**	**10.**
11–12. Discounted at the bank a non–interest–bearing note..................			**11.**	**12.**
13–14. Paid for settlement of note and interest....................................			**13.**	**14.**
15–16. Issued check in payment of a discounted note			**15.**	**16.**

UNIT C—Analyzing Notes and Interest

DIRECTIONS: For each of the following items, select the choice that best completes the statement. Print the letter identifying your choice in the Answers column.

	Answers	For Scoring
0. Notes Payable are classified as **(A)** assets **(B)** liabilities **(C)** stockholders' equity **(D)** other expenses...	B	**0.** ✓
1. The maturity date of a 3-month note dated August 22 is **(A)** November 19 **(B)** November 20 **(C)** November 21 **(D)** November 22		**1.**
2. The source document for recording payment received from a customer in settlement of a note is a **(A)** check **(B)** receipt **(C)** memorandum **(D)** copy of the note		**2.**
3. The interest on a 6-month, 10% interest-bearing note of $1,000.00 is **(A)** $10.00 **(B)** $40.00 **(C)** 50.00 **(D)** $100.00....................................		**3.**
4. When a business issues a note payable, the face amount of the note is credited to a(an) **(A)** asset account **(B)** liability account **(C)** owner's equity account **(D)** expense account..		**4.**
5. The maturity value of a 3-month, 12% interest-bearing note of $600.00, **(A)** 528.00 **(B)** 582.00 **(C)** 672.00 **(D)** $618.00..................................		**5.**
6. The source document for recording the issuance of a note payable is a **(A)** check **(B)** receipt **(C)** memorandum **(D)** copy of the note.............		**6.**
7. Interest expense of a business is a **(A)** financial expense **(B)** normal operations expense **(C)** contra revenue account **(D)** additional cost of merchandise...		**7.**
8. Notes receivable are classified as **(A)** assets **(B)** liabilities **(C)** stockholders' equity **(D)** other revenue..		**8.**
9. The bank discount on a 3-month, non-interest-bearing note of $800.00, discounted at 12% is **(A)** zero **(B)** $24.00 **(C)** $96.00 **(D)** none of these....		**9.**
10. The proceeds on a 4-month, non-interest-bearing note of $1,000.00, discounted at 12% is **(A)** $40.00 **(B)** $960.00 **(C)** $1,000.00 **(D)** $1,040.00		**10.**
11. The maturity value of a 6-month, non-interest-bearing note of $800.00, discounted at 12% is **(A)** $48.00 **(B)** $752.00 **(C)** $800.00 **(D)** $848.00......		**11.**

Calculating interest on notes

No. of Note	Principal of Note	Interest Rate	Time of Note	Interest
1	$ 700.00	8%	1 year	
2	1,200.00	12%	6 months	
3	500.00	15%	30 days	
4	800.00	9%	4 months	
5	600.00	10%	60 days	

Calculating maturity dates of notes

DRILL 24-D2, p. 613

No. of Note	Date of Note	Time of Note	Maturity Date
1	Jan. 11	90 days	
2	Feb. 5	1 year	
3	May 17	30 days	
4	July 1	3 months	
5	Oct. 20	6 months	

Calculating maturity dates and interest on notes

DRILL 24-D3, p. 613

No. of Note	Date of Note	Principal of Note	Interest Rate	Time of Note	Maturity Date	Interest
1	Jan. 4	$ 400	9%	30 days		
2	Mar. 21	800	11%	1 year		
3	May 8	1,200	13%	60 days		
4	July 15	1,700	12%	6 months		
5	Sept. 1	2,000	10%	90 days		

Analyzing recording notes payable transactions

DRILL 24-D4, p. 613

Trans. No.	Account Title	Debit	Credit
1.	Cash	✓	
	Interest Expense	✓	
	Notes Payable		✓
2.			
3.			
4.			
5.			
6.			
7.			
8.			

Name ______________________ Date ________ Class ________ *DRILL 24-D5, p. 613*

Analyzing recording notes receivable transactions

Trans. No.	Account Title	Debit	Credit
1.	Notes Receivable	✓	
	Accounts Receivable		✓
2.			
3.			
4.			
5.			
6.			
7.			
8.			

[1]

GENERAL JOURNAL

PAGE 10

DATE		ACCOUNT TITLE	DOC. NO.	POST. REF.	DEBIT	CREDIT

[1, 2]

CASH RECEIPTS JOURNAL

PAGE 20

	DATE	ACCOUNT TITLE	DOC. NO.	POST. REF.	1 GENERAL DEBIT	2 GENERAL CREDIT	3 ACCOUNTS RECEIVABLE CREDIT	4 SALES CREDIT	5 SALES TAX PAYABLE DEBIT	6 SALES TAX PAYABLE CREDIT	7 SALES DISCOUNT DEBIT	8 CASH DEBIT	
1													1
2													2
3													3
4													4
5													5
6													6

[1, 2]

CASH PAYMENTS JOURNAL

PAGE 18

	DATE	ACCOUNT TITLE	CK. NO.	POST. REF.	1 GENERAL DEBIT	2 GENERAL CREDIT	3 ACCOUNTS PAYABLE DEBIT	4 PURCHASES DISCOUNT CREDIT	5 CASH CREDIT	
1										1
2										2
3										3
4										4
5										5
6										6
7										7
8										8
9										9
10										10
11										11
12										12
13										13

PROBLEM 24-2, p. 615

[1]

GENERAL JOURNAL

PAGE 16

DATE		ACCOUNT TITLE	DOC. NO.	POST. REF.	DEBIT	CREDIT

[1, 2]

CASH RECEIPTS JOURNAL

PAGE 23

	DATE	ACCOUNT TITLE	DOC. NO.	POST. REF.	1 GENERAL DEBIT	2 GENERAL CREDIT	3 ACCOUNTS RECEIVABLE CREDIT	4 SALES CREDIT	5 SALES TAX PAYABLE DEBIT	6 SALES TAX PAYABLE CREDIT	7 SALES DISCOUNT DEBIT	8 CASH DEBIT	
1													1
2													2
3													3
4													4
5													5
6													6
7													7

[1, 2]

CASH PAYMENTS JOURNAL

PAGE 20

	DATE	ACCOUNT TITLE	CK. NO.	POST. REF.	1 GENERAL DEBIT	2 GENERAL CREDIT	3 ACCOUNTS PAYABLE DEBIT	4 PURCHASES DISCOUNT CREDIT	5 CASH CREDIT	
1										1
2										2
3										3
4										4
5										5
6										6
7										7
8										8
9										9
10										10
11										11
12										12
13										13

Journalizing notes receivable transactions [1]

GENERAL JOURNAL

PAGE 19

	DATE		ACCOUNT TITLE	DOC. NO.	POST. REF.	DEBIT	CREDIT	
1								1
2								2
3								3
4								4
5								5
6								6
7								7
8								8
9								9
10								10

[1, 2]

CASH RECEIPTS JOURNAL

PAGE 22

	DATE		ACCOUNT TITLE	DOC. NO.	POST. REF.	1 GENERAL	2	3	4	5 SALES TAX PAYABLE	6	7	8	
						DEBIT	CREDIT	ACCOUNTS RECEIVABLE CREDIT	SALES CREDIT	DEBIT	CREDIT	SALES DISCOUNT DEBIT	CASH DEBIT	
1														1
2														2
3														3
4														4
5														5
6														6
7														7
8														8
9														9
10														10

Name ______________________ Date ________ Class ______

MASTERY PROBLEM 24-M, p. 616
[1]

Journalizing notes payable and notes receivable transactions

GENERAL JOURNAL

PAGE 14

	DATE		ACCOUNT TITLE	DOC. NO.	POST. REF.	DEBIT	CREDIT	
1								1
2								2
3								3
4								4
5								5
6								6
7								7
8								8
9								9
10								10
11								11
12								12
13								13
14								14
15								15
16								16
17								17
18								18
19								19
20								20
21								21
22								22
23								23
24								24
25								25
26								26
27								27
28								28
29								29
30								30
31								31
32								32

[1, 2]

CASH RECEIPTS JOURNAL

PAGE 20

					1	2	3	4	5	6	7	8	
	DATE	ACCOUNT TITLE	DOC. NO.	POST. REF.	GENERAL		ACCOUNTS RECEIVABLE CREDIT	SALES CREDIT	SALES TAX PAYABLE		SALES DISCOUNT DEBIT	CASH DEBIT	
					DEBIT	CREDIT			DEBIT	CREDIT			
1													1
2													2
3													3
4													4
5													5
6													6
7													7
8													8
9													9
10													10

[1, 2]

CASH PAYMENTS JOURNAL

PAGE 16

					1	2	3	4	5	
	DATE	ACCOUNT TITLE	CK. NO.	POST. REF.	GENERAL		ACCOUNTS PAYABLE DEBIT	PURCHASES DISCOUNT CREDIT	CASH CREDIT	
					DEBIT	CREDIT				
1										1
2										2
3										3
4										4
5										5
6										6
7										7
8										8
9										9
10										10

Name ______________________ Date ________ Class ______

CHALLENGE PROBLEM 24-C, p. 616

[1]

Journalizing notes payable and notes receivable transactions

GENERAL JOURNAL

PAGE 20

DATE		ACCOUNT TITLE	DOC. NO.	POST. REF.	DEBIT	CREDIT

[1, 2]

CASH RECEIPTS JOURNAL

PAGE 27

	DATE		ACCOUNT TITLE	DOC. NO.	POST. REF.	1 GENERAL DEBIT	2 GENERAL CREDIT	3 ACCOUNTS RECEIVABLE CREDIT	4 SALES CREDIT	5 SALES TAX PAYABLE DEBIT	6 SALES TAX PAYABLE CREDIT	7 SALES DISCOUNT DEBIT	8 CASH DEBIT	
1														1
2														2
3														3
4														4
5														5
6														6
7														7
8														8
9														9

[1, 2]

CASH PAYMENTS JOURNAL

PAGE 31

	DATE		ACCOUNT TITLE	CK. NO.	POST. REF.	1 GENERAL DEBIT	2 GENERAL CREDIT	3 ACCOUNTS PAYABLE DEBIT	4 PURCHASES DISCOUNT CREDIT	5 CASH CREDIT	
1											1
2											2
3											3
4											4
5											5
6											6
7											7
8											8
9											9
10											10
11											11

Perfect Score..... 45 Name ____________________

Deduct......... ___ Date ____________ Class ____________

Your Score..... ___ Checked by ____________________

STUDY GUIDE 25

UNIT A—Identifying Accounting Terms

DIRECTIONS: Select the one term in Column I that best fits each definition in Column II. Print the letter identifying your choice in the Answers column.

Column I

A. accrued expenses
B. accrued interest expense
C. accrued interest income
D. accrued revenue
E. notes receivable
F. reversing entry

Column II	Answers	For Scoring
0. Promissory notes that a business accepts from customers	E	**0.** ✓
1. Revenue earned in one fiscal period but not received until a later fiscal period		**1.**
2. An entry made at the beginning of one fiscal period to reverse an adjusting entry made in the previous fiscal period		**2.**
3. Expenses incurred in one fiscal period but not paid until a later fiscal period		**3.**
4. Interest incurred but not yet paid		**4.**
5. Interest earned but not yet received		**5.**

UNIT B—Examining Accrued Revenue and Accrued Expenses

DIRECTIONS: For each of the following items, select the choice that best completes the statement. Print the letter identifying your choice in the Answers column.

	Answers	For Scoring
0. At the end of a fiscal period, each expense that has been incurred but not paid should be recorded as a(an) **(A)** Adjusting entry **(B)** closing entry **(C)** opening entry **(D)** reversing entry	A	**0.** ✓
1. At the end of a fiscal period, any revenue that has been earned but not received should be debited to an appropriate **(A)** revenue account **(B)** expense account **(C)** asset account **(D)** liability account		**1.**
2. At the end of a fiscal period, any revenue that has been earned but not received should be credited to an appropriate **(A)** revenue account **(B)** expense account **(C)** asset account **(D)** liability account		**2.**
3. Recording reversing entries for the fiscal period in which the revenue has been earned but will not be received until a later fiscal period is an application of the concept **(A)** Objective Evidence **(B)** Historical Cost **(C)** Adequate Disclosure **(D)** Realization of Revenue		**3.**
4. A reversing entry for accrued interest income results in a debit to **(A)** Interest Income **(B)** Interest Receivable **(C)** Income Summary **(D)** Notes Receivable		**4.**
5. A reversing entry for accrued interest income will result in an account balance of **(A)** Interest Receivable Debit **(B)** Interest Receivable Credit **(C)** Interest Income Debit **(D)** Interest Income Credit		**5.**
6. An adjusting entry normally is reversed if the adjusting entry creates a balance in a(an) **(A)** revenue or expense account **(B)** revenue and liability account **(C)** expense and asset account **(D)** asset or liability account		**6.**
7. At the end of a fiscal period, each expense that has been incurred but not paid should be debited to an appropriate **(A)** revenue account **(B)** expense account **(C)** asset account **(D)** liability account		**7.**
8. At the end of a fiscal period, each expense that has been incurred but not paid should be credited to an appropriate **(A)** revenue account **(B)** expense account **(C)** asset account **(D)** liability account		**8.**
9. A reversing entry for an adjusting entry for accrued interest expense will result in an account balance of **(A)** Interest Payable Debit **(B)** Interest Payable Credit **(C)** Interest Expense Debit **(D)** Interest Expense Credit		**9.**

UNIT C—Analyzing Accounts Affected by Accrued Revenue and Accrued Expenses

DIRECTIONS: Analyze each of the following entries into debit and credit parts. Print the letters identifying your choice in the proper Answers columns.

Account Titles

A. Cash
B. Income Summary
C. Interest Expense
D. Interest Income
E. Interest Payable
F. Interest Receivable
G. Notes Payable
H. Notes Receivable

Transactions	Answers Debit	Answers Credit	For Scoring Debit	For Scoring Credit
0–0. Closing entry for interest expense account	B	C	**0.** ✓	**0.** ✓
1–2. Adjusting entry for interest income earned but not received at the end of a fiscal period			**1.**	**2.**
3–4. Pay principal and interest for a note payable issued in a previous fiscal period			**3.**	**4.**
5–6. Reversing entry for accrued interest expense			**5.**	**6.**
7–8. Closing entry for interest income account			**7.**	**8.**
9–10. Adjusting entry for interest expense incurred but not paid at the end of a fiscal period			**9.**	**10.**
11–12. Reversing entry for accrued interest income			**11.**	**12.**
13–14. Receive principal and interest for a note receivable accepted in a previous fiscal period			**13.**	**14.**

UNIT D—Analyzing Accrued Revenue and Accrued Expenses

DIRECTIONS: Place a check mark in the proper Answers column to show whether each of the following statements is true or false.

	Answers True	Answers False	For Scoring
0. The adjustment for accrued interest income is planned on a work sheet	✓		**0.** ✓
1. Interest Income is closed into the retained earnings account			**1.**
2. Reporting all liabilities on a balance sheet, including accrued expenses, is an application of the concept Adequate Disclosure			**2.**
3. When an adjusting entry for accrued interest expense is made, the account Interest Receivable is debited			**3.**
4. A reversing entry for accrued interest expense reduces the amount of interest expense incurred			**4.**
5. Revenue usually is recorded when the revenue is earned			**5.**
6. Adjusting entries are made at the beginning of each fiscal period			**6.**
7. Accrued interest is figured by multiplying principal times interest rate times time as a fraction of a year			**7.**
8. Reversing entries are made on the last day of the fiscal period			**8.**
9. At the end of a fiscal period, the Interest Expense debit balance after adjustments shows the amount of interest expense that has been incurred in that fiscal period			**9.**
10. The interest income account normally is used only during the closing process			**10.**
11. Accrued revenue receivable is reported on a balance sheet			**11.**
12. Information used to journalize an adjustment for accrued interest income is obtained from the Trial Balance columns of a work sheet			**12.**
13. Information needed to record closing entries for interest income is obtained from the Income Statement columns of a work sheet			**13.**
14. The balance of Interest Payable on a work sheet is extended to the Income Statement Credit column			**14.**
15. Information needed to record closing entries for interest expense is obtained from the Income Statement columns of a work sheet			**15.**
16. An Interest Payable credit balance is accrued interest expense incurred in the current year but to be paid in the next year			**16.**
17. When reversing entries are used for accrued interest income, no credit entry is required to recognize collection of the balance of Interest Receivable			**17.**

Analyzing entries for notes receivable and accrued revenue

Entry No.	Cash		Notes Receivable		Accounts Receivable		Interest Receivable		Interest Income		Income Summary	
	Debit	**Credit**	**Debit**	**Credit**	**Debit**	**Credit**	**Debit**	**Credit**	**Debit**	**Credit**	**Debit**	**Credit**
1.												
2.												
3.												
4.												
5.												

Analyzing entries for notes payable and accrued expenses

DRILL 25-D2, p. 633

Entry No.	Cash		Notes Payable		Accounts Payable		Interest Payable		Interest Expense		Income Summary	
	Debit	**Credit**	**Debit**	**Credit**	**Debit**	**Credit**	**Debit**	**Credit**	**Debit**	**Credit**	**Debit**	**Credit**
1.												
2.												
3.												
4.												
5.												

Problem 25-1 begins on page 417.

PROBLEM 25-1, *continued*
[1–4]

GENERAL LEDGER

ACCOUNT Notes Receivable — ACCOUNT NO. 1115

DATE		ITEM	POST. REF.	DEBIT	CREDIT	BALANCE DEBIT	BALANCE CREDIT
19X1 Dec.	31	Balance	✓			800 00	

ACCOUNT Interest Receivable — ACCOUNT NO. 1120

DATE		ITEM	POST. REF.	DEBIT	CREDIT	BALANCE DEBIT	BALANCE CREDIT

ACCOUNT Income Summary — ACCOUNT NO. 3120

DATE		ITEM	POST. REF.	DEBIT	CREDIT	BALANCE DEBIT	BALANCE CREDIT

ACCOUNT Interest Income — ACCOUNT NO. 7110

DATE		ITEM	POST. REF.	DEBIT	CREDIT	BALANCE DEBIT	BALANCE CREDIT
19X1 Dec.	31	Balance	✓				226 00

Name ______________________ Date ________ Class ________

PROBLEM 25-1, p. 634

[1, 2]

Journalizing and posting entries for accrued revenue

GENERAL JOURNAL

PAGE 14

	DATE		ACCOUNT TITLE	DOC. NO.	POST. REF.	DEBIT	CREDIT	
1								1
2								2
3								3
4								4
5								5
6								6
7								7
8								8
9								9
10								10
11								11
12								12

[3]

GENERAL JOURNAL

PAGE 15

	DATE		ACCOUNT TITLE	DOC. NO.	POST. REF.	DEBIT	CREDIT	
1								1
2								2
3								3
4								4
5								5
6								6
7								7
8								8
9								9
10								10
11								11
12								12

PROBLEM 25-1, concluded

[4]

CASH RECEIPTS JOURNAL

PAGE 18

					1	2	3	4	5	6	7	8	
	DATE	ACCOUNT TITLE	DOC. NO.	POST. REF.	GENERAL		ACCOUNTS RECEIVABLE CREDIT	SALES CREDIT	SALES TAX PAYABLE		SALES DISCOUNT DEBIT	CASH DEBIT	
					DEBIT	CREDIT			DEBIT	CREDIT			
1													1
2													2
3													3
4													4
5													5
6													6
7													7
8													8
9													9
10													10
11													11
12													12
13													13
14													14
15													15
16													16
17													17
18													18
19													19
20													20
21													21
22													22
23													23
24													24
25													25

Name ______________________ Date ________ Class ________

PROBLEM 25-2, p. 634

[1, 2]

Journalizing and posting entries for accrued expenses

GENERAL JOURNAL

PAGE 15

DATE		ACCOUNT TITLE	DOC. NO.	POST. REF.	DEBIT	CREDIT

[3]

GENERAL JOURNAL

PAGE 16

DATE		ACCOUNT TITLE	DOC. NO.	POST. REF.	DEBIT	CREDIT

[4]

CASH PAYMENTS JOURNAL

PAGE 20

	DATE	ACCOUNT TITLE	CK. NO.	POST. REF.	1 GENERAL DEBIT	2 GENERAL CREDIT	3 ACCOUNTS PAYABLE DEBIT	4 PURCHASES DISCOUNT CREDIT	5 CASH CREDIT	
1										1
2										2
3										3
4										4
5										5
6										6
7										7
8										8
9										9
10										10
11										11
12										12
13										13
14										14
15										15
16										16
17										17
18										18
19										19
20										20
21										21
22										22
23										23
24										24
25										25

[1–4]

GENERAL LEDGER

ACCOUNT Notes Payable **ACCOUNT NO.** 2105

DATE		ITEM	POST. REF.	DEBIT	CREDIT	BALANCE DEBIT	BALANCE CREDIT
19X1 Dec.	31	Balance	✓				4 000 00

ACCOUNT Interest Payable **ACCOUNT NO.** 2110

DATE		ITEM	POST. REF.	DEBIT	CREDIT	BALANCE DEBIT	BALANCE CREDIT

ACCOUNT Income Summary **ACCOUNT NO.** 3120

DATE		ITEM	POST. REF.	DEBIT	CREDIT	BALANCE DEBIT	BALANCE CREDIT

ACCOUNT Interest Expense **ACCOUNT NO.** 8110

DATE		ITEM	POST. REF.	DEBIT	CREDIT	BALANCE DEBIT	BALANCE CREDIT
19X1 Dec.	31	Balance	✓			634 00	

Journalizing and posting entries for accrued revenue and expenses

MASTERY PROBLEM 25-M, p. 635

[1, 2]

GENERAL JOURNAL

PAGE 15

	DATE		ACCOUNT TITLE	DOC. NO.	POST. REF.	DEBIT	CREDIT	
1								1
2								2
3								3
4								4
5								5
6								6
7								7
8								8
9								9
10								10
11								11
12								12

[3]

GENERAL JOURNAL

PAGE 16

	DATE		ACCOUNT TITLE	DOC. NO.	POST. REF.	DEBIT	CREDIT	
1								1
2								2
3								3
4								4
5								5
6								6
7								7
8								8
9								9
10								10
11								11
12								12

[1–4]

GENERAL LEDGER

ACCOUNT Notes Receivable ACCOUNT NO. 1115

DATE		ITEM	POST. REF.	DEBIT	CREDIT	BALANCE DEBIT	BALANCE CREDIT
19X1 Dec.	31	Balance	✓			600 00	

ACCOUNT Interest Receivable ACCOUNT NO. 1120

DATE		ITEM	POST. REF.	DEBIT	CREDIT	BALANCE DEBIT	BALANCE CREDIT

ACCOUNT Notes Payable ACCOUNT NO. 2105

DATE		ITEM	POST. REF.	DEBIT	CREDIT	BALANCE DEBIT	BALANCE CREDIT
19X1 Dec.	31	Balance	✓				2,400 00

ACCOUNT Interest Payable ACCOUNT NO. 2110

DATE		ITEM	POST. REF.	DEBIT	CREDIT	BALANCE DEBIT	BALANCE CREDIT

[1–4]

GENERAL LEDGER

ACCOUNT Income Summary ACCOUNT NO. 3120

DATE		ITEM	POST. REF.	DEBIT	CREDIT	BALANCE DEBIT	BALANCE CREDIT

ACCOUNT Interest Income ACCOUNT NO. 7110

DATE		ITEM	POST. REF.	DEBIT	CREDIT	BALANCE DEBIT	BALANCE CREDIT
19X1 Dec.	31	Balance	✓				104 00

ACCOUNT Interest Expense ACCOUNT NO. 8110

DATE		ITEM	POST. REF.	DEBIT	CREDIT	BALANCE DEBIT	BALANCE CREDIT
19X1 Dec.	31	Balance	✓			325 00	

ACCOUNT ACCOUNT NO.

DATE		ITEM	POST. REF.	DEBIT	CREDIT	BALANCE DEBIT	BALANCE CREDIT

[4]

CASH RECEIPTS JOURNAL

PAGE 19

	DATE	ACCOUNT TITLE	DOC. NO.	POST. REF.	1 GENERAL DEBIT	2 GENERAL CREDIT	3 ACCOUNTS RECEIVABLE CREDIT	4 SALES CREDIT	5 SALES TAX PAYABLE DEBIT	6 SALES TAX PAYABLE CREDIT	7 SALES DISCOUNT DEBIT	8 CASH DEBIT	
1													1
2													2
3													3
4													4
5													5
6													6
7													7
8													8
9													9

[5]

CASH PAYMENTS JOURNAL

PAGE 25

	DATE	ACCOUNT TITLE	CK. NO.	POST. REF.	1 GENERAL DEBIT	2 GENERAL CREDIT	3 ACCOUNTS PAYABLE DEBIT	4 PURCHASES DISCOUNT CREDIT	5 CASH CREDIT	
1										1
2										2
3										3
4										4
5										5
6										6
7										7
8										8
9										9

Journalizing and posting entries for accrued revenue and expenses

CHALLENGE PROBLEM 25-C, p. 636

[1, 2]

GENERAL JOURNAL

PAGE 13

DATE		ACCOUNT TITLE	DOC. NO.	POST. REF.	DEBIT	CREDIT

[3]

GENERAL JOURNAL

PAGE 14

DATE		ACCOUNT TITLE	DOC. NO.	POST. REF.	DEBIT	CREDIT

[4]

GENERAL JOURNAL

PAGE 16

	DATE		ACCOUNT TITLE	DOC. NO.	POST. REF.	DEBIT	CREDIT	
1								1
2								2
3								3
4								4
5								5
6								6
7								7
8								8
9								9
10								10
11								11
12								12
13								13
14								14
15								15
16								16
17								17
18								18
19								19
20								20
21								21
22								22
23								23
24								24
25								25
26								26
27								27
28								28
29								29
30								30
31								31
32								32

[5]

CASH PAYMENTS JOURNAL

PAGE 33

	DATE		ACCOUNT TITLE	CK. NO.	POST. REF.	1 GENERAL DEBIT	2 GENERAL CREDIT	3 ACCOUNTS PAYABLE DEBIT	4 PURCHASES DISCOUNT CREDIT	5 CASH CREDIT	
1											1
2											2
3											3
4											4
5											5
6											6
7											7
8											8
9											9
10											10
11											11
12											12
13											13
14											14
15											15
16											16
17											17
18											18
19											19
20											20
21											21
22											22
23											23
24											24
25											25

[1–5]

GENERAL LEDGER

ACCOUNT Notes Receivable — ACCOUNT NO. 1115

DATE		ITEM	POST. REF.	DEBIT	CREDIT	BALANCE DEBIT	BALANCE CREDIT
19X1 Dec.	31	Balance	✓			4 0 0 00	

ACCOUNT Interest Receivable — ACCOUNT NO. 1120

DATE		ITEM	POST. REF.	DEBIT	CREDIT	BALANCE DEBIT	BALANCE CREDIT

ACCOUNT Accounts Receivable — ACCOUNT NO. 1125

DATE		ITEM	POST. REF.	DEBIT	CREDIT	BALANCE DEBIT	BALANCE CREDIT

ACCOUNT Notes Payable — ACCOUNT NO. 2105

DATE		ITEM	POST. REF.	DEBIT	CREDIT	BALANCE DEBIT	BALANCE CREDIT
19X1 Dec.	31	Balance	✓				2 5 0 0 00

[1–5]

GENERAL LEDGER

ACCOUNT Interest Payable — ACCOUNT NO. 2110

DATE		ITEM	POST. REF.	DEBIT	CREDIT	BALANCE DEBIT	BALANCE CREDIT

ACCOUNT Income Summary — ACCOUNT NO. 3120

DATE		ITEM	POST. REF.	DEBIT	CREDIT	BALANCE DEBIT	BALANCE CREDIT

ACCOUNT Interest Income — ACCOUNT NO. 7110

DATE		ITEM	POST. REF.	DEBIT	CREDIT	BALANCE DEBIT	BALANCE CREDIT
19X1 Dec.	31	Balance	✓				326 50

ACCOUNT Interest Expense — ACCOUNT NO. 8110

DATE		ITEM	POST. REF.	DEBIT	CREDIT	BALANCE DEBIT	BALANCE CREDIT
19X1 Dec.	31	Balance	✓			1248 00	

Perfect Score..... 44 Name ______________________

Deduct......... ___ Date ______________ Class ______________

Your Score..... ___ Checked by ______________________

STUDY GUIDE 26

UNIT A—Analyzing Dividend Transactions and Adjusting Entries for a Corporation

DIRECTIONS: Analyze each of the following entries into debit and credit parts. Print the letters identifying your choices in the proper Answers column.

Account Titles

A. Accumulated Depreciation—Office Equipment
B. Accumulated Depreciation—Store Equipment
C. Allowance for Uncollectible Accounts
D. Cash
E. Depreciation Expense—Office Equipment
F. Depreciation Expense—Store Equipment
G. Dividends
H. Dividends Payable
I. Federal Income Tax Expense
J. Federal Income Tax Payable
K. Income Summary
L. Insurance Expense
M. Interest Expense
N. Interest Income
O. Interest Payable
P. Interest Receivable
Q. Merchandise Inventory
R. Prepaid Insurance
S. Retained Earnings
T. Supplies
U. Supplies Expense
V. Uncollectible Accounts Expense

Transactions	Answers Debit	Answers Credit	For Scoring Debit	For Scoring Credit
0–0. Adjusting entry for supplies..............	U	T	**0.** ✓	**0.** ✓
1–2. Adjusting entry for accrued interest expense..			**1.**	**2.**
3–4. Adjusting entry for prepaid insurance ..			**3.**	**4.**
5–6. Declared stockholders' dividend.........			**5.**	**6.**
7–8. Adjusting entry for a decrease in merchandise inventory			**7.**	**8.**
9–10. Adjusting entry for an increase in merchandise inventory			**9.**	**10.**
11–12. Adjusting entry for uncollectible accounts expense for the period.........			**11.**	**12.**
13–14. Adjusting entry for accrued interest income..			**13.**	**14.**
15–16. Paid cash for dividends declared			**15.**	**16.**
17–18. Adjusting entry for federal income tax.			**17.**	**18.**
19–20. Adjusting entry for depreciation expense—store equipment			**19.**	**20.**
21–22. Adjusting entry for depreciation expense—office equipment..............			**21.**	**22.**

UNIT B—Identifying Accounting Terms

DIRECTIONS: Select the one term in Column I that best fits each definition in Column II. Print the letter identifying your choice in the Answers column.

Column I	Column II	Answers	For Scoring
A. accrued revenue	0. Revenue earned in one fiscal period but not received until a later fiscal period	A	0. ✓
B. board of directors	1. Action by a board of directors to distribute corporate earnings to stockholders		1.
C. declaring a dividend	2. A group of persons elected by the stockholders to manage a corporation		2.
D. dividends	3. An owner of one or more shares of a corporation		3.
E. retained earnings	4. An amount earned by a corporation and not yet distributed to stockholders		4.
F. stockholder	5. Earnings distributed to stockholders		5.

UNIT C—Analyzing Dividend Transactions and End-of-Fiscal-Period Adjustments for a Corporation

DIRECTIONS: Place a check mark in the proper Answers column to show whether each of the following statements is true or false.

	Answers True	Answers False	For Scoring
0. Each unit of ownership in a corporation is known as a share of stock	✓		0. ✓
1. Most accounting procedures used for a corporation differ from the procedures used for a proprietorship or a partnership			1.
2. A dividends account is listed under the major chart of accounts division titled Operating Expenses			2.
3. A dividends account has a normal debit balance and is increased by a debit			3.
4. Separate general ledger accounts are kept for each owner of a corporation			4.
5. Both partnerships and corporations use accounts for federal income tax			5.
6. No income can be distributed to stockholders except by formal action of a corporation's board of directors			6.
7. A check is the source document for declaring a dividend			7.
8. Work sheet adjustments for interest expense are made for corporations but not for proprietorships			8.
9. The two accounts used to make an uncollectible accounts expense adjustment are Uncollectible Accounts Expense and Accounts Receivable			9.
10. A corporation's dividend account is a temporary account similar to a proprietorship's capital account			10.
11. The balance of Federal Income Tax Payable is the amount of income tax expense still unpaid at the end of a fiscal period			11.
12. When the total of a work sheet's Income Statement Credit column is larger than the total of the Income Statement Debit column, the difference represents net income of the business			12.
13. The amount of federal income tax depends on net income before the tax is recorded			13.
14. Work sheets for corporations, proprietorships, and partnerships are similar			14.
15. A declared dividend is classified as an expense			15.
16. The merchandise inventory balance in a trial balance is the beginning inventory for a fiscal period			16.
17. Federal income tax is an expense of a corporation			17.

Name ______________ Date ________ Class ________

DRILL 26-D1, p. 650

Analyzing adjustments on a work sheet

Adjustment No.	Work Sheet Adjustment	
	Account Debited	Account Credited
1.	Supplies Expense	Supplies
2.		
3.		
4.		
5.		
6.		
7.		
8.		
9.		

Extending account balances on a work sheet

DRILL 26-D2, p. 650

Account	Work Sheet Columns			
	Income Statement		Balance Sheet	
	Debit	Credit	Debit	Credit
1. Allowance for Uncollectible Accts.				✓
2. Sales Returns and Allowances				
3. Notes Payable				
4. Retained Earnings				
5. Accounts Receivable				
6. Purchases Discount				
7. Merchandise Inventory				
8. Dividends				
9. Federal Income Tax Expense				
10. Accum. Depr.— Store Equip.				

Journalizing dividends [1]

GENERAL JOURNAL

PAGE 12

	DATE		ACCOUNT TITLE	DOC. NO.	POST. REF.	DEBIT	CREDIT	
1								1
2								2
3								3
4								4
5								5
6								6
7								7
8								8
9								9
10								10

[2]

CASH PAYMENTS JOURNAL

PAGE 15

	DATE		ACCOUNT TITLE	CK. NO.	POST. REF.	1 GENERAL DEBIT	2 GENERAL CREDIT	3 ACCOUNTS PAYABLE DEBIT	4 PURCHASES DISCOUNT CREDIT	5 CASH CREDIT	
1											1
2											2
3											3
4											4
5											5
6											6
7											7
8											8
9											9
10											10

PROBLEM 26-1, p. 651

Name ________________ Date ________________ Class ________________

Extra form

	ACCOUNT TITLE	TRIAL BALANCE		ADJUSTMENTS		INCOME STATEMENT		BALANCE SHEET		
		1	2	3	4	5	6	7	8	
		DEBIT	CREDIT	DEBIT	CREDIT	DEBIT	CREDIT	DEBIT	CREDIT	
1										1
2										2
3										3
4										4
5										5
6										6
7										7
8										8
9										9
10										10
11										11
12										12
13										13
14										14
15										15
16										16
17										17
18										18
19										19
20										20
21										21
22										22
23										23
24										24
25										25
26										26
27										27
28										28
29										29
30										30
31										31
32										32

Preparing a work sheet for a corporation

PROBLEM 26-2, p. 651

Eagle System Corporation

Work Sheet

For Year Ended December 31, 19--

	ACCOUNT TITLE	1 TRIAL BALANCE DEBIT	2 TRIAL BALANCE CREDIT	3 ADJUSTMENTS DEBIT	4 ADJUSTMENTS CREDIT	5 INCOME STATEMENT DEBIT	6 INCOME STATEMENT CREDIT	7 BALANCE SHEET DEBIT	8 BALANCE SHEET CREDIT	
1	Cash	95,052.23								1
2	Petty Cash	300.00								2
3	Notes Receivable	10,952.00								3
4	Interest Receivable									4
5	Accounts Receivable	70,094.10								5
6	Allow. for Uncollectible Accts.		44.64							6
7	Merchandise Inventory	64,316.30								7
8	Supplies	2,552.08								8
9	Prepaid Insurance	9,071.60								9
10	Office Equipment	26,940.00								10
11	Accum. Depr.—Office Equip.		6,735.00							11
12	Store Equipment	21,199.20								12
13	Accum. Depr.—Store Equip.		6,357.40							13
14	Notes Payable		14,400.00							14
15	Interest Payable									15
16	Accounts Payable		62,016.18							16
17	Employee Income Tax Payable		1,652.40							17
18	Federal Income Tax Payable									18
19	FICA Tax Payable		1,906.70							19
20	Sales Tax Payable		6,652.60							20
21	Unemploy. Tax Pay.—Federal		33.44							21
22	Unemploy. Tax Pay.—State		225.72							22
23	Health Insurance Premiums Pay.		702.60							23
24	Dividends Payable		10,800.00							24
25	Capital Stock		100,000.00							25
26	Retained Earnings		59,241.54							26
27	Dividends	43,200.00								27
28	Income Summary									28
29	Sales		1078,888.30							29
30	Sales Discount	2,002.80								30
31	Sales Returns and Allowances	8,347.20								31
32	Purchases	737,482.80								32

Eagle System Corporation

Work Sheet (continued)

For Year Ended December 31, 19--

	ACCOUNT TITLE	1 TRIAL BALANCE DEBIT	2 TRIAL BALANCE CREDIT	3 ADJUSTMENTS DEBIT	4 ADJUSTMENTS CREDIT	5 INCOME STATEMENT DEBIT	6 INCOME STATEMENT CREDIT	7 BALANCE SHEET DEBIT	8 BALANCE SHEET CREDIT	
33	Purchases Discount		5463 60							33
34	Purchases Returns and Allow.		2716 14							34
35	Advertising Expense	15948 00								35
36	Credit Card Fee Expense	11066 94								36
37	Depr. Expense—Office Equip.									37
38	Depr. Expense—Store Equip.									38
39	Insurance Expense									39
40	Miscellaneous Expense	9682 20								40
41	Payroll Taxes Expense	14966 00								41
42	Rent Expense	32400 00								42
43	Salary Expense	158964 00								43
44	Supplies Expense									44
45	Uncollectible Accounts Expense									45
46	Utilities Expense	2661 00								46
47	Gain on Plant Assets		110 00							47
48	Interest Income		894 48							48
49	Cash Short and Over	8 15								49
50	Interest Expense	2086 14								50
51	Loss on Plant Assets	248 00								51
52	Federal Income Tax Expense	19300 00								52
53		1358840 74	1358840 74							53
54	Net Income after Fed. Inc. Tax									54
55										55
56										56
57										57
58										58
59										59
60										60
61										61
62										62
63										63
64										64

Journalizing dividends and preparing a work sheet for a corporation [1]

MASTERY PROBLEM 26-M, p. 652

Universal Corporation

Work Sheet

For Year Ended December 31, 19--

	ACCOUNT TITLE	1 TRIAL BALANCE DEBIT	2 TRIAL BALANCE CREDIT	3 ADJUSTMENTS DEBIT	4 ADJUSTMENTS CREDIT	5 INCOME STATEMENT DEBIT	6 INCOME STATEMENT CREDIT	7 BALANCE SHEET DEBIT	8 BALANCE SHEET CREDIT	
1	Cash	45 194 00								1
2	Petty Cash	300 00								2
3	Notes Receivable	3 938 00								3
4	Interest Receivable									4
5	Accounts Receivable	53 724 00								5
6	Allow. for Uncollectible Accts.		351 00							6
7	Merchandise Inventory	112 331 00								7
8	Supplies	7 484 00								8
9	Prepaid Insurance	14 175 00								9
10	Office Equipment	12 383 00								10
11	Accum. Depr.—Office Equip.		2 486 00							11
12	Store Equipment	75 224 00								12
13	Accum. Depr.—Store Equip.		14 439 00							13
14	Notes Payable		2 494 00							14
15	Interest Payable									15
16	Accounts Payable		55 691 00							16
17	Employee Income Tax Payable		1 481 00							17
18	Federal Income Tax Payable									18
19	FICA Tax Payable		1 798 00							19
20	Sales Tax Payable		6 043 00							20
21	Unemploy. Tax Pay.—Federal		31 00							21
22	Unemploy. Tax Pay.—State		209 25							22
23	Health Insurance Premiums Pay.		506 00							23
24	Dividends Payable		10 500 00							24
25	Capital Stock		100 000 00							25
26	Retained Earnings		92 842 75							26
27	Dividends	42 000 00								27
28	Income Summary									28
29	Sales		1369 987 00							29
30	Sales Discount	6 903 00								30
31	Sales Returns and Allowances	16 243 00								31
32	Purchases	979 468 00								32

[1]

Universal Corporation
Work Sheet (continued)
For Year Ended December 31, 19--

	ACCOUNT TITLE	1 TRIAL BALANCE DEBIT	2 TRIAL BALANCE CREDIT	3 ADJUSTMENTS DEBIT	4 ADJUSTMENTS CREDIT	5 INCOME STATEMENT DEBIT	6 INCOME STATEMENT CREDIT	7 BALANCE SHEET DEBIT	8 BALANCE SHEET CREDIT	
33	Purchases Discount		5 355 00							33
34	Purchases Returns and Allow.		3 570 00							34
35	Advertising Expense	18 857 00								35
36	Credit Card Fee Expense	12 323 00								36
37	Depr. Expense—Office Equip.									37
38	Depr. Expense—Store Equip.									38
39	Insurance Expense									39
40	Miscellaneous Expense	25 718 00								40
41	Payroll Taxes Expense	15 778 00								41
42	Rent Expense	42 840 00								42
43	Salary Expense	167 864 00								43
44	Supplies Expense									44
45	Uncollectible Accounts Expense									45
46	Utilities Expense	3 290 00								46
47	Gain on Plant Assets		205 00							47
48	Interest Income		355 00							48
49	Cash Short and Over	11 00								49
50	Interest Expense	281 00								50
51	Loss on Plant Assets	315 00								51
52	Federal Income Tax Expense	11 700 00								52
53		1668 344 00	1668 344 00							53
54	Net Income after Fed. Inc. Tax									54
55										55

[2]

CASH PAYMENTS JOURNAL

PAGE 36

	DATE	ACCOUNT TITLE	CK. NO.	POST. REF.	1 GENERAL DEBIT	2 GENERAL CREDIT	3 ACCOUNTS PAYABLE DEBIT	4 PURCHASES DISCOUNT CREDIT	5 CASH CREDIT	
1										1
2										2
3										3

	ACCOUNT TITLE	TRIAL BALANCE 1 DEBIT	TRIAL BALANCE 2 CREDIT	ADJUSTMENTS 3 DEBIT	ADJUSTMENTS 4 CREDIT	INCOME STATEMENT 5 DEBIT	INCOME STATEMENT 6 CREDIT	BALANCE SHEET 7 DEBIT	BALANCE SHEET 8 CREDIT	
1										1
2										2
3										3
4										4
5										5
6										6
7										7
8										8
9										9
10										10
11										11
12										12
13										13
14										14
15										15
16										16
17										17
18										18
19										19
20										20
21										21
22										22
23										23
24										24
25										25
26										26
27										27
28										28
29										29
30										30
31										31
32										32

Name ______________________ Date ________ Class ______

Challenge problem 26-C begins on page 444.

Center

(continued)

December 31, 19--

	5	6	7	8	9	10	
	ADJUSTED TRIAL BALANCE		INCOME STATEMENT		BALANCE SHEET		
	DEBIT	CREDIT	DEBIT	CREDIT	DEBIT	CREDIT	
33							33
34							34
35							35
36							36
37							37
38							38
39							39
40							40
41							41
42							42
43							43
44							44
45							45
46							46
47							47
48							48
49							49
50							50
51							51
52							52
53							53
54							54
55							55
56							56
57							57
58							58
59							59
60							60
61							61
62							62
63							63
64							64

Austin Sports

Work

For Year Ended

	ACCOUNT TITLE	1 TRIAL BALANCE DEBIT	2 TRIAL BALANCE CREDIT	3 ADJUSTMENTS DEBIT	4 ADJUSTMENTS CREDIT	
1	Cash	47609 00				1
2	Petty Cash	250 00				2
3	Notes Receivable	3180 00				3
4	Interest Receivable					4
5	Accounts Receivable	50562 00				5
6	Allowance for Uncollectible Accounts		344 00			6
7	Merchandise Inventory	78670 00				7
8	Supplies	7024 00				8
9	Prepaid Insurance	13320 00				9
10	Office Equipment	11656 00				10
11	Accumulated Depreciation—Office Equipment		2340 00			11
12	Store Equipment	70800 00				12
13	Accumulated Depreciation—Store Equipment		13590 00			13
14	Notes Payable		1500 00			14
15	Interest Payable					15
16	Accounts Payable		52680 00			16
17	Employee Income Tax Payable		1396 00			17
18	Federal Income Tax Payable					18
19	FICA Tax Payable		733 00			19
20	Sales Tax Payable		5688 00			20
21	Unemployment Tax Payable—Federal		35 00			21
22	Unemployment Tax Payable—State		236 25			22
23	Health Insurance Premiums Payable		478 00			23
24	Dividends Payable		7500 00			24
25	Capital Stock		100000 00			25
26	Retained Earnings		69828 00			26
27	Dividends	30000 00				27
28	Income Summary					28
29	Sales		1312692 00			29
30	Sales Discount	4029 00				30
31	Sales Returns and Allowances	15925 00				31
32	Purchases	960264 00				32

Center

Sheet

December 31, 19--

	5	6	7	8	9	10	
	ADJUSTED TRIAL BALANCE		INCOME STATEMENT		BALANCE SHEET		
	DEBIT	CREDIT	DEBIT	CREDIT	DEBIT	CREDIT	
1							1
2							2
3							3
4							4
5							5
6							6
7							7
8							8
9							9
10							10
11							11
12							12
13							13
14							14
15							15
16							16
17							17
18							18
19							19
20							20
21							21
22							22
23							23
24							24
25							25
26							26
27							27
28							28
29							29
30							30
31							31
32							32

Austin Sports

Work Sheet

For Year Ended

	ACCOUNT TITLE	1 TRIAL BALANCE DEBIT	2 TRIAL BALANCE CREDIT	3 ADJUSTMENTS DEBIT	4 ADJUSTMENTS CREDIT	
33	Purchases Discount		7113 00			33
34	Purchases Returns and Allowances		3500 00			34
35	Advertising Expense	21232 00				35
36	Credit Card Fee Expense	11850 00				36
37	Depreciation Expense—Office Equipment					37
38	Depreciation Expense—Store Equipment					38
39	Insurance Expense					39
40	Miscellaneous Expense	25214 00				40
41	Payroll Taxes Expense	14811 00				41
42	Rent Expense	42000 00				42
43	Salary Expense	164574 00				43
44	Supplies Expense					44
45	Uncollectible Accounts Expense					45
46	Utilities Expense	3150 00				46
47	Gain on Plant Assets		240 00			47
48	Interest Income		357 75			48
49	Cash Short and Over	8 00				49
50	Interest Expense	168 00				50
51	Loss on Plant Assets	155 00				51
52	Federal Income Tax Expense	3800 00				52
53		1580251 00	1580251 00			53
54	Net Income after Fed. Inc. Tax					54
55						55
56						56
57						57
58						58
59						59
60						60
61						61
62						62
63						63
64						64

Perfect Score..... 57 Name ______________________

Deduct......... ___ Date ______________ Class ______________

Your Score..... ___ Checked by ______________________

STUDY GUIDE 27

UNIT A—Identifying Accounting Terms

DIRECTIONS: Select the one term in Column I that best fits each definition in Column II. Print the letter identifying your choice in the Answers column.

Column I	*Column II*	Answers	For Scoring
A. book value	**0.** Liabilities due within a short time, usually within a year	B	**0.** ✓
B. current liabilities	**1.** The difference between an asset's account balance and its related contra account balance		**1.**
C. current ratio	**2.** Liabilities owed for more than a year		**2.**
D. long-term liabilities	**3.** A comparison between two numbers showing how many times one number exceeds the other		**3.**
E. net purchases	**4.** A ratio that shows the numeric relationship of current assets to current liabilities		**4.**
F. net sales	**5.** A financial statement that shows changes in a corporation's ownership for a fiscal period		**5.**
G. ratio	**6.** Total purchases less purchases discount and purchases returns and allowances		**6.**
H. statement of stockholders' equity	**7.** The amount of total current assets less total current liabilities		**7.**
I. working capital	**8.** Total sales less sales discount and sales returns and allowances		**8.**

UNIT B—Analyzing End-of-Fiscal-Period Work for a Corporation

DIRECTIONS: Place a check mark in the proper Answers column to show whether each of the following statements is true or false.

Statement	Answers: True	Answers: False	For Scoring
0. Corporations prepare financial statements that report financial information similar to proprietorships and partnerships	✓		**0.** ✓
1. If an adjusting entry creates a balance in an asset or liability account, a reversing entry is necessary			**1.**
2. For a business to determine whether it is progressing satisfactorily, results of operations are compared with the balance sheet			**2.**
3. A corporation's preparation of financial statements at the end of each year is an application of the Accounting Period Cycle concept			**3.**
4. An example of a long-term liability is Mortgage Payable			**4.**
5. The balance of Federal Income Tax Payable is the amount of income tax expense reported for the fiscal period			**5.**
6. Both partnerships and corporations use accounts for federal income tax			**6.**
7. A declared dividend is reported on the income statement as an expense			**7.**
8. Net purchases is reported in the Operating Expenses section of an income statement			**8.**
9. A corporation's capital stock plus retained earnings always equals total assets			**9.**
10. Reporting net income before and after federal income tax is unique to corporation income statements			**10.**
11. A corporation's dividend account is a temporary account similar to a proprietorship's capital account			**11.**
12. The stockholders' equity section of a balance sheet contains accounts related to capital stock and earnings kept in the business			**12.**
13. Net sales is reported in the Operating Revenue section of an income statement			**13.**
14. To calculate the component percentage of cost of merchandise sold, divide net sales by cost of merchandise sold			**14.**
15. A corporation balance sheet reports assets, liabilities, and dividends paid			**15.**

UNIT C—Analyzing End-of-Fiscal-Period Entries for a Corporation

DIRECTIONS: For each closing or reversing entry described, decide which accounts are debited and credited. Print the letter identifying your choice in the proper Answers column.

A. Cash Short and Over
B. Depreciation Expense—Store Equipment
C. Dividends
D. Dividends Payable
E. Federal Income Tax Expense
F. Federal Income Tax Payable
G. Gain on Plant Assets
H. Income Summary
I. Insurance Expense
J. Interest Expense
K. Interest Income
L. Interest Payable
M. Interest Receivable
N. Loss on Plant Assets
O. Merchandise Inventory
P. Purchases
Q. Purchases Returns and Allowances
R. Prepaid Insurance
S. Retained Earnings
T. Sales
U. Sales Discount
V. Supplies
W. Supplies Expense
X. Uncollectible Accounts Expense

	Answers Debit	Answers Credit	For Scoring Debit	For Scoring Credit
0–0. Closing entry for the sales discount account	H	U	**0.** ✓	**0.** ✓
1–2. Closing entry for the gain on plant assets account			**1.**	**2.**
3–4. Closing entry for the cash short and over account (cash is short)			**3.**	**4.**
5–6. Closing entry for the purchases account			**5.**	**6.**
7–8. Closing entry for the uncollectible expense account			**7.**	**8.**
9–10. Closing entry for the interest expense account			**9.**	**10.**
11–12. Closing entry for the purchases returns and allowances account			**11.**	**12.**
13–14. Closing entry for the sales account			**13.**	**14.**
15–16. Closing entry for the interest income account			**15.**	**16.**
17–18. Reversing entry for the accrued interest expense			**17.**	**18.**
19–20. Closing entry for the cash short and over account (cash is over)			**19.**	**20.**
21–22. Closing entry for the income summary account (net income)			**21.**	**22.**
23–24. Closing entry for the depreciation expense—store equipment account			**23.**	**24.**
25–26. Closing entry for the federal income tax expense account			**25.**	**26.**
27–28. Closing entry for the dividends account			**27.**	**28.**
29–30. Closing entry for the income summary account (net loss)			**29.**	**30.**
31–32. Reversing entry for the accrued interest income account			**31.**	**32.**
33–34. Closing entry for the loss on plant assets account			**33.**	**34.**

Classifying a corporation's revenue, cost, and expense accounts

Account No.	Operating Revenue	Contra Account of Operating Revenue	Cost of Merchandise	Contra Account of Cost of Merchandise	Operating Expense	Other Revenue	Other Expense
1.					✓		
2.							
3.							
4.							
5.							
6.							
7.							
8.							
9.							
10.							
11.							
12.							
13.							
14.							
15.							

Classifying a corporation's assets, liabilities, and stockholders' equity accounts

DRILL 27-D2, p. 678

Account No.	Current Asset	Contra Account of a Current Asset	Plant Asset	Contra Account of a Plant Asset	Current Liability	Long-Term Liability	Stockholders' Equity
1.	✓						
2.							
3.							
4.							
5.							
6.							
7.							
8.							
9.							
10.							
11.							
12.							
13.							
14.							
15.							
16.							
17.							
18.							
19.							
20.							

Name ______________________ Date ________ Class ______

PROBLEM 27-1, p. 679
[1, 2]

Preparing financial statements for a corporation

					% OF NET SALES

[1, 2]

					% OF NET SALES

[3, 4]

[4, 5]

Income Statement Analysis

[2]

	Acceptable %	**Actual %**	**Positive Result Yes**	**Positive Result No**	**Recommended Action If Needed**
Cost of merchandise sold	Not more than 73.0%				
Gross profit on operations	Not less than 27.0%				
Total operating expenses	Not more than 24.9%				
Income from operations	Not less than 2.1%				
Net deduction from other revenue and expenses	Not more than 0.1%				
Net income before federal income tax	Not less than 2.0%				

Balance Sheet Analysis

[5]

	Acceptable	**Actual**	**Positive Result Yes**	**Positive Result No**	**Recommended Action If Needed**
Working capital	Not less than $100,000.00				
Current ratio	Between 2.2 to 1 and 2.8 to 1				

Name ______________ Date ________ Class ________

PROBLEM 27-2, p. 682
[1]

Journalizing adjusting, closing, and reversing entries for a corporation

GENERAL JOURNAL

PAGE 18

	DATE		ACCOUNT TITLE	DOC. NO.	POST. REF.	DEBIT	CREDIT	
1								1
2								2
3								3
4								4
5								5
6								6
7								7
8								8
9								9
10								10
11								11
12								12
13								13
14								14
15								15
16								16
17								17
18								18
19								19
20								20
21								21
22								22
23								23
24								24
25								25
26								26
27								27
28								28
29								29
30								30
31								31
32								32

[2]

GENERAL JOURNAL

PAGE 19

DATE		ACCOUNT TITLE	DOC. NO.	POST. REF.	DEBIT	CREDIT

[3]

GENERAL JOURNAL

PAGE 20

DATE		ACCOUNT TITLE	DOC. NO.	POST. REF.	DEBIT	CREDIT

Preparing financial statements and end-of-fiscal-period entries for a corporation

MASTERY PROBLEM 27-M, p. 682
[1, 2]

Accent, Inc.

Income Statement

For Year Ended December 31, 19--

					% OF NET SALES
Operating Revenue:					
Sales					
Less: Sales Discount					
Sales Returns and Allowances					
Net Sales					
Cost of Merchandise Sold:					
Merchandise Inventory, Jan. 1, 19--					
Purchases					
Less: Purchases Discount					
Purchases Returns and Allow.					
Net Purchases					
Total Cost of Mdse. Avail. for Sale					
Less Mdse. Inventory, Dec. 31, 19--					
Cost of Merchandise Sold					
Gross Profit on Operations					
Operating Expenses:					
Advertising Expense					
Credit Card Fee Expense					
Depr. Expense—Office Equipment					
Depr. Expense—Store Equipment					
Insurance Expense					
Miscellaneous Expense					
Payroll Taxes Expense					
Rent Expense					
Salary Expense					
Supplies Expense					
Uncollectible Accounts Expense					
Utilities Expense					
Total Operating Expenses					
Income from Operations					
Other Revenue:					
Gain on Plant Assets					

[1, 2]

Accent, Inc.

Income Statement (continued)

For Year Ended December 31, 19--

					% OF NET SALES
Interest Income					
Total Other Revenue					
Other Expenses:					
Cash Short and Over					
Interest Expense					
Loss on Plant Assets					
Total Other Expenses					
Net Deduction					
Net Income before Fed. Income Tax					
Less Federal Income Tax Expense					
Net Income after Federal Income Tax					

[3, 4]

Accent, Inc.

Statement of Stockholders' Equity

For Year Ended December 31, 19--

Capital Stock:			
$10.00 Per Share			
January 1, 19--, 15,000 Shares Issued			
Issued during Current Year, None			
Balance, December 31, 19--, 15,000 Shares Issued			
Retained Earnings:			
Balance, January 1, 19--			
Net Income after Federal Income Tax for 19--			
Less Dividends Declared during 19--			
Net Increase during 19--			
Balance, December 31, 19--			
Total Stockholders' Equity, December 31, 19--			

[4, 5]

Accent, Inc.

Balance Sheet

December 31, 19--

ASSETS			
Current Assets:			
Cash			
Petty Cash			
Notes Receivable			
Interest Receivable			
Accounts Receivable			
Less Allowance for Uncollectible Accounts			
Merchandise Inventory			
Supplies			
Prepaid Insurance			
Total Current Assets			
Plant Assets:			
Office Equipment			
Less Accumulated Depreciation—Office Equipment			
Store Equipment			
Less Accumulated Depreciation—Store Equipment			
Total Plant Assets			
Total Assets			
LIABILITIES			
Current Liabilities:			
Notes Payable			
Interest Payable			
Accounts Payable			
Employee Income Tax Payable			
Federal Income Tax Payable			
FICA Tax Payable			
Sales Tax Payable			
Unemployment Tax Payable—Federal			
Unemployment Tax Payable—State			
Health Insurance Premiums Payable			
Dividends Payable			

[4, 5]

Accent, Inc.

Balance Sheet (continued)

December 31, 19--

Total Liabilities			
STOCKHOLDERS' EQUITY			
Capital Stock			
Retained Earnings			
Total Stockholders' Equity			
Total Liabilities and Stockholders' Equity			

Income Statement Analysis **[2]**

	Acceptable %	Actual %	Positive Result Yes	Positive Result No	Recommended Action If Needed
Cost of merchandise sold	Not more than 72.0%				
Gross profit on operations	Not less than 28.0%				
Total operating expenses	Not more than 22.0%				
Income from operations	Not less than 6.0%				
Net deduction from other revenue and expenses	Not more than 0.1%				
Net income before federal income tax	Not less than 5.9%				

Balance Sheet Analysis **[5]**

	Acceptable	Actual	Positive Result Yes	Positive Result No	Recommended Action If Needed
Working capital	Not less than $125,000.00				
Current ratio	Between 2.0 to 1 and 2.6 to 1				

[6]

GENERAL JOURNAL

PAGE 20

DATE		ACCOUNT TITLE	DOC. NO.	POST. REF.	DEBIT	CREDIT

[7]

GENERAL JOURNAL

PAGE 21

DATE		ACCOUNT TITLE	DOC. NO.	POST. REF.	DEBIT	CREDIT

[8]

GENERAL JOURNAL

PAGE 22

DATE		ACCOUNT TITLE	DOC. NO.	POST. REF.	DEBIT	CREDIT

Name ______________________ Date ________ Class ______

Begin Challenge Problem 27-C on page 464.

CHALLENGE PROBLEM 27-C, p. 682

[1]

Preparing financial statements and end-of-fiscal-period entries for a corporation

Design

(continued)

December 31, 19--

	5	6	7	8	9	10	
	ADJUSTED TRIAL BALANCE		INCOME STATEMENT		BALANCE SHEET		
	DEBIT	CREDIT	DEBIT	CREDIT	DEBIT	CREDIT	
33							33
34							34
35							35
36							36
37							37
38							38
39							39
40							40
41							41
42							42
43							43
44							44
45							45
46							46
47							47
48							48
49							49
50							50
51							51
52							52
53							53
54							54
55							55
56							56
57							57
58							58
59							59
60							60
61							61
62							62

[1]

Glass

Work

For Year Ended

	ACCOUNT TITLE	TRIAL BALANCE (1) DEBIT	TRIAL BALANCE (2) CREDIT	ADJUSTMENTS (3) DEBIT	ADJUSTMENTS (4) CREDIT	
1	Cash	86817 00				1
2	Petty Cash	300 00				2
3	Notes Receivable	9850 00				3
4	Interest Receivable					4
5	Accounts Receivable	63085 00				5
6	Allowance for Uncollectible Accounts		40 00			6
7	Merchandise Inventory	61884 60				7
8	Supplies	2296 90				8
9	Prepaid Insurance	8164 00				9
10	Office Equipment	24246 00				10
11	Accumulated Depreciation—Office Equipment		6061 50			11
12	Store Equipment	19080 00				12
13	Accumulated Depreciation—Store Equipment		5721 00			13
14	Notes Payable		12960 00			14
15	Interest Payable					15
16	Accounts Payable		69809 72			16
17	Employee Income Tax Payable		1488 00			17
18	Federal Income Tax Payable					18
19	FICA Tax Payable		1716 00			19
20	Sales Tax Payable		5988 00			20
21	Unemployment Tax Payable—Federal		30 00			21
22	Unemployment Tax Payable—State		202 50			22
23	Health Insurance Premiums Payable		632 34			23
24	Dividends Payable		10000 00			24
25	Capital Stock		100000 00			25
26	Retained Earnings		33028 87			26
27	Dividends	38000 00				27
28	Income Summary					28
29	Sales		970998 47			29
30	Sales Discount	1802 52				30
31	Sales Returns and Allowances	7512 48				31
32	Purchases	663734 50				32

Name ______________________ Date ________ Class ________

CHALLENGE PROBLEM 27-C, continued
[1]

Design

Sheet

December 31, 19--

	5	6	7	8	9	10	
	ADJUSTED TRIAL BALANCE		INCOME STATEMENT		BALANCE SHEET		
	DEBIT	CREDIT	DEBIT	CREDIT	DEBIT	CREDIT	
1							1
2							2
3							3
4							4
5							5
6							6
7							7
8							8
9							9
10							10
11							11
12							12
13							13
14							14
15							15
16							16
17							17
18							18
19							19
20							20
21							21
22							22
23							23
24							24
25							25
26							26
27							27
28							28
29							29
30							30
31							31
32							32

CHALLENGE PROBLEM 27-C, continued

[1]

Glass

Work Sheet

For Year Ended

	ACCOUNT TITLE	1 TRIAL BALANCE DEBIT	2 TRIAL BALANCE CREDIT	3 ADJUSTMENTS DEBIT	4 ADJUSTMENTS CREDIT	
33	Purchases Discount		4917 24			33
34	Purchases Returns and Allowances		2444 52			34
35	Advertising Expense	14353 20				35
36	Credit Card Fee Expense	9960 24				36
37	Depreciation Expense—Office Equipment					37
38	Depreciation Expense—Store Equipment					38
39	Insurance Expense					39
40	Miscellaneous Expense	8714 00				40
41	Payroll Taxes Expense	13469 40				41
42	Rent Expense	30000 00				42
43	Salary Expense	143067 60				43
44	Supplies Expense					44
45	Uncollectible Accounts Expense					45
46	Utilities Expense	2394 90				46
47	Gain on Plant Assets		99 00			47
48	Interest Income		805 00			48
49	Cash Short and Over	7 30				49
50	Interest Expense	1877 52				50
51	Loss on Plant Assets	225 00				51
52	Federal Income Tax Expense	16100 00				52
53		1226942 16	1226942 16			53
54	Net Income after Fed. Inc. Tax					54
55						55
56						56
57						57
58						58
59						59
60						60
61						61
62						62
63						63
64						64

Name ______________________ Date ________ Class ________

CHALLENGE PROBLEM 27-C, continued

[2, 3]

Glass Design

Income Statement

For Year Ended December 31, 19--

					% OF NET SALES
Operating Revenue:					
Sales					
Less: Sales Discount					
Sales Returns and Allowances					
Net Sales					
Cost of Merchandise Sold:					
Merchandise Inventory, Jan. 1, 19--					
Purchases					
Less: Purchases Discount					
Purchases Returns and Allow.					
Net Purchases					
Total Cost of Mdse. Avail. for Sale					
Less Mdse. Inventory, Dec. 31, 19--					
Cost of Merchandise Sold					
Gross Profit on Operations					
Operating Expenses:					
Advertising Expense					
Credit Card Fee Expense					
Depr. Expense—Office Equipment					
Depr. Expense—Store Equipment					
Insurance Expense					
Miscellaneous Expense					
Payroll Taxes Expense					
Rent Expense					
Salary Expense					
Supplies Expense					
Uncollectible Accounts Expense					
Utilities Expense					
Total Operating Expenses					
Income from Operations					
Other Revenue:					
Gain on Plant Assets					

[2, 3]

Glass Design

Income Statement (continued)

For Year Ended December 31, 19--

					% OF NET SALES
Interest Income					
Total Other Revenue					
Other Expenses:					
Cash Short and Over					
Interest Expense					
Loss on Plant Assets					
Total Other Expenses					
Net Deduction					
Net Income before Fed. Income Tax					
Less Federal Income Tax Expense					
Net Income after Federal Income Tax					

[4, 5]

Glass Design

Statement of Stockholders' Equity

For Year Ended December 31, 19--

Capital Stock:			
$10.00 Per Share			
January 1, 19--, 10,000 Shares Issued			
Issued during Current Year, None			
Balance, December 31, 19--, 10,000 Shares Issued			
Retained Earnings:			
Balance, January 1, 19--			
Net Income after Federal Income Tax for 19--			
Less Dividends Declared during 19--			
Net Increase during 19--			
Balance, December 31, 19--			
Total Stockholders' Equity, December 31, 19--			

Name ______________________ Date ________ Class ________

CHALLENGE PROBLEM 27-C, continued
[5, 6]

Glass Design

Balance Sheet

December 31, 19--

ASSETS			
Current Assets:			
Cash			
Petty Cash			
Notes Receivable			
Interest Receivable			
Accounts Receivable			
Less Allowance for Uncollectible Accounts			
Merchandise Inventory			
Supplies			
Prepaid Insurance			
Total Current Assets			
Plant Assets:			
Office Equipment			
Less Accumulated Depreciation—Office Equipment			
Store Equipment			
Less Accumulated Depreciation—Store Equipment			
Total Plant Assets			
Total Assets			
LIABILITIES			
Current Liabilities:			
Notes Payable			
Interest Payable			
Accounts Payable			
Employee Income Tax Payable			
Federal Income Tax Payable			
FICA Tax Payable			
Sales Tax Payable			
Unemployment Tax Payable—Federal			
Unemployment Tax Payable—State			
Health Insurance Premiums Payable			
Dividends Payable			

[5, 6]

Glass Design

Balance Sheet (continued)

December 31, 19--

Total Liabilities			
STOCKHOLDERS' EQUITY			
Capital Stock			
Retained Earnings			
Total Stockholders' Equity			
Total Liabilities and Stockholders' Equity			

Income Statement Analysis

[3]

	Acceptable %	**Actual %**	**Positive Result**		**Recommended Action If Needed**
			Yes	**No**	
Cost of merchandise sold	Not more than 70.0%				
Gross profit on operations	Not less than 30.0%				
Total operating expenses	Not more than 24.0%				
Income from operations	Not less than 6.0%				
Net deduction from other revenue and expenses	Not more than 0.1%				
Net income before federal income tax	Not less than 5.9%				

Balance Sheet Analysis

[6]

	Acceptable	**Actual**	**Positive Result**		**Recommended Action If Needed**
			Yes	**No**	
Working capital	Not less than $125,000.00				
Current ratio	Between 2.0 to 1 and 2.5 to 1				

[7]

GENERAL JOURNAL

PAGE 13

DATE		ACCOUNT TITLE	DOC. NO.	POST. REF.	DEBIT	CREDIT

[8]

GENERAL JOURNAL

PAGE 14

DATE		ACCOUNT TITLE	DOC. NO.	POST. REF.	DEBIT	CREDIT

Name ______________________ Date ________ Class ________

CHALLENGE PROBLEM 27-C, concluded

[9]

GENERAL JOURNAL

PAGE 15

DATE		ACCOUNT TITLE	DOC. NO.	POST. REF.	DEBIT	CREDIT

GENERAL JOURNAL

PAGE

DATE		ACCOUNT TITLE	DOC. NO.	POST. REF.	DEBIT	CREDIT

Name ______ Date ______ Class ______

AN ACCOUNTING CYCLE FOR A CORPORATION: END-OF-FISCAL-PERIOD WORK [12, 13, 16, 18, 19]

The general ledger used in Reinforcement Activity 3, Part A, is needed to complete Part B.

Hardware Mart

Work Sheet

For Year Ended December 31, 19--

		1	2	3	4	5	6	7	8	
	ACCOUNT TITLE	TRIAL BALANCE		ADJUSTMENTS		INCOME STATEMENT		BALANCE SHEET		
		DEBIT	CREDIT	DEBIT	CREDIT	DEBIT	CREDIT	DEBIT	CREDIT	
1	Cash									1
2	Petty Cash									2
3	Notes Receivable									3
4	Interest Receivable									4
5	Accounts Receivable									5
6	Allowance for Uncollectible Accts.									6
7	Merchandise Inventory									7
8	Supplies									8
9	Prepaid Insurance									9
10	Office Equipment									10
11	Accum. Depr.—Office Equip.									11
12	Store Equipment									12
13	Accum. Depr.—Store Equip.									13
14	Notes Payable									14
15	Interest Payable									15
16	Accounts Payable									16
17	Employee Income Tax Payable									17
18	Federal Income Tax Payable									18
19	FICA Tax Payable									19
20	Sales Tax Payable									20
21	Unemploy. Tax Payable—Fed.									21
22	Unemploy. Tax Payable—State									22
23	Health Insurance Premiums Pay.									23
24	Dividends Payable									24
25	Capital Stock									25
26	Retained Earnings									26
27	Dividends									27
28	Income Summary									28
29	Sales									29
30	Sales Discount									30
31	Sales Returns and Allowances									31
32	Purchases									32

[12, 13, 16, 18, 19]

Hardware Mart

Work Sheet (continued)

For Year Ended December 31, 19--

		1	2	3	4	5	6	7	8	
	ACCOUNT TITLE	TRIAL BALANCE		ADJUSTMENTS		INCOME STATEMENT		BALANCE SHEET		
		DEBIT	CREDIT	DEBIT	CREDIT	DEBIT	CREDIT	DEBIT	CREDIT	
33	Purchases Discount									33
34	Purchases Returns and Allow.									34
35	Advertising Expense									35
36	Credit Card Fee Expense									36
37	Deprec. Expense—Office Equip.									37
38	Deprec. Expense—Store Equip.									38
39	Insurance Expense									39
40	Miscellaneous Expense									40
41	Payroll Taxes Expense									41
42	Rent Expense									42
43	Salary Expense									43
44	Supplies Expense									44
45	Uncollectible Accounts Expense									45
46	Utilities Expense									46
47	Gain on Plant Assets									47
48	Interest Income									48
49	Cash Short and Over									49
50	Interest Expense									50
51	Loss on Plant Assets									51
52	Federal Income Tax Expense									52
53										53
54	Net Income after Fed. Inc. Tax									54
55										55
56										56
57										57
58										58
59										59
60										60
61										61
62										62
63										63
64										64

Name ______________ Date ________ Class ________

REINFORCEMENT ACTIVITY 3
PART B, continued

[13, 14]

Hardware Mart

Income Statement

For Year Ended December 31, 19--

					% OF NET SALES
Operating Revenue:					
Sales					
Less: Sales Discount					
Sales Returns and Allowances					
Net Sales					
Cost of Merchandise Sold:					
Merchandise Inventory, Jan. 1, 19--					
Purchases					
Less: Purchases Discount					
Purchases Returns and Allow.					
Net Purchases					
Total Cost of Mdse. Avail. for Sale					
Less Mdse. Inventory, Dec. 31, 19--					
Cost of Merchandise Sold					
Gross Profit on Operations					
Operating Expenses:					
Advertising Expense					
Credit Card Fee Expense					
Depr. Expense—Office Equipment					
Depr. Expense—Store Equipment					
Insurance Expense					
Miscellaneous Expense					
Payroll Taxes Expense					
Rent Expense					
Salary Expense					
Supplies Expense					
Uncollectible Accounts Expense					
Utilities Expense					
Total Operating Expenses					
Income from Operations					
Other Revenue:					
Gain on Plant Assets					

[13, 14]

Hardware Mart

Income Statement (continued)

For Year Ended December 31, 19--

					% OF NET SALES
Interest Income					
Total Other Revenue					
Other Expenses:					
Cash Short and Over					
Interest Expense					
Loss on Plant Assets					
Total Other Expenses					
Net Deduction					
Net Income before Fed. Income Tax					
Less Federal Income Tax Expense					
Net Income after Federal Income Tax					

[15, 16]

Hardware Mart

Statement of Stockholders' Equity

For Year Ended December 31, 19--

Capital Stock:			
$10.00 Per Share			
January 1, 19--, 4,000 Shares Issued			
Issued during Current Year, None			
Balance, December 31, 19--, 4,000 Shares Issued			
Retained Earnings:			
Balance, January 1, 19--			
Net Income after Federal Income Tax for 19--			
Less Dividends Declared during 19--			
Net Increase during 19--			
Balance, December 31, 19--			
Total Stockholders' Equity, December 31, 19--			

[16, 17]

Hardware Mart

Balance Sheet

December 31, 19--

ASSETS			
Current Assets:			
Cash			
Petty Cash			
Notes Receivable			
Interest Receivable			
Accounts Receivable			
Less Allowance for Uncollectible Accounts			
Merchandise Inventory			
Supplies			
Prepaid Insurance			
Total Current Assets			
Plant Assets:			
Office Equipment			
Less Accumulated Depreciation—Office Equipment			
Store Equipment			
Less Accumulated Depreciation—Store Equipment			
Total Plant Assets			
Total Assets			
LIABILITIES			
Current Liabilities:			
Notes Payable			
Interest Payable			
Accounts Payable			
Employee Income Tax Payable			
Federal Income Tax Payable			
FICA Tax Payable			
Sales Tax Payable			
Unemployment Tax Payable—Federal			
Unemployment Tax Payable—State			
Health Insurance Premiums Payable			
Total Liabilities			

[16, 17]

Hardware Mart

Balance Sheet (continued)

December 31, 19--

STOCKHOLDERS' EQUITY			
Capital Stock			
Retained Earnings			
Total Stockholders' Equity			
Total Liabilities and Stockholders' Equity			

Income Statement Analysis **[14]**

	Acceptable %	Actual %	Positive Result Yes	Positive Result No	Recommended Action If Needed
Cost of merchandise sold	Not more than 66.0%				
Gross profit on operations	Not less than 34.0%				
Total operating expenses	Not more than 25.0%				
Income from operations	Not less than 9.0%				
Net addition from other revenue and expenses	Not more than 0.5%				
Net income before federal income tax	Not less than 8.5%				

Balance Sheet Analysis **[17]**

	Acceptable	Actual	Positive Result Yes	Positive Result No	Recommended Action If Needed
Working capital	Not less than $50,000.00				
Current ratio	Between 2.0 to 1 and 2.5 to 1				

[18]

GENERAL JOURNAL

PAGE 13

DATE		ACCOUNT TITLE	DOC. NO.	POST. REF.	DEBIT	CREDIT

[19]

GENERAL JOURNAL

PAGE 14

DATE		ACCOUNT TITLE	DOC. NO.	POST. REF.	DEBIT	CREDIT

[20]

Hardware Mart

Post-Closing Trial Balance

December 31, 19--

ACCOUNT TITLE	DEBIT	CREDIT
Cash		
Petty Cash		
Notes Receivable		
Interest Receivable		
Accounts Receivable		
Allowance for Uncollectible Accounts		
Merchandise Inventory		
Supplies		
Prepaid Insurance		
Office Equipment		
Accumulated Depreciation—Office Equipment		
Store Equipment		
Accumulated Depreciation—Store Equipment		
Notes Payable		
Interest Payable		
Accounts Payable		
Employee Income Tax Payable		
Federal Income Tax Payable		
FICA Tax Payable		
Sales Tax Payable		
Unemployment Tax Payable—Federal		
Unemployment Tax Payable—State		
Health Insurance Premiums Payable		
Capital Stock		
Retained Earnings		
Totals		

[21]

GENERAL JOURNAL

PAGE 15

DATE		ACCOUNT TITLE	DOC. NO.	POST. REF.	DEBIT	CREDIT

Name ______________________ Date ________ Class ______

COMPUTER APPLICATION 6, p. 688
[3]

AUTOMATED ACCOUNTING CYCLE FOR A CORPORATION:
END-OF-FISCAL-PERIOD WORK

RUN DATE ___/___/___
MM DD YY

BATCH NO. [ ]

GENERAL LEDGER
Input Form

Problem No. __________

FORM GL-2

	1	2	3	4	5	
	DAY	DOC. NO.	ACCOUNT NUMBER	DEBIT AMOUNT	CREDIT AMOUNT	
1						1
2						2
3						3
4						4
5						5
6						6
7						7
8						8
9						9
10						10
11						11
12						12
13						13
14						14
15						15
16						16
17						17
18						18
19						19
20						20
21						21
22						22
23						23
24						24
25						25
			BATCH TOTALS			

RUN DATE ____/____/____
MM DD YY

BATCH NO. [ ]

GENERAL LEDGER
Input Form

Problem No. ________

FORM GL-2

	1	2	3	4	5	
	DAY	DOC. NO.	ACCOUNT NUMBER	DEBIT AMOUNT	CREDIT AMOUNT	
1						1
2						2
3						3
4						4
5						5
6						6
7						7
8						8
9						9
10						10
11						11
12						12
13						13
14						14
15						15
16						16
17						17
18						18
19						19
20						20
21						21
22						22
23						23
24						24
25						25
			BATCH TOTALS			

Perfect Score..... 50	Name ______________
Deduct......... ___	Date ________ Class ________
Your Score..... ___	Checked by ______________

STUDY GUIDE 28

UNIT A—Identifying Accounting Terms

DIRECTIONS: Select the one term in Column I that best fits each definition in Column II. Print the letter identifying your choice in the Answers column.

Column I

A. check register
B. voucher
C. voucher check
D. voucher register
E. voucher system

Column II	Answers	For Scoring
0. A check with space for writing details about a cash payment	C	**0.** ✔
1. A journal used to record vouchers		**1.**
2. A journal used in a voucher system to record cash payments		**2.**
3. A set of procedures for controlling cash payments by preparing and approving vouchers before payments are made		**3.**
4. A business form used to show an authorized person's approval for a cash payment		**4.**

UNIT B—Analyzing Concepts and Practices in a Voucher System

DIRECTIONS: For each of the following items, select the choice that best completes the statement. Print the letter identifying your choice in the Answers column.

	Answers	For Scoring
0. The source document for an entry in a voucher register is a(an) **(A)** debit memorandum **(B)** invoice **(C)** voucher **(D)** none of these	C	**0.** ✔
1. The source document for an entry in a check register is a(an) **(A)** copy of check **(B)** voucher **(C)** check **(D)** none of these		**1.**
2. The liability account that is used in a voucher system in place of accounts payable is **(A)** notes payable **(B)** vouchers receivable **(C)** vouchers payable **(D)** none of these		**2.**
3. Vouchers to be paid are filed in the unpaid vouchers file according to the **(A)** date of the invoice **(B)** date the voucher must be paid **(C)** voucher number **(D)** name of the vendor		**3.**
4. When an account has no special columns in the voucher register, information is recorded in the **(A)** delivery expense debit column **(B)** general columns **(C)** purchases debit column **(D)** vouchers payable credit column		**4.**
5. A check register is similar to and replaces a **(A)** purchases journal **(B)** voucher register **(C)** cash receipts journal **(D)** cash payments journal ..		**5.**
6. Paid vouchers are filed by the **(A)** voucher number **(B)** date of the voucher **(C)** name of the vendor **(D)** date of payment		**6.**

UNIT C—Analyzing Voucher Transactions

DIRECTIONS: Decide in which register the following transactions will be recorded and analyze the transactions into their debit and credit parts. In Answers Column 1, print the abbreviation for the register in which each transaction is to be recorded. In Columns 2 and 3 print the letters identifying the accounts to be debited and credited for each transaction.

CR—check register VR—voucher register

Account Title

A. Cash
B. Delivery Expense
C. Purchases
D. Purchases Discount
E. Purchases Returns and Allowances
F. Office Equipment
G. Supplies
H. Vouchers Payable

Transaction	Answers 1 Reg.	Answers 2 Debit	Answers 3 Credit	For Scoring 1 Reg.	For Scoring 2 Debit	For Scoring 3 Credit
0-0-0. Purchased merchandise on account	VR	C	H	**0.** ✓	**0.** ✓	**0.** ✓
1-2-3. Received invoice for delivery expense				**1.**	**2.**	**3.**
4-5-6. Bought office equipment on account				**4.**	**5.**	**6.**
7-8-9. Paid voucher for delivery expense				**7.**	**8.**	**9.**
10-11-12. Issued a debit memorandum				**10.**	**11.**	**12.**
13-14-15. Paid a voucher, no discount......................				**13.**	**14.**	**15.**
16-17-18. Bought supplies on account......................				**16.**	**17.**	**18.**
19-20-21. Paid voucher less a discount......................				**19.**	**20.**	**21.**

UNIT D—Analyzing Accounting Practices in a Voucher System

DIRECTIONS: Place a check mark in the proper Answers column to show whether each of the following statements is true or false.

	Answers True	Answers False	For Scoring
0. Invoices are verified before a voucher is prepared............................	✓		**0.** ✓
1. Cash control procedures include storing cash in a safe place...............			**1.**
2. Vouchers are prepared only for bills other than invoices			**2.**
3. The source document for an entry in the voucher register is the approved invoice..			**3.**
4. In a voucher system, the account Vouchers Payable is used only for purchases of merchandise on account..			**4.**
5. A voucher is sometimes known as a voucher jacket...........................			**5.**
6. Vouchers must be approved before being recorded in the voucher register..			**6.**
7. When a voucher is recorded, a notation is made on the voucher..........			**7.**
8. Vouchers are placed in the unpaid file according to the due date			**8.**
9. When an amount is recorded in a special column in the voucher register, an account title must be written in the Account Title column..			**9.**
10. Separate amounts recorded in the General Debit column of a voucher register are posted individually during the month............................			**10.**
11. Separate amounts recorded in special amount columns of a voucher register are posted individually during the month............................			**11.**
12. A voucher check has a detachable stub			**12.**
13. When a voucher is paid, a notation is made on the voucher and in the voucher register..			**13.**
14. Paid vouchers are filed according to the date paid...........................			**14.**
15. A check register replaces a cash receipts journal			**15.**
16. In addition to journalizing cash payments, a check register can also be used to maintain the checking account balance...............................			**16.**
17. Each check recorded in a check register includes a debit to Vouchers Payable and a credit to Cash			**17.**
18. When a debit memo is issued for the return of merchandise purchased, the original voucher is discarded			**18.**
19. The amount of net salaries is credited to Vouchers Payable to record the voucher for payroll			**19.**

Name ______________________ Date ________ Class ________ *DRILL 28-D1, p. 719*

Preparing vouchers

Vchr. No. **42**

Date ________ Due Date ________ Payment Date ________

To ______________________

Address ______________________
Street

____
City State ZIP

ACCOUNTS DEBITED	AMOUNT	
PURCHASES		
SUPPLIES		
PREPAID INSURANCE		
ADVERTISING EXPENSE		
DELIVERY EXPENSE		
MISCELLANEOUS EXPENSE		
RENT EXPENSE		
SALARY EXPENSE		
UTILITIES EXPENSE		
TOTAL DEBITS		

ACCOUNTS CREDITED	AMOUNT	
VOUCHERS PAYABLE		
EMPLOYEE INC. TAX PAY. - FEDERAL		
EMPLOYEE INC. TAX PAY. - STATE		
FICA TAX PAYABLE		
TOTAL CREDITS		

Voucher Approved by ______________________

Recorded in Voucher Register Page ________ by ________

Paid { Date ______________________ Check No. ________ Amount $ ________ Approved by ______________________

Vchr. No. **43**

Date ________ Due Date ________ Payment Date ________

To ______________________

Address ______________________
Street

____
City State ZIP

ACCOUNTS DEBITED	AMOUNT	
PURCHASES		
SUPPLIES		
PREPAID INSURANCE		
ADVERTISING EXPENSE		
DELIVERY EXPENSE		
MISCELLANEOUS EXPENSE		
RENT EXPENSE		
SALARY EXPENSE		
UTILITIES EXPENSE		
TOTAL DEBITS		

ACCOUNTS CREDITED	AMOUNT	
VOUCHERS PAYABLE		
EMPLOYEE INC. TAX PAY. - FEDERAL		
EMPLOYEE INC. TAX PAY. - STATE		
FICA TAX PAYABLE		
TOTAL CREDITS		

Voucher Approved by ______________________

Recorded in Voucher Register Page ________ by ________

Paid { Date ______________________ Check No. ________ Amount $ ________ Approved by ______________________

Vchr. No. **44**

Date ________ Due Date ________ Payment Date ________

To ______________________

Address ______________________
Street

____
City State ZIP

ACCOUNTS DEBITED	AMOUNT	
PURCHASES		
SUPPLIES		
PREPAID INSURANCE		
ADVERTISING EXPENSE		
DELIVERY EXPENSE		
MISCELLANEOUS EXPENSE		
RENT EXPENSE		
SALARY EXPENSE		
UTILITIES EXPENSE		
TOTAL DEBITS		

ACCOUNTS CREDITED	AMOUNT	
VOUCHERS PAYABLE		
EMPLOYEE INC. TAX PAY. - FEDERAL		
EMPLOYEE INC. TAX PAY. - STATE		
FICA TAX PAYABLE		
TOTAL CREDITS		

Voucher Approved by ______________________

Recorded in Voucher Register Page ________ by ________

Paid { Date ______________________ Check No. ________ Amount $ ________ Approved by ______________________

Analyzing journalizing transactions in a voucher register

DRILL 28-D2, p. 719

Item No.	Amount Columns in a Voucher Register					
	Vouchers Payable Credit	Purchases Debit	Delivery Expense Debit	Supplies Debit	General Debit	General Credit
1.	✓	✓				
2.						
3.						
4.						
5.						
6.						
7.						

Analyzing journalizing transactions in a check register

DRILL 28-D3, p. 720

Item No.	Amount Columns in a Check Register				
	Vouchers Payable Debit	Purchases Discount Credit	Cash Credit	Bank	
				Deposits	Balance
1.	✓		✓		✓
2.					
3.					

Journalizing cash payments and deposits in a check register [1–3]

Problem 28-1 begins on page 492. The voucher register prepared in Problem 28-1 is needed to complete Problem 28-2.

CHECK REGISTER

PAGE 9

	DATE		PAYEE	CK. NO.	VCHR. NO.	1 VOUCHERS PAYABLE DEBIT	2 PURCHASES DISCOUNT CREDIT	3 CASH CREDIT	4 BANK DEPOSITS	5 BANK BALANCE	
1											1
2											2
3											3
4											4
5											5
6											6
7											7
8											8
9											9
10											10
11											11
12											12
13											13
14											14
15											15
16											16
17											17
18											18
19											19
20											20
21											21
22											22
23											23
24											24
25											25

Journalizing vouchers in a voucher register

PROBLEM 28-1, p. 720

[1, 2]

The voucher register prepared in Problem 28-1 is needed to complete Problem 28-2.

PAGE 9

VOUCHER

	DATE		PAYEE	VCHR. NO.	PAID		1 VOUCHERS PAYABLE CREDIT	
					DATE	CK. NO.		
1								1
2								2
3								3
4								4
5								5
6								6
7								7
8								8
9								9
10								10
11								11
12								12
13								13
14								14
15								15

Journalizing purchases returns and allowances in a voucher register

PROBLEM 28-3, p. 721

PAGE 2

VOUCHER

	DATE		PAYEE	VCHR. NO.	PAID		1 VOUCHERS PAYABLE CREDIT	
					DATE	CK. NO.		
1								1
2								2
3								3
4								4
5								5
6								6
7								7
8								8
9								9
10								10
11								11
12								12

PROBLEM 28-1, concluded
[1, 2]

REGISTER

PAGE 9

2	3	4			5	6
			GENERAL			
PURCHASES DEBIT	DELIVERY EXPENSE DEBIT	SUPPLIES DEBIT	ACCOUNT TITLE	POST. REF.	DEBIT	CREDIT

PROBLEM 28-3, concluded

REGISTER

PAGE 2

2	3	4			5	6
			GENERAL			
PURCHASES DEBIT	DELIVERY EXPENSE DEBIT	SUPPLIES DEBIT	ACCOUNT TITLE	POST. REF.	DEBIT	CREDIT

Preparing and journalizing a voucher for payroll

PROBLEM 28-4, p. 721
[1, 2]

Vchr.
No. **51**

Date ________ Due Date ________ Payment Date ________

To ____________________

Address ____________________
Street

____
City State ZIP

ACCOUNTS DEBITED	AMOUNT	
PURCHASES		
SUPPLIES		
PREPAID INSURANCE		
ADVERTISING EXPENSE		
DELIVERY EXPENSE		
MISCELLANEOUS EXPENSE		
RENT EXPENSE		
SALARY EXPENSE		
UTILITIES EXPENSE		
TOTAL DEBITS		

ACCOUNTS CREDITED	AMOUNT	
VOUCHERS PAYABLE		
EMPLOYEE INC. TAX PAY. - FEDERAL		
EMPLOYEE INC. TAX PAY. - STATE		
FICA TAX PAYABLE		
TOTAL CREDITS		

Voucher Approved by *Jason Conway*

Recorded in Voucher
Register Page ________ by ________

Paid { Date ________
Check No. ________ Amount $ ________
Approved by ________

[2]

PAGE 5 VOUCHER

	DATE		PAYEE	VCHR. NO.	PAID		VOUCHERS PAYABLE CREDIT (1)	
					DATE	CK. NO.		
1								1
2								2
3								3
4								4
5								5

[1, 2]

VOUCHER

Vchr. No. **51**

Payment Date ______________ 19 ______

Date ____________ 19 ______ Terms ________ Due ____________ 19 ______

To ________________________________

Address ________________________________

City ______________________ State ____________ Zip ________

For the following: Enclose all invoices or other papers.

DATE	VOUCHER DETAILS	AMOUNT

[2]

REGISTER

PAGE 5

	2	3	4			5	6	
	PURCHASES DEBIT	DELIVERY EXPENSE DEBIT	SUPPLIES DEBIT	GENERAL				
				ACCOUNT TITLE	POST. REF.	DEBIT	CREDIT	
1								1
2								2
3								3
4								4
5								5

[2, 3]

PAGE 22

VOUCHER

DATE		PAYEE	VCHR. NO.	PAID		1 VOUCHERS PAYABLE CREDIT
				DATE	CK. NO.	

[2, 3]

REGISTER

PAGE 22

2	3	4			5	6
			GENERAL			
PURCHASES DEBIT	DELIVERY EXPENSE DEBIT	SUPPLIES DEBIT	ACCOUNT TITLE	POST. REF.	DEBIT	CREDIT

[1–3]

CHECK REGISTER

PAGE 20

	DATE		PAYEE	CK. NO.	VCHR. NO.	1 VOUCHERS PAYABLE DEBIT	2 PURCHASES DISCOUNT CREDIT	3 CASH CREDIT	4 BANK DEPOSITS	5 BANK BALANCE	
1											1
2											2
3											3
4											4
5											5
6											6
7											7
8											8
9											9
10											10
11											11
12											12
13											13
14											14
15											15
16											16
17											17
18											18
19											19
20											20
21											21
22											22
23											23
24											24
25											25

Name ______________________ Date ________ Class ______ *CHALLENGE PROBLEM 28-C, p. 722*

Journalizing purchase invoices at the net amount in a voucher system [1–3]

CHECK REGISTER

PAGE 20

	DATE	PAYEE	CK. NO.	VCHR. NO.	1 VOUCHERS PAYABLE DEBIT	2 CASH CREDIT	3 BANK DEPOSITS	4 BANK BALANCE	
1									1
2									2
3									3
4									4
5									5
6									6
7									7
8									8
9									9
10									10
11									11
12									12
13									13
14									14
15									15
16									16
17									17
18									18
19									19
20									20
21									21
22									22
23									23
24									24
25									25

[2, 3]

PAGE 25

VOUCHER

DATE		PAYEE	VCHR. NO.	PAID		1 VOUCHERS PAYABLE CREDIT
				DATE	CK. NO.	

Name ______________________ Date ________ Class ______

CHALLENGE PROBLEM 28-C, concluded

[2, 3]

REGISTER

PAGE 25

	2	3	4			5	6	
	PURCHASES DEBIT	DISCOUNTS LOST DEBIT	SUPPLIES DEBIT	GENERAL				
				ACCOUNT TITLE	POST. REF.	DEBIT	CREDIT	
1								1
2								2
3								3
4								4
5								5
6								6
7								7
8								8
9								9
10								10
11								11
12								12
13								13
14								14
15								15
16								16
17								17
18								18
19								19
20								20
21								21
22								22
23								23
24								24
25								25
26								26
27								27
28								28
29								29
30								30
31								31
32								32

CHECK REGISTER

PAGE

	DATE		PAYEE	CK. NO.	VCHR. NO.	1 VOUCHERS PAYABLE DEBIT	2 PURCHASES DISCOUNT CREDIT	3 CASH CREDIT	4 BANK DEPOSITS	5 BANK BALANCE	
1											1
2											2
3											3
4											4
5											5
6											6
7											7
8											8
9											9
10											10
11											11
12											12
13											13
14											14
15											15
16											16
17											17
18											18
19											19
20											20
21											21
22											22
23											23
24											24
25											25

Perfect Score..... 34 Name ______________________

Deduct......... ___ Date ______________ Class ______________

Your Score..... ___ Checked by ______________________

STUDY GUIDE 29

UNIT A—Identifying Accounting Terms

DIRECTIONS: Select the one term in Column I that best fits each definition in Column II. Print the letter identifying your choice in the Answers column.

Column I

- **A.** first-in, first-out inventory costing method
- **B.** gross profit method of estimating inventory
- **C.** inventory record
- **D.** last-in, first-out inventory costing method
- **E.** periodic inventory
- **F.** perpetual inventory
- **G.** stock ledger
- **H.** stock record
- **I.** weighted-average inventory costing method

Column II	Answers	For Scoring
0. A file of stock records for all merchandise on hand ..	G	**0.** ✓
1. Using the price of merchandise purchased last to calculate the cost of merchandise sold first		**1.**
2. A merchandise inventory determined by keeping a continuous record of increases, decreases, and balance on hand...		**2.**
3. Using the average cost of beginning inventory plus merchandise purchased during a fiscal period to calculate the cost of merchandise sold...................		**3.**
4. A form used to show kind of merchandise, quantity received, quantity sold, and balance on hand...........		**4.**
5. Estimating inventory by using previous year's percentage of gross profit on operations.................		**5.**
6. A form used during a periodic inventory to record information about each item of merchandise on hand		**6.**
7. Using the price of merchandise purchased first to calculate the cost of merchandise sold first		**7.**
8. Merchandise inventory determined by counting, weighing, or measuring items of merchandise on hand..		**8.**

UNIT B—Analyzing Inventory Systems

DIRECTIONS: Place a check mark in the proper Answers column to show whether each of the following statements is true or false.

	Answers		For Scoring
	True	False	
0. Merchandise inventory on hand is typically the largest asset and cost of a merchandising business..	✓		**0.** ✓
1. The only financial statement on which the value of merchandise on hand is reported is the income statement.......................................			**1.**
2. A minimum inventory balance is the amount of merchandise that will typically last until ordered merchandise can be received from vendors...			**2.**
3. A perpetual inventory is sometimes known as a physical inventory.......			**3.**
4. Net income of a business can be decreased by maintaining merchandise inventory that is larger than needed..			**4.**
5. A periodic inventory should be taken at least once a month even when perpetual inventory records are kept..			**5.**
6. A perpetual inventory stock record always shows quantity and value of the merchandise on hand..			**6.**
7. Some cash registers use optical scanners to read the UPC codes marked on products...			**7.**
8. First-in, first-out is a method used to determine the quantity of each type of merchandise on hand..			**8.**
9. Using the same inventory method for all fiscal periods provides financial statements that can be compared with other fiscal-period statements...			**9.**
10. The gross profit method makes it possible to prepare monthly income statements without taking a periodic inventory			**10.**
11. Using the gross profit method, the first step in figuring the value of ending inventory is to determine the cost of merchandise sold............			**11.**

UNIT C—Analyzing Lifo, Fifo, and Weighted-Average Methods

DIRECTIONS: For each of the following items, select the choice that best completes the statement. Print the letter identifying your choice in the Answers column.

0. The fifo method is based on the assumption that the merchandise purchased first is the merchandise **(A)** sold first **(B)** sold last **(C)** in beginning inventory **(D)** none of these ....

1. The weighted-average method is based on the assumption that the cost of merchandise sold should be calculated using the **(A)** average price per unit of beginning inventory **(B)** average price of ending inventory **(C)** average price of beginning inventory plus purchases during the fiscal period **(D)** average price of ending inventory plus purchases during the fiscal period...

2. The lifo method is based on the assumption that the merchandise purchased last is the merchandise **(A)** sold first **(B)** sold last **(C)** in ending inventory **(D)** none of these ....

3. A business that uses the same inventory costing method for all fiscal periods is applying the concept **(A)** Accounting Period Cycle **(B)** Adequate Disclosure **(C)** Perpetual Inventory **(D)** Consistent Reporting..........

4. When the fifo method is used, cost of merchandise sold is valued at the **(A)** average price **(B)** earliest price **(C)** most recent price **(D)** none of these ..

5. When the lifo method is used, cost of merchandise sold is priced at the **(A)** average price **(B)** earliest price **(C)** most recent price **(D)** none of these ..

6. When the fifo method is used, ending inventory units are priced at the **(A)** average price **(B)** earliest price **(C)** most recent price **(D)** none of these ..

7. When the weighted-average method is used, ending inventory units are priced at the **(A)** average price **(B)** earliest price **(C)** most recent price **(D)** none of these ....

8. In a year of rising prices, the inventory method that gives the lowest possible value for ending inventory is **(A)** fifo **(B)** lifo **(C)** weighted-average **(D)** gross profit ....

9. Inventory information for Adams Company is shown below:

	Units	*Unit Price*
Beginning inventory	20	$20.00
Purchases during year	40	$30.00
Ending inventory	30	

Under the fifo method, ending inventory is **(A)** $700.00 **(B)** $750.00 **(C)** $900.00 **(D)** none of these ....

10. Using the inventory information in Question 9, ending inventory under the lifo method is **(A)** $700.00 **(B)** $750.00 **(C)** $900.00 **(D)** none of these....

11. Using the inventory information in Question 9, ending inventory under the weighted-average method is **(A)** $700.00 **(B)** $750.00 **(C)** $900.00 **(D)** none of these ....

12. In a year of falling prices, the inventory method that gives the lowest possible value for ending inventory is **(A)** fifo **(B)** lifo **(C)** weighted-average **(D)** gross profit ....

13. Inventory information for Pate Company is shown below:

	Units	*Unit Price*
Beginning inventory	30	$5.00
Purchases during year	20	$4.00
Ending inventory	40	

Under the fifo method ending inventory is **(A)** $180.00 **(B)** $184.00 **(C)** $200.00 **(D)** none of these ....

14. Using the inventory information in Question 13, ending inventory under the lifo method is **(A)** $180.00 **(B)** $184.00 **(C)** $200.00 **(D)** none of these....

15. Using the inventory information in Question 13, ending inventory under the weighted-average method is **(A)** $180.00 **(B)** $184.00 **(C)** $200.00 **(D)** none of these ....

Answers	For Scoring
A	0. ✓
	1.
	2.
	3.
	4.
	5.
	6.
	7.
	8.
	9.
	10.
	11.
	12.
	13.
	14.
	15.

Name ______________________ Date ________ Class ________

DRILL 29-D1, p. 736
[1, 2]

Determining quantities of merchandise on hand using a perpetual inventory

Increases		**Decreases**		**Balance**
Date	**Quantity**	**Date**	**Quantity**	**Quantity**
July 1				68

Determining cost of inventory using the fifo, lifo, and weighted-average methods

PROBLEM 29-1, p. 737
[1]

fifo method

Model No.	**No. of Units on Hand**	**Unit Price**	**Cost of Ending Inventory**
A48	29	16 @ \$18.00 13 @ 15.00	\$ 483.00
		TOTAL *fifo* COST →	

[2]

lifo method

Model No.	No. of Units on Hand	Unit Price	Cost of Ending Inventory
		TOTAL *lifo* COST→	

weighted-average method

[3]

Model No.	No. of Units on Hand	Unit Price	Cost of Ending Inventory
		TOTAL *weighted-average* COST→	

[4] The inventory costing method that resulted in the lowest total cost of ending inventory is ________

Name ____________________ Date ________ Class ______

PROBLEM 29-2, p. 738

[1]

Estimating inventory using the gross profit method of estimating inventory

STEP 1

Beginning inventory, July 1	$
Plus net purchases for July 1 to July 31	+
Equals cost of merchandise available for sale	$

STEP 2

Net sales for July 1 to July 31	$
Times previous year's gross profit percentage	×
Equals estimated gross profit on operations	$

STEP 3

Net sales for July 1 to July 31	$
Less estimated gross profit on operations	–
Equals estimated cost of merchandise sold	$

STEP 4

Cost of merchandise available for sale	$
Less estimated cost of merchandise sold	–
Equals estimated ending merchandise inventory	$

[2]

Daniel Company

Income Statement

For Month Ended July 31, 19--

			% OF SALES
Operating Revenue:			
Net Sales			
Cost of Merchandise Sold:			
Estimated Beginning Inventory, July 1			
Net Purchases			
Merchandise Available for Sale			
Less Estimated Ending Inventory, July 31			
Cost of Merchandise Sold			
Gross Profit on Operations			
Operating Expenses			
Net Income			

[1]

STEP 1

Beginning inventory, July 1	$
Plus net purchases, July 1 to July 31	+
Equals cost of merchandise available for sale	$

STEP 2

Net sales for July 1 to July 31	$
Times previous year's gross profit percentage	×
Equals estimated gross profit on operations	$

STEP 3

Net sales for July 1 to July 31	$
Less estimated gross profit on operations	−
Equals estimated cost of merchandise sold	$

STEP 4

Cost of merchandise available for sale	$
Less estimated cost of merchandise sold	−
Equals estimated ending merchandise inventory	$

[2]

Pearson Company

Income Statement

For Month Ended July 31, 19--

			% OF SALES
Operating Revenue:			
Net Sales			
Cost of Merchandise Sold:			
Estimated Beginning Inventory, July 1			
Net Purchases			
Merchandise Available for Sale			
Less Estimated Ending Inventory, July 31			
Cost of Merchandise Sold			
Gross Profit on Operations			
Operating Expenses			
Net Income			

Name ______________________ Date ________ Class ________

MASTERY PROBLEM 29-M, p. 738

Determining cost of ending inventory using the fifo, lifo, and weighted-average methods

[1]

fifo method

Model No.	No. of Units on Hand	Unit Price	Cost of Ending Inventory
23B2	22	15 @ $5.20 7 @ 4.90	$112.30
		TOTAL *fifo* COST→	

[2]

lifo method

Model No.	No. of Units on Hand	Unit Price	Cost of Ending Inventory
		TOTAL *lifo* COST→	

[3]

weighted-average method

Model No.	No. of Units on Hand	Unit Price	Cost of Ending Inventory
		TOTAL *weighted-average* COST→	

[4] The inventory costing method that resulted in the lowest total cost of ending inventory is ________

Extra form

Model No.	No. of Units on Hand	Unit Price	Cost of Ending Inventory
		TOTAL COST→	

Name ______________________ Date ________ Class ______ CHALLENGE PROBLEM 29-C, p. 739

Determining the cost of merchandise inventory destroyed in a fire

[1]

Gross profit on operations	$
Divided by net sales	÷
Equals gross profit percentage of net sales (prior year)	

[2]

STEP 1

Beginning inventory, August 1	$
Plus net purchases, August 1 to October 12	+
Equals cost of merchandise available for sale, August 1–October 12	$

STEP 2

Net sales, August 1 to October 12	$
Times previous year's gross profit percentage	×
Equals estimated gross profit on operations	$

STEP 3

Net sales, August 1 to October 12	$
Less estimated gross profit on operations	–
Equals estimated cost of merchandise sold	$

STEP 4

Cost of merchandise available for sale	$
Less estimated cost of merchandise sold	–
Equals estimated ending merchandise inventory	$

[3]

Estimated merchandise inventory, October 12	$
Less cost of merchandise inventory	–
Equals estimated cost of merchandise inventory destroyed	$

[4]

Fleming Lighting Company

Income Statement

For the Period August 1 to October 12, 19--

			% OF SALES
Operating Revenue:			
Net Sales			
Cost of Merchandise Sold:			
Estimated Beginning Inventory, August 1			
Net Purchases			
Merchandise Available for Sale			
Less Estimated Ending Inventory, October 12			
Cost of Merchandise Sold			
Gross Profit on Operations			
Operating Expenses			
Net Income			

Extra form